D1607469

International Perspectives on Designing Professional Practice Doctorates

International Perspectives on Designing Professional Practice Doctorates

Applying the Critical Friends Approach to the EdD and Beyond

Edited by
Valerie A. Storey

palgrave
macmillan

WITHDRAWN
McConnell Library Radford University

INTERNATIONAL PERSPECTIVES ON DESIGNING PROFESSIONAL PRACTICE DOCTORATES
Selection and editorial content © Valerie A. Storey 2016
Individual chapters © their respective contributors 2016

All rights reserved. No reproduction, copy or transmission of this publication may be made without written permission. No portion of this publication may be reproduced, copied or transmitted save with written permission. In accordance with the provisions of the Copyright, Designs and Patents Act 1988, or under the terms of any licence permitting limited copying issued by the Copyright Licensing Agency, Saffron House, 6-10 Kirby Street, London EC1N 8TS.

Any person who does any unauthorized act in relation to this publication may be liable to criminal prosecution and civil claims for damages.

First published 2016 by
PALGRAVE MACMILLAN

The authors have asserted their rights to be identified as the authors of this work in accordance with the Copyright, Designs and Patents Act 1988.

Palgrave Macmillan in the UK is an imprint of Macmillan Publishers Limited, registered in England, company number 785998, of Houndmills, Basingstoke, Hampshire, RG21 6XS.

Palgrave Macmillan in the US is a division of Nature America, Inc., One New York Plaza, Suite 4500, New York, NY 10004-1562.

Palgrave Macmillan is the global academic imprint of the above companies and has companies and representatives throughout the world.

Hardback ISBN: 978–1–137–52705–9
E-PUB ISBN: 978–1–137–52707–3
E-PDF ISBN: 978–1–137–52706–6
DOI: 10.1057/9781137527066

Distribution in the UK, Europe and the rest of the world is by Palgrave Macmillan®, a division of Macmillan Publishers Limited, registered in England, company number 785998, of Houndmills, Basingstoke, Hampshire RG21 6XS.

Library of Congress Cataloging-in-Publication Data

Names: Storey, Valerie Anne, editor of compilation.
Title: International perspectives on designing professional practice doctorates : applying the critical friends approach to the EdD and beyond /edited by Valerie A. Storey.
Description: New York, NY : Palgrave Macmillan, 2016. | Includes index.
Identifiers: LCCN 2015022085 | ISBN 9781137527059 (hardback)
Subjects: LCSH: Doctor of education degree. | BISAC: EDUCATION / Higher. | EDUCATION / Comparative. | EDUCATION / Leadership. | EDUCATION / Professional Development.
Classification: LCC LB1742 .I67 2016 | DDC 378.2—dc23 LC record available at http://lccn.loc.gov/2015022085

A catalogue record for the book is available from the British Library.

To Critical Friends who recognize that doctoral education is an international activity and that we never cease to learn from each other.

Contents

List of Illustrations

Tables

Figures

Foreword

The dogmas of the quiet past are inadequate to the stormy present. The occasion is piled high with difficulty. As our case is new, so we must think anew and act anew. We must disenthrall ourselves and then we shall save our country.

Abraham Lincoln, 1862

Today we are living in a world that socially, politically, culturally, and economically changes faster than ever before. Uncertainty and unpredictability now present some of the biggest challenges to organizations. There was never a greater need for us all to have the ability to disenthrall ourselves, to think anew and act anew, yet our educational systems have not changed quickly enough in response to this need. That is why this is an important book, because it challenges the way we view education, and doctoral education in particular. In doing so it poses some very timely questions to those of us who lead and teach on doctoral programs, and offers a valuable model for those of us who are eager to embrace change.

All through history, some of the greatest advances have been by ordinary people thinking outside the box, with creativity and imagination, to dream "what might be": The Wright brothers had the vision and belief that their bicycle-making skills could be used to develop a machine that could fly, ultimately changing the world forever. Physician John Snow defied the miasma theory of disease transmission to identify the true transmission route of cholera in the lethal London epidemic of 1854. Ridiculed and vilified both by his profession and by the authorities, he nevertheless went on to make one of the most important scientific discoveries of his age. Jenny Clack (now Professor and Curator of Vertebrate Palaeontology at the University of Cambridge, UK) was working as a young researcher early in her career when the conventional wisdom at the time was that land animals had evolved from fish that crawled out of the water using their fins, and that over time fins developed into legs. However, a newly discovered fossil made Jenny curious—it seemed to contradict the theory and suggested that some species had developed legs to help propel themselves along the seabed, before they ever emerged onto land. Jenny's theory was rejected by the eminent scientists of the day, unwilling to have their own research and theories contradicted, but finally her curiosity prevailed and after the discovery of further fossils that supported her theory she was able to rewrite part of the story of evolution and in doing so make a significant contribution to scientific understanding.

All these people have one thing in common—they had the ability to "disenthrall" themselves. Through imagination, curiosity, creativity, and an ability to open their minds to the possibility of something new, they were able to free themselves from the constraints of established ideas, and in doing so they were able to develop new knowledge that was more relevant to the times.

Professional doctorate programs are designed to produce research- ing professionals who similarly can bring new insights to their profession through consideration of fresh perspectives, new ideas, and alternative approaches. They are encouraged to view their profession through a "fresh lens." While few of them will make the sort of world-changing discoveries described above, the hope is that they can be instrumental in helping our society cope with the pace of twenty-first century change.

However, the demands that the challenges of change place upon practi- tioners should not be underestimated; encouraged to adapt to the specific norms, language, and behaviors of their chosen profession, they now have to break out of that mold, learn different ways of communicating, and new ways of thinking when all of this is at odds with the way they have been educated and trained. Langer (1997) proposes a mindful approach to learning which requires three characteristics: the continuous creation of new categories, openness to new information, and an implicit aware- ness of more than one perspective. Godfrey et al. (2014) offer a solution by making a case for a systems approach to learning that is embedded in context-driven enquiry rather than the acquisition of specialized subject knowledge. Learners progress through a formative, dynamic learning process which draws on higher order creative and critical thinking that begins with observation and concludes with a product which is the unique application of knowledge for a particular purpose. This process is pro- foundly interdisciplinary.

The unfreezing of established ways of professional thinking in order to open minds to different ideas can be a very difficult challenge for educators, especially as the established practices of teaching and assessment have been designed largely to reinforce discipline or professional-specific knowledge and behaviors. After all, as educators we ourselves are subject to the strong discipline-based boundaries that can restrict our own ability to think in different ways. Yet, the challenges we face are not unique. Many are cur- rently being addressed by colleagues around the world in a variety of ways depending on culture and context. Our learning occurs when our eyes are open to the fact that there is not always one best approach and that we may need to look beyond our own borders for solutions. We no longer have to work in isolation as this book contributes to a more holistic view of doctoral programs.

This is where the notion of a "critical friends" approach is so appealing. Bambino (2002) explains how critical friends groups create communities of learners who can collaborate to share feedback and develop new solutions. They change the dynamic of the learning process and offer a vehicle for educators and learners to become co-creators of knowledge. This is important.

Some time ago, the training manager of a large organization was speaking to me about the possibility of developing a program of higher education for his account managers. He told me,

> These guys are really clever. They average £100,000 a year. They can work out a deal in their heads quicker than any accountant, and yet none of them have formal qualifications. They are guys who spent their years at school looking out of the window because they were bored. If you're going to teach them you need to do something different, or you'll bore them too.

I believe this book offers the reader that opportunity to consider how to do something different for our clever, professional learners. Our critical friends who have contributed to this book have shared their experiences, and I hope that may just be the start of a growing community of critical friends who can help transform doctoral education to meet the modern challenges that our society faces.

Gail Sanders,
Professor of Management Education and Development,
University of Sunderland, UK

References

Bambino, D. (2002). Critical friends. *Educational Leadership, 59*(6), 25–27.

Godfrey, P., Deakin Crick, R., & Huang, S. (2014). Systems thinking, systems design, and learning power in engineering education. *International Journal of Engineering Education, 30*(1), 112–127.

Langer, E. J. (1997). *The power of mindful learning.* Cambridge, MA: Perseus Books.

Acknowledgments

A book offering insights on current important global issues in professional practice doctoral programs could not have been written without outstanding critical friends around the world who embody the essence of critical friendship by continually challenging and supporting each other. The rapid increase in the number and variety of professional practice doctorates in the twenty-first century has resulted in a proliferation of programs utilizing a variety of pedagogical models focused on practicing professionals. Inevitably the leadership and management of such a complex landscape are not without challenges and issues.

Critical friends from Australia, Canada, England, Ireland, New Zealand, Israel, and the United States have worked collaboratively across national boundaries in different settings to address identified trends and themes in international professional practice doctoral programs. Their willingness to share research, work, experiences, insights, and self-reflections in the interest of improving professional practice doctoral program design, impact, and outcomes is greatly appreciated and applauded.

Introduction—Crossing Borders with Critical Friends: Applying an International Lens to Innovative Professional Practice Doctorates

Valerie A. Storey

The number of professional doctorates in the United States, the United Kingdom, Australia, and New Zealand has skyrocketed in the past 50 years (Adams, Bondy, Ross, Dana, & Kennedy-Lewis, 2014; Kot & Hendel, 2012; Zusman, 2013). Doctoral education is becoming more collaborative on a global scale as ease of communication, sharing of data, and physical mobility has improved drastically in recent decades (European University Association, 2013). What seems like a diffuse landscape for the provision of doctoral education is actually driven by strong currents of convergence in which the same issues can be seen across different continents. However, how these issues are addressed tends to be contextually based and influenced by factors such as cultural history, politics, and economics (Kot & Hendel, 2012; Zusman, 2013).

Doctoral education has taken a new direction, incorporating a varied landscape as PhDs are being challenged to reinvent themselves. An observable trend in some countries has been the design of new doctoral degree programs, referred to as professional doctorates, applied doctorates, practitioner doctorates, or clinical doctorates in various disciplines (Kot & Hendel, 2012; Zusman, 2013). The degrees include, among others, the doctor of education (EdD), doctor of psychology (PsyD), doctor of engineering (EngD), doctor of music art (DMA), doctor of dental surgery (DDS), doctor of juridical science (SJD), and doctor of public health (DPH). The world of academia is no longer the distant "ivory tower." Rather it is seeking to place itself very firmly at the core of knowledge creation and application in practice. In summarizing characteristics of professional doctorates and PhD programs, Kot and Hendel (2012) conclude that professional doctorates are varied and elude a standard definition.

The purpose of this book is to enable critical friends acting on an international stage to collaborate, enhance capacity, and explicitly describe the international agenda relating to doctoral programs and the manner in which it is evidenced in their countries. Chapter authors highlight the increased recognition of the importance of doctoral education, while doctoral level of study continues to be the subject of debate, discussion, study, amendments, revision, and restructuring. Common issues identified include the purpose of the various doctoral programs, entry requirements, program outcomes, skills to be demonstrated, and career possibilities of graduate; of course, underpinning all discussion is the concern as to how in this varied mix we ensure quality: the quality of the students, research, the capstone produced, the examiners, and the examination process, as well as the quality of the supervisors and supervision.

This book highlights the fact that in the second decade of the twenty-first century, doctorates are shifting shape. In America, the research and professional development undertaken through the Carnegie Foundation, specifically the work of the Carnegie Project on the Education Doctorate (CPED), saw the development of a professional practice education doctorate for education professionals and the PhD as more a pathway to a career in the academy. The professional doctorate in the United Kingdom continues to grow while the situation in Australia is in flux. The PhD also seems to be morphing. The irony is that while doctoral design work in North America has as a motivational drive, in Europe the design of the structured PhD, the professional PhD, and the interdisciplinary PhD is in fact converging with rather than diverging from professional doctorates in a desire to differentiate the PhD from the EdD.

By adding nuanced complexity to the issue of doctoral program design, the authors in this book seek to identify trends and challenges to those involved in doctoral programs and to provide guideposts for future research, policy, and practice.

Critical Friends

Critical to organizational change and program (re)design are changes in mindset and practices (Fullan, 2001; Gardner, 2006; Leithwood, Harris, & Strauss, 2010). Experienced faculty working in collaborative settings involving trust, access to information, and collective norms to accomplish agreed goals create the potential for changing organizational mindset through the generation of intellectual capital (Nahapiet & Ghoshal, 1998). The reciprocal exchange of knowledge that occurs in a socially bounded group can lead to new understandings, alternative viewpoints, co-construction of new knowledge, and, ultimately, mindset change.

A central theme of *Redesigning Professional Education Doctorates: Application of Critical Friendship Theory to the EdD* is the concept of critical friends in fostering trust among students, faculty, and stakeholders as they contribute to constructive dialogue that provides the basis for continuous improvement.

In the foreword, Sanders, Program Leader for the Professional Doctorate, University of Sunderland, United Kingdom, highlights the importance of critical friends from around the world sharing their experiences and suggests that this may just be the start of a growing community of critical friends who can help transform doctoral education to meet the modern challenges that our society faces.

In chapter 1, "Critical Friends and the Evolving Terminal Degree," Storey and Reardon provide an overview of professional practice doctorates in the United States. First, they explore the knowledge creation path and the knowledge incorporation path, which lead to the final destination of contributing to the knowledge-based economy. Second, they turn their attention to the evolution of doctoral program structure in the United States and Europe, and the program's unique role in knowledge creation and knowledge incorporation. Third, they examine the role of Critical Friend Groups (CFGs) in facilitating change in terminal degree programs by focusing on the improvement science approach. They conclude the chapter by suggesting that society in general and the academy specifically need to acknowledge that there may be an element of academic elitism involved in the consideration of those who create knowledge and those who incorporate knowledge. This thought-provoking chapter sets the stage for the remaining chapters in the book.

The next three chapters are authored by scholars in Australasia. Chapter 2, "Psychology and Medicine Professional Doctorates in New Zealand and Australia: Context of Development and Characteristics," by Mpofu moves the reader from a global issue to a specific issue focused on psychology and medical professional doctorates in New Zealand and Australia. Given the close geographical, economic, and sociopolitical ties between these countries, Mpofu argues that a cross-country case study methodology seeking to identify the characteristics of these professional doctorates will add a new dimension to scholarship in this subject.

Chapters 3 and 4 focus specifically on professional practice doctorates in Australia. First, Malloch in "Trends in Doctoral Education in Australia" describes how Australia took a lead in the 1990s by contributing ideas and models for professional doctorates and influencing England in particular. The focus then shifts to the impact of national government policy goals, which has resulted in strands of doctoral study, the PhD, and the professional doctorate becoming entwined and blurred. From interviews with course leaders and program graduates and from participant observation as a practitioner leading postgraduate education programs, Malloch concludes that Australia is now moving away from professional doctorates to a more generic PhD, which draws upon the professional doctorate. In chapter 4, "Australian EdDs: At a Crossroad?," Maxwell further unpacks the current doctoral landscape in Australia. He articulates the outcome of conversations with EdD program coordinators and examines EdD websites and programs to identify the state of play of the EdD and what the future might hold for their program.

In chapter 5, "Professional Doctorate as a Means to Impacting Practice: Reflections from Critical Friends in New Zealand," Smythe, Rolfe, and Larmer take a philosophical approach to professional doctorate program design. They highlight how critical friends from across health disciplines (midwifery, nursing, and physiotherapy) and countries (New Zealand and the United Kingdom) have sparked insights related to doctoral education for health professionals by exploring the nature of thinking that integrates the process of learning, scholarship, and practice development. The authors suggest that there is a moral imperative to reclaim and reassert a mode of doctoral education for health care professionals that privileges thinking and asserts the primary function of research as making a real and substantive difference in the local context of practice.

Chapters 6 and 7 transition the reader from Australasia to the United Kingdom by outlining current doctoral program design issues in England and Ireland. In chapter 6, "Redesigning the EdD at the Institute of Education, London, England: Thoughts of the Incoming EdD Program Leader," Hawkes and Taylor focus on their experience as program leaders of an EdD that draws students from around the world. They describe how recent program innovation has increasingly blurred the line between PhD and EdD students in an attempt to enhance the EdD recognition as a valid route to a doctorate. Hawkes and Taylor explore the motivation of this move to promote the integration of the education professional practice doctorate (EdD) students within the wider research student body (PhD) and the potential gains and losses of such an approach. In chapter 7, "A Different Practice? Professional Identity and Doctoral Education in Art and Design in England," Taylor and Vaughan examine the relationship between the PhD and the professional practice doctorate by focusing on a specific subject domain (i.e., art and design). They argue that the ethos underpinning the professional doctorate in art and design is in fact encapsulated in the very nature of the art and design PhD. They conclude that art and design doctoral study and the professional doctorate in other disciplines can play the role of critical friends to one another, stimulating reflections of the self within the other in relation to concepts of professionalism, practice, identity, and cohorts.

Chapters 8 to 13 highlight critical friends theory as an appropriate strategy to facilitate change. In chapter 8, "Pedagogical Strategy Design and Positioning of Practitioner Doctorates: Grounding Business Practice in Subjectivism and First-Person Research in an Irish Institution," the reader is required to cross the Irish Sea from the British mainland (chapters 6 and 7) to Ireland. Doyle provides a detailed summary of the theory and practices underpinning the pedagogy of the practitioner doctorate at the School of Economics, University College Cork, Ireland. The approach outlined is grounded in the areas of subjectivism, foundations of business growth, and first-person research. Doyle highlights the role of CFGs as fundamental to scaffolding the change process through which engagement and transformation of faculty mindset and program design unfold. Nikolou-Walker in chapter 9, "Postgraduate Work-Based Learning for 'Nontraditional' Learners: Focused across All Four UK Regions," also applies critical friends theory to support the design of innovative professional practice in postgraduate study in work-based learning (WBL) education. The intention is to dissolve the traditional boundaries between the workplace, higher education, and doctoral studies by developing high-quality learning opportunities within a university context. The focus of the chapter is on the small number of postgraduate university WBL programs across all four UK regions that cater to such nontraditional learners. While postgraduate WBL has previously been the object of both analysis and critique, this chapter's objective involves undertaking empirical study into the specific case of postgraduate WBL for nontraditional learners. Readers of this chapter will want to consider the relationship between WBL and professional practice doctorates particularly as programs move to individualized or personalized learning.

In chapter 10, "Transforming Doctoral Leadership Program Design through Cross-National Dialog," Kochhar-Bryant focuses the reader's attention on the United States and Israel. She examines a new EdD program initiative for educational leaders resulting from a dialogue between the United States and Israeli critical friends. The redesigned framework emphasizes development of leaders and inquiry as practice in authentic settings. Candidates are challenged to (1) define an educational "identity"; (2) reflect on their capacity to attack complex education policies; and (3) explore their commitment to seek imaginative solutions to today's challenges.

In chapter 11, "The Transition from Discipline-Based Scholarship to Interdisciplinarity: Implications for Faculty," Pulla and Schissel focus on a challenge that many of us in Canada face as we develop transdisciplinary doctorates: the complexity of faculty transitioning from discipline-based scholarship to interdisciplinarity. They explore the implications of this transition for faculty research, faculty evaluation, and faculty professional development. In addition, they note that such a transition has profound implications for pedagogical approaches. Not only do faculty have to meet the requirements of online pedagogy, but there is the additional complexity of a shift in response to interdisciplinary teaching and learning. This chapter also focuses on career implications including research funding, research development, and the role of critical friends in program dissemination, colleague approval, colleague collaboration, and internal university acknowledgment. In addition, it explores pedagogical implications for faculty including teacher satisfaction, skill development, student–teacher challenges, and transformative approaches to doctoral supervision.

In chapter 12, "Dissertation in Practice: Reconceptualizing the Nature and Role of the Practitioner-Scholar," Storey and Maughan ask whether an EdD degree in United States can be designed in a way that is indicative and reflective of contemporary thought as a practical degree embedded with professional practice, such as the case of a medical doctor or lawyer. They note that many innovative (re)designed professional practice EdDs have been driven by improvement science, particularly in redefining the scope of the professional practice–based degree's culminating exercise. Small CFGs working within the Improvement Science Research Network have developed theoretical frameworks and models in which problem-driven solutions are sought. This chapter attempts to answer two questions: "Is there a 'best' model for a dissertation in practice?" and "Is there evidence of an alignment between dissertations in practice and the guiding working principles of consortia, such as the Carnegie Project for the Education Doctorate (http://cpedinitiative.org), that are influential in moving to reconceptualize the nature and role of the practitioner-scholar?"

In chapter 13, "Critical Friendship as a Pedagogical Strategy," Smith, Wood, Lewis, and Burgess outline an action research project in England in which strategies to develop EdD students' critical writing and peer reviewing skills, by being engaged with students in a process of peer assessment, were trialed. They consider the implications of the project for professional practice doctorate program design and apply the critical friends approach to the EdD and beyond.

In the concluding chapter of the book, "Indigenizing the EdD in New Zealand: Te Puna Wānanga EdD," Bol Jun Lee describes the inaugural Māori- and indigenous-focused EdD program launched at Te Puna

Wānanga (TPW, School of Māori Education), Faculty of Education, at the University of Auckland, New Zealand. She explains how "indigenizing" an EdD program is not just about growing a critical mass of Māori and indigenous students in a cohort-based program; rather, it requires a culturally located pedagogy that includes an indigenous theoretical framework and analysis. In the spirit of a critical friends approach, this chapter seeks to explain the indigenizing nature and aim of the TPW EdD, as well as contribute to understanding the wider educational space, of which the EdD is a part, from an indigenous lens.

In the epilogue, Holley highlights the importance of this edited volume in collecting information on the range of doctoral programs globally and in revealing how the forces of globalization are influencing multiple higher education systems. She offers three lessons learned from this global examination of the doctorate: (1) A changing social, economic, and political culture requires changes to the ways in which higher education institutions structure and deliver a curriculum. (2) Innovations should be sensitive to the local, institutional, and national contexts, although these variations make it a challenge to define the degree and wholly grasp its impact. (3) An application of the critical friends approach requires recognition of multiple communities of practice, including the profession that supports the degree. Holley concludes by suggesting that the biggest challenge facing doctoral education in the future is maintaining the integrity of the degree while being open to innovation, change, and new directions.

References

Adams, A., Bondy, E., Ross, D. D., Dana, N. F., & Kennedy-Lewis, B. (2014). Implementing an online professional practice doctoral program in a PhD environment: Managing the dilemmas. *Journal of School Public Relations, 35*(Summer), 363–382.

European University Association. (2013). Annual Report. Retrieved from http://www.eua.be/Home.aspx

Fullan, M. (2001). *Leading in a culture of change*. San Francisco: Jossey-Bass.

Gardner, H. (2006). *Multiple intelligences: New horizons*. New York: BasicBooks.

Kot, F. C., & Hendel, D. D. (2012). Emergence and growth of professional doctorates in the United States, United Kingdom, Canada, and Australia: A comparative analysis. *Studies in Higher Education, 37*(3), 345–364.

Leithwood, K., Harris, A., & Strauss, T. (2010). *Leading school turn-around: How successful leaders transform low-performing schools*. San Francisco: Jossey-Bass.

Nahapiet, J., & Ghoshal, S. (1998). Social capital, intellectual capital, and the organizational advantage. *Academy of Management Review, 23*(2), 242–266.

Zusman, A. (2013). *How new kinds of professional doctorates are changing higher education institutions*. Research & Occasional Paper Series: 8.13. University of California, Berkeley: Center for Studies in Higher Education.

1

Critical Friends and the Evolving Terminal Degree

Valerie A. Storey and R. Martin Reardon

Doctoral level programs (known in the United Kingdom as "level 8," in Australia as "level 10," and within the European area's Bologna Agreement as "third cycle") make possible an institution's capacity to produce innovative research and new knowledge (Holley, 2013). The focus on innovative research fuels an emphasis on creativity in research, which Walsh, Anders, Hancock, and Elvidge (2011) juxtaposed against the focus on impact—especially in the "'strategically important' science, technology, engineering and mathematics (STEM) disciplines" (p. 1260). The current international policy debate on higher education and more specifically the doctoral program is delineated by two paths—the knowledge creation path and the knowledge incorporation path—both of which lead to the final destination of contributing to the knowledge-based economy. Our decision to juxtapose knowledge creation against knowledge incorporation dynamically recognizes the changing doctoral landscape and the evolving relationship between societal needs and doctoral programs.

Juxtaposing knowledge creation against knowledge incorporation invokes the utilization of research to inform applications of research to practice. In choosing the word incorporation, we also intentionally allude to the corporatization and/or commercialization of the benefits of the knowledge creation process in the course of such application. To a great extent the two "paths" are complementary and, as such, contribute to confusion both within the academy and among participants in doctoral programs. The two paths are further confounded by the fact that the awarding of doctoral status is intrinsically linked to the history of universities which has contextually determined the varying paths taken in Europe, Australia, and North America.

In this chapter we first explore the knowledge creation path and the knowledge incorporation path, which lead to the final destination of contributing to the knowledge-based economy. Second, we explore the evolution of the doctoral program structure in the United States and Europe, and the program's unique role in knowledge creation and knowledge incorporation. Third, we examine the role of Critical Friend Groups (CFGs) in facilitating change in terminal degree programs by focusing on the improvement science approach. Finally, we conclude the chapter by suggesting that society in general and the academy in particular need to acknowledge that there may be an element of academic elitism involved in the consideration of those who create knowledge and those who incorporate knowledge.

The Knowledge Pathway

The traditional view is that the creation of new knowledge is the raison d'être of a PhD program. The PhD program prepares students for an academic career in the sense that students do research: theorize a topic, review the literature, collect data, analyze the collected data, and write up the dissertation. Therefore, the university shows a commitment to the creation of knowledge, as well as academic and research training. The researcher is, in essence, separate and remote from practice with the locus of enquiry being within the university. But, particularly in the twenty-first century, it would be problematic to generalize this description to all PhD programs. In England, for example, PhD programs now provide a wide array of training for doctoral students, which includes transferable skills that are more oriented toward the needs of the market than the academy (Park, 2007). As a consequence, the locus of enquiry has transitioned from the academy to the profession or organization, thereby characterizing the PhD as knowledge incorporation rather than knowledge creation.

The 2010 position paper from the League of European Research Universities (LERU; Bogle, Dron, Eggermont, & van Henten, 2010) substantiates the characterization of academic research that we are invoking. Writing on behalf of LERU, Bogle et al. state that the "prime function of leading-edge research is to develop new understanding and the creative people who will carry it into society" (p. 2). In this endeavor, they declare, the "seed corn" of basic research, facilitated by "the best talents of the rising generation and the creative influence of the irreverent young" (p. 2), culminates in the "modern doctorate" which provides "excellent training for those who go into roles beyond research and education, in the public, charitable and private sectors" (p. 3). This engagement in "the business of research and innovation in the knowledge economy," Bogle et al. claim, is vital to Europe's objective "to become the most competitive and dynamic knowledge-based economy in the world" (Lisbon European Council, 2000, Strategic goal, para. 5).

We contend that appropriately preparing creative PhD graduates to carry research into society (Bogle et al., 2010) implicates many of the epistemological stances traditionally associated with the professional doctorate (PD). For example, knowledge incorporation in PD programs is driven by "real world" and "real time" imperatives (Costley, 2013; Murphy, 2014a; Murphy, 2014b; Storey & Richard, 2013). Program candidates have dual postionality: (1) a doctoral program cohort and (2) a specific role within their work context. Further, they sustain a duality of identity: (1) practitioner in the field and (2) scholar in the academy. This duality influences knowledge incorporation as conceptualized in Schön's (1983) view of the interdependence of knowledge and practice with each enriching the other.

To further investigate the apparent increasing overlap in program design between PhDs and PDs, an ongoing research project in the United Kingdom and Australia is currently exploring the nature of doctorates (Costley, 2013). The research is specifically focused on the status and knowledge contributions of PhD and PD researchers, the kinds of knowledge they deal with, and how their doctoral learning is recognized in communities other than the academy. The researchers reported overlap between different doctoral programs but found that, generally, PDs provide a way of addressing knowledge that is to an extent outside disciplinary cultures, and that offers alternative views and values that resonate with practice, thereby engaging higher education more coherently with learning at work.

Knowledge-Based Economy

In terms of the knowledge-based economy, in 2002, the World Bank, reflecting that it was "commonly viewed as supporting only basic education" (p. xviii), declared its aspiration to "apply its extensive knowledge base and financial resources toward increased efforts in the tertiary education sector" (p. xxxi). This apparent change of policy was driven by a belief that "knowledge accumulation and application have become major factors in economic development and are increasingly at the core of a country's competitive advantage in the global economy" (p. xvii).

Consistent with the Lisbon European Council (2000) goal-setting, many changes in Europe have been driven by the imperative to secure Europe's place in the knowledge economy. For example, a decade ago,

Table 1.1   Identified Problem Issues

The place of doctoral studies in the overall structure of programs offered by higher
education institutions.
The status of persons undertaking studies and research leading to doctoral qualifications:
Are they still students, or already researchers?
The role of institutions other than those of higher education, bearing in mind that in a
number of countries doctoral qualifications can also be earned in academies of science
or other research organizations—including the evaluation of doctoral degrees and
qualifications obtained abroad.
The procedures for the award of doctoral qualifications, and the role of external bodies in
validating them.
The costs of the research generally required for the award of doctoral qualifications.

Source: CEPES (2004). Studies on higher education.

the United Nations Educational, Scientific and Cultural Organization's
(UNESCO) Center Européen pour l'Enseignment Supérieur (CEPES)
and the Elias Foundation of the Romanian Academy (2004) initiated
a project leading to the International Seminar on Doctoral Degrees
and Qualifications in the Contexts of the European Higher Education
Area. Thirteen national case studies, Austria, France, Germany, Italy, the
Netherlands, Norway, Poland, Romania, the Russian Federation, Spain,
Sweden, the United Kingdom, and the United States, were commissioned and analyzed in detail. The analysis (see Table 1.1) describes general trends, legal and institutional arrangements, and specific program
problems.

Changes in Formal Structures of Doctoral Education

The CEPES (2004) analysis highlighted a trend, among the case study
countries, of developing a relatively formal structure for doctoral education, including abolishing the traditional "apprenticeship model" (consisting of a professorial supervisor and independent research) in favor of more
structured research education and training within disciplinary or interdisciplinary programs or graduate schools, thereby reducing the duration of
doctoral education, reducing dropout rates, and providing more targeted
research training. Typically, the changes include course work plus a plan
for undertaking supervised research for a thesis.

The change to a more structured model has not gone uncontested.
For example, Wastl-Walter and Wintzer (2012) reference student unrest
in particularly the German-speaking universities in autumn 2009.
Protestors objected to both the formalization of education and its market orientation—changes that Wastl-Walter and Wintzer characterized

as "valuing the commodification of learning driven by economic forces rather than critical thinking skills" (p. 36). Today, both traditional and formal systems of doctoral education exist in parallel in some European countries (e.g., Germany, Austria, Russia, Poland, Italy, and Norway). The CEPES (2004) study found that many of the case study countries were redesigning their degree structures, with the shape of the doctoral program being dependent on whether the master's degree included a research option. For programs preceded by a research option, the taught elements of doctoral studies (or some part of them) were waived. CEPES also identified an emerging distinction between research doctorates and professional doctorates (e.g., in the United Kingdom, Austria, and the United States) and highlighted the problem of definition and distinction in most countries in terms of the role of research training in doctoral education.

From a broader perspective, Boud and Lee (2009) discerned a shift from "postgraduate education" in the decade or so preceding their edited volume to "doctoral education" as the "organizing idea" (p. 1) underpinning the education of participants in doctoral programs. They portrayed this shift in organizing the idea as contributing to clarity about the purpose of doctoral programs—specifically, as to whether the primary focus is the products of the participant's research endeavors or the graduation of a licensed researcher. The majority of Boud and Lee's contributing authors responded from Australia (16), followed by England (8), Canada (3), with one each from Slovakia (by way of Belgium) and the United States. (The sole contributor from the United States highlighted the Carnegie Initiative on the Doctorate [CID], which will be discussed shortly.) The range of disciplinary perspectives included archaeology, architecture, astronomy, immunology, medicine and health sciences, science and technology, social anthropology, rhetoric and writing, as well as a range of subfields of education (e.g., management, curriculum, and pedagogy). The above litany serves to substantiate that concerns regarding doctoral education exist in many fields, nor are they confined to the United States and countries under the European umbrella.

Green (2009) concludes Boud and Lee's (2009) volume by asserting that, from a global perspective, we are in a time of momentous change—partly driven by forces external to higher education, and partly driven by our own conviction that change is warranted. In terms of external forces, Boud and Lee in their introduction and Green in his conclusion refer to the change in the relationship between disciplinary knowledge production and knowledge production that transcends the conventional disciplinary boundaries, where the former corresponds to the Gibbons et al. (1994) "Mode 1" knowledge and the latter to their "Mode 2" knowledge. Green goes so far as to postulate the marginalization of the modern research university in the face of "the accelerated opening up of a new dynamic sociotechnical space of flows of knowledge, and new global networks of research and education" (p. 239).

The flows of knowledge and expansive networks envisaged by Green (2009) are exemplified in the European doctoral program discussed below. On a less radical scale, Jones (2009) characterized CID as engendering collaborative interdependence among traditional disciplinary fields. Walker, Golde, Jones, Bueschel, and Hutchins's (2008) expansive discussion of CID begins with an epigraph tentatively attributed to Will Rogers to the effect that failure to move with the times leads to being overrun by challenging circumstances. Writing in the context of doctoral training in clinical psychology, McFall (2006) put it succinctly in asserting that "we cannot continue to train doctoral students the same old way simply because we've always done things this way. If evolving circumstances render past approaches, no longer defensible or sustainable, then we must face this reality and deal with it forthrightly" (p. 23).

Long-standing, well-recognized challenges enumerated by Shulman, Golde, Bueschel, & Garabedian (2006) include (1) the high attrition rates in doctoral programs, coupled with the somewhat jaundiced perspective among the initially passionate participants who persist; (2) suboptimal opportunities for participants to grow in their proficiency in the field, partly accounting for the overall poor preparation for the full range of roles graduates will be expected to fill; (3) underrepresentation of women and minority participants in programs; and (4) exacerbating all of the aforementioned challenges, inadequate processes for evaluating the effectiveness of graduate education programs—leading to either complacency, denial, or a tendency to blame the participant.

In terms of the evolving circumstances highlighted by McFall (2006), newer challenges that Shulman et al.'s (2006) list includes (1) new technologies (in accord with Green's [2009] dynamic sociotechnical space of flows of knowledge); (2) global marketplace for scholars and scholarship (in accord with Green's [2009] global networks of research and education); (3) "borderlands between fields" where groundbreaking research is taking place; (4) greater salience to everyday issues being demanded of researchers; and (5) increasing pressures for accountability and shrinking public funding highlight issues of purpose, vision, and quality. Nearly a decade after Shulman et al.'s (2006) study, there is evidence of diversification in the structure of doctoral programs that have moved away from the traditional to a new-route PhD, and the professional practice doctorates (Jackson & Kelley, 2002; Murphy, 2006; Shulman, 2005; Storey & Richard, 2013; Walker et al., 2008).

European Doctoral Education Evolution

In the European arena, the transition from Bologna Process to the European Higher Education Area has encouraged a range of innovative doctorate programs to respond to the changing demands of a global labor market (European University Association, 2007). Despite doctoral program diversity, there is a degree of consistency, as the European University Association requires that original research remains the main component of all doctorates, and that no matter what their type or form they should be based on a core of processes and outcomes.

An example of innovative format and structure is the European Doctoral Program for the Human and Social Sciences developed in 2010 with five partner institutions—École des Hautes Études en Sciences Sociales and the École Pratique des Hautes Études in Paris, the Humboldt-Universität in Berlin, the Central European University in Budapest, and the Istituto Italiano di Scienze Umane in Florence—developed a PhD program which enables doctoral students engaged in the program to move from one academic institution to another and experience firsthand multifocal doctoral training. The doctoral students are enrolled in one of the partner institutions, but also work in the other institutions, each of which contributes a specific seminar module. The program requires four intensive rotations of six weeks between partnering institutions—rotating between the various partners' institutions—during the first two years on methodological and thematic issues. Students can spend the rest of the time where it is most convenient for their work, while the third year is mainly devoted to writing the doctoral thesis. The development of other curricula is foreseen for the future.

This interinstitutional, interdisciplinary doctoral program model holds promise that the dissertation might contribute to large-scale impact as it enables the doctoral student to (1) pursue a bespoke program instructed and mentored by professors in the field with an active research agenda; (2) accumulate knowledge across fields; (3) develop common interdisciplinary, interinstitutional, and international research agendas; and (4) facilitate a continuum of research on identified issues that are recognized by broad swaths of the field.

European Professional Practice Doctorates

The European University Association (EUA, 2007) defined professional doctorates or "practice related doctorates" as "doctorates that focus on embedding research in a reflective manner into another professional practice" (EUA, 2007, p. 14). The EUA requires that professional doctorates meet the same core standards as PhDs. Consequently, the professional practice doctorate continues to evolve from a first-generation model of course work plus dissertation to a second generation that is characterized by a learning environment focused on the facilitation of the learning of scholar-practitioners (Shulman et al., 2006). Scholar-practitioners thrive in a learning environment in which they collaborate with critical friends to identify problems of practice, discern appropriate responses, and evaluate the outcome of actions taken to address those problems—appropriately crafting the documentation of work into a dissertation (Archbald, 2008).

US Doctoral Program Evolution

Almost a century ago, in his study of engineering education, Mann (1918) developed statistics that were subsequently extrapolated into the oft-cited assertion that 85% of an individual's job success is related to interpersonal skills and only 15% is related to technical knowledge. While not wishing to invest inordinate confidence in these percentages, figures such as these align with the putative benefit of education in how to lead change. One evolutionary step in the context of a professional practice doctorate program (outlined subsequently by way of example) grounds the development of educational leaders in the real world of education by engaging program participants as critical friends. This innovative approach privileges relevance to practice (Gutiérrez & Penuel, 2014) by casting program participants from early stages of their program as critical friends who collaborate with small groups of teachers in a selected school to address high-leverage problems of practice of mutual interest.

Critical Friendship

In overview, this informal school–university collaborative research initiative accords with the analogy that Costa and Kallick (1993) drew between critical friendship and the dialog that transpires during a visit to the ophthalmologist: the ophthalmologist is unable to know which set of lenses he or she interposes in the client's line of sight represents an improvement until the client replies to the "better or worse" query. Similarly, the critical friend, although familiar with similar situations from his or her experiential base, relies on the feedback from the "befriended" (Swaffield, 2005, p. 44) to guide the trajectory of the dialog. The doctoral program participants bring "the enlightened eye of accumulated wisdom" (Reardon & Shakeshaft, 2013) from their prior practice in similar situations, but would be unwise to project from their experience into the contexts of the teachers with whom they collaborate in the absence of the continual feedback from the teachers. Thus, the collaboration between the doctoral program participants and the teachers benefits the school from the sounding board of critical friendship among the teachers and the doctoral program participants as the teachers elaborate on their perspectives of the problem of practice. The learning of the doctoral program participants is enriched as they change the lenses through which teachers view the problem of practice and learn from the teachers' feedback (Andreu, Canós, de Juana, Manresa, Rienda, & Tarí, 2003). The intended outcome is the conduct of action-oriented research in which collaborative teams apply the concepts of improvement science in the conduct of multiple plan-do-study-act cycles.

Critical Friendship and Improvement Science

Law (2005) raises the question of whether a school as an institution can be moral. He answers this question in the affirmative, and highlights the role of CFGs in assisting "moral leaders to create moral schools" (p. 53). CFGs, Law suggests, constitute "vehicles for creating collective intentionality that reaches a shared end: increased opportunity for the disadvantaged to create equality of opportunity" (p. 56). He typifies collective intentionality as representing "a collective end to which each teacher contributes individual decisions" (p. 54). Law distinguishes collective intentionality both from coordinated activity (e.g., alignment of teachers' actions with a centrally issued timetable for classes) and from an aggregate of individual intentionality (individual teachers' moral actions may not be directed toward a collectively determined end). He proposes that the CFG is a vehicle for engaging stakeholders in the determination of moral purpose for an institution that is explicit about the agreements upon which it was founded, and that will "both shape and reflect individual thinking and practices" (p. 57).

There are many drivers of the evolution of the terminal degree (Golde & Walker, 2006; Murphy, 2014a; Murphy, 2014b; Walker et al., 2008). The contributors to Storey (2013) catalog many ways in which CFGs have been implemented in order to facilitate change in terminal degree programs. The improvement science approach (Langley et al., 2009) offers a blueprint of how CFGs can collaborate with leaders of change in institutions to ensure that, in the course of several iterative cycles, change is improvement. Bryk, Gomez, and Grunow (2011) have shown the feasibility of adopting an improvement science approach in confronting persistent problems related to developmental mathematics courses in the community college

environment at the national level. The Carnegie Project on the Education
Doctorate (http://cpedinitiative.org/) continues to refine an implementation of improvement science approach to the redesign of the doctor of
education (EdD) among some 87 university programs.

The Whole Cloth

The role of critical friend embraces a wide range of scales in the refine-
ment of terminal degree programs. The tendency for graduate programs
to steadfastly keep on doing what they have always done has been acer-
bically highlighted by Grafton and Grossman (2011) who observed that
"graduate programs have proved achingly reluctant to see the world as it
is" (para. 11). While this malaise seems particularly ironic in Grafton and
Grossman's field of history, it appears to be quite pervasive. For example,
the Council of Graduate Schools and Educational Testing Service (CGS &
ETS, 2012) lamented the finding that "very few employers indicated that
they collaborate with graduate schools or programs regarding the development of or revisions to courses or curriculum" (p. 11).

At the policy level, the imperative for change in how doctoral education is conducted is driven by a clear call for both knowledge creation
and knowledge incorporation. Casting the Council of Graduate Schools
and Educational Testing Service (CGS & ETS, 2010) in the role of critical
friend to the graduate education community, there is credit given to "some
U.S. universities [that] have adopted policies and practices designed to
enhance their role in transforming our society [by a focus] on conducting
use-inspired research" (p. 42). CGS and ETS give equal prominence to the
imperative to prepare future faculty as well as future professionals. They
conceded that "doctoral education has not typically included a strong
professional development component" (p. 43). Recent CGS and ETS
(2010, 2012) reports highlight the Vitae program, which has been active
in the United Kingdom since 1968 in supporting the transition of doctoral
researchers to industry (https://www.vitae.ac.uk/about-us) as a model.
Without in any way diminishing the rigor of the doctoral degree, to be
globally competitive, CGS and ETS suggest that universities "encourage the
development of skills that enhance research impact" (2010, p. 45). Another
collaboration of critical friends, The Conference Board, the Partnership
for 21st Century Skills, Corporate Voices for Working Families, and the
Society for Human Resource Management (Casner-Lotto & Barrington,
2006) has defined the requisite skills as including "(a) professionalism and
work ethic, (b) oral and written communication, (c) teamwork and collaboration, (d) critical thinking and problem solving, (e) ethics and social
responsibility" (CGS & ETS, 2012, p. 8).

A sense of the extent of the change in perception which may be required at the individual program level to implement such a globally competitive approach is indicated by a recent study of doctoral-level biomedical science graduates—a field in which academic positions for the increasing number of PhD-trained scientists are scarce. Fuhrmann, Halme, O'Sullivan, and Lindstaedt (2011) referred to those graduates "who have pursued paths outside of academia" as being considered as "leaks" from the pipeline (p. 239). According to Fuhrmann et al., these "leaks" are considered "outside the norm and represent failures within the system" (p. 239). To conclude this introductory chapter in an appropriately enigmatic fashion, we dare to suggest that there may be an element of academic elitism involved in the consideration of those who incorporate knowledge as potential pipeline "leaks," and representing "failures within the system." The Fuhrmann et al. characterization of the situation in biomedical science calls to mind Gardner's (1984) assertion that

> the society that scorns excellence in plumbing because plumbing is a humble activity and tolerates shoddiness in philosophy because it is an exalted activity will have neither good plumbing nor good philosophy: neither its pipes nor its theories will hold water. (p. 86)

References

Andreu, R., Canós, L., de Juana, S., Manresa, E., Rienda, L., & Tarí, J. J. (2003). Critical friends: A tool for quality improvement in universities. *Quality Assurance in Education, 11*(1), 31–36.

Archbald, D. (2008). Research versus problem solving for the educational leadership doctoral thesis: Implications for form and function. *Educational Administration Quarterly, 44*(5), 704–739. doi:10.1177/0013161X07313288

Bogle, D., Dron, M., Eggermont, J., & van Henten, J. W. (2010, March). *Doctoral degrees beyond 2000: Training talented researchers for society* (Position Paper). League of European Research Universities. Retrieved from http://www.leru.org/files/publications/LERU_Doctoral_degrees_beyond_2010.pdf

Boud, D., & Lee, A. (Eds.). (2009). *Changing practices of doctoral education.* London: Routledge.

Bryk, A. S., Gomez, L. M., & Grunow, A. (2011). *Getting ideas into action: Building networked improvement communities in education* (Essay). Stanford, CA: Carnegie Foundation for the Advancement of Teaching.

Casner-Lotto, J., & Barrington, L. (2006). *Are they really ready to work?.* Retrieved from http://www.p21.org/storage/documents/FINAL_REPORT_PDF09-29-06.pdf

Center Européen pour l'Enseignment Supérieur (CEPES). (2004). *Studies on higher education. Doctoral studies and education in Europe and the United States: Status and prospectus.* Bucharest: UNESCO-CEPES.

Costa, A. L., & Kallick, B. (1993). Through the lens of a critical friend. *Educational Leadership, 51*(2), 49–51.

Costley, C. (2013). Evaluation of the current status and knowledge contributions of professional doctorates. *Quality in Higher Education, 19*(1), 7–27. Retrieved from http://eprints.mdx.ac.uk/11307/

Council of Graduate Schools and Educational Testing Service. (2010). *The path forward: The future of graduate education in the United States. Report from the Commission on the Future of Graduate Education in the United States.* Princeton, NJ: Educational Testing Service.

Council of Graduate Schools and Educational Testing Service. (2012). *Pathways through graduate schools and into careers. Report from the Commission on Pathways through Graduate School and into Careers.* Princeton, NJ: Educational Testing Service.

European University Association. (2007). *Doctoral programmes in Europe's universities: Achievements and challenges.* Brussels, Belgium: EUA Publications.

Fuhrmann, C. N., Halme, D. G., O'Sullivan, P. S., & Lindstaedt, B. (2011). Improving graduate education to support a branching career pipeline: Recommendations based on a survey of doctoral students in the basic biomedical sciences. *CBE-Life Sciences Education, 10*(3), 239–249. doi:10.1187/cbe.11-02-0013

Gardner, J. W. (1984). *Excellence. Can we be equal and excellent too?* (Rev. ed.). New York, NY: W. W. Norton.

Gibbons, M., Limoges, C., Nowotny, H., Schwartzman, S., Scott, P., & Trow, M. (1994). *The new production of knowledge: The dynamics of science and research in contemporary societies.* London: Sage.

Golde, C. M., & Walker, G. E. (2006). *Envisioning the future of doctoral education: Preparing stewards of the discipline.* San Francisco, CA: Jossey Bass.

Grafton, A. T., & Grossman, J. (2011). *No more Plan B: A very modest proposal for graduate programs in history.* Retrieved from http://www.historians.org/perspectives/issues/2011/1110/1110pre1.cfm

Green, B. (2009). Challenging perspectives, changing practices: Doctoral education in transition. In D. Boud & A. Lee (Eds.), *Changing practices of doctoral education* (pp. 239–248). London: Routledge.

Gutiérrez, K. D., & Penuel, W. R. (2014). Relevance to practice as a criterion for rigor. *Educational Researcher, 43*(1), 19–23. doi:10.3102/0013189X13520289

Holley, K. A. (2013). Doctoral education and the development of an interdisciplinary identity. *Innovations in Education and Teaching International.* Taylor & Francis Online. http://dx.doi.org/10.1080/14703297.2013.847796

Jackson, B., & Kelley, C. (2002). Exceptional and innovative programs in educational leadership. *Educational Administration Quarterly, 38*(2), 192–212. doi:10.1177/0013161X02382005

Jones, L. (2009). Converging paradigms for doctoral training in the sciences and humanities. In D. Boud & A. Lee (Eds.), *Changing practices of doctoral education* (pp. 29–41). London: Routledge.

Langley, G. J., Moen, R. D., Nolan, K. M., Nolan, T. W., Norman, C. L., & Provost, L. P. (2009). *The improvement guide.* San Francisco, CA: Jossey-Bass.

Law, B. (2005). Creating moral schools: The enabling potential of critical friends groups. *Educational Horizons, 84*(1), 53–57.

Lisbon European Council. (2000, March 23–24). *Presidency conclusions.* Retrieved from http://www.europarl.europa.eu/summits/lis1_en.htm

Mann, C. R. (1918). *A study of engineering education* (pp. 106–107). Carnegie Foundation. Retrieved from http://www.carnegiefoundation.org/faqs/recently-read-somewhere-carnegie-foundation-report-said-85-persons-job-success-product-interpersonal-skills-15-success-result-technical-knowle/

McFall, R. M. (2006). Doctoral training in clinical psychology. *Annual Review of Clinical Psychology, 2,* 21–49. doi:0.1146/annurev.clinpsy.2.022305.095245

Murphy, J. (2006). *Preparing school leaders: An agenda for research and action.* Lantham, MD: Rowman and Littlefield Education.

Murphy, J. (2014a). Notes on the EdD/PhD discussion in the UCEA review: The essential question. *UCEA Review, 55*(1), 25–26.

Murphy, J. (2014b). Insights about the profession: Questionable norms and the marginalization of practice. *On the Horizon, 22*(3), 192–198.

Park, C. (2007). *Redefining the doctorate.* York: The Higher Education Academy.

Reardon, R. M., & Shakeshaft, C. (2013). Criterion-inspired, emergent design in doctoral education: A critical friends perspective. In V. Storey (Ed.), *Redesigning professional education doctorates: Applications of critical friendship theory to the EdD* (pp. 177–193). New York, NY: Palgrave Macmillan.

Schön, D. A. (1983). *The reflective practitioner: How professionals think in action.* New York: Basic Books.

Shulman, L. S. (2005). Signature pedagogies in the professions. *Daedalus, 134*(3), 52–59.

Shulman, L. S., Golde, C. M., Bueschel, A. C., & Garabedian, K. J. (2006). Reclaiming education's doctorate: A critique and a proposal. *Educational Researcher, 35*(3), 25–32. doi:10.3102/0013189X035003025

Storey, V. A. (Ed.). (2013). *Redesigning professional education doctorates: Applications of critical friendship theory to the EdD.* New York, NY: Palgrave Macmillan.

Storey, V. A., & Richard, B. (2013). Critical friend groups: Moving beyond mentoring. In V. A. Storey (Ed.), *Redesigning professional education doctorates: Applications of critical friendship theory to the EdD* (pp. 9–25). New York, NY: Palgrave Macmillan.

Swaffield, S. (2005). No sleeping partners: Relationships between head teachers and critical friends. *School Leadership & Management, 25*(1), 45–57.

Walker, G. E., Golde, C. M., Jones, L., Bueschel, A. C., & Hutchins, P. (2008). *The formation of scholars: Rethinking doctoral education for the twenty-first century.* San Francisco, CA: Jossey-Bass.

Walsh, E., Anders, K., Hancock, S., & Elvidge, L. (2011). Reclaiming creativity in the era of impact: Exploring ideas about creative research in science and engineering. *Studies in Higher Education, 38*(9), 1259–1273. doi:10.1080/03075079.2011.620091

Wastl-Walter, D., & Wintzer, J. (2012). Rethinking postgraduate education in Europe: Bologna and its implications for geography. *Journal of Geography in Higher Education, 36*(1), 35–41. doi:10.1080/03098265.2011.641115

2

Professional Doctorates in Psychology and Medicine in New Zealand and Australia: Context of Development and Characteristics

Charles Mpofu[1]

Introduction

Policy reforms and calls for the need to link university ends with national economic priorities in government reports of the 1990s–2000s provided a context for the subsequent proliferation of professional doctorates in New Zealand and Australia. In these two countries with a unique context of close geographical, economic, and sociopolitical ties, the professional doctorates in psychology and medicine have taken different forms in the development process (Zurn & Dumont, 2008). Given such a transnational context, it is argued that a cross-country case study methodology seeking to identify the characteristics of these professional doctorates will add a new dimension to scholarship in this subject. The findings of this study can be used as a platform for enquiry or discussion about other countries that have similar sociopolitical or geographical ties and health professional regulation mechanisms as is the case between Canada and the United States.

The chapter contributes to wider issues on professional doctorates that are discussed in this book and therefore adds to the critical friendship discourse. This is because the thinking around this study was that knowledge of different forms of professional doctorates in the international arena might inform the development of similar programs in other countries. Such a conception is consistent with the critical friendship theory that knowledge building is a community endeavor (Scardamalia & Bereiter, 2006).

Critical friendship groups in various countries need resources in the form of case studies from other contexts in order to develop innovative programs. The case of the characteristics of professional doctorates in psychology and medicine in New Zealand and Australia is even more important to countries such as the United States, United Kingdom, and Canada, as these countries often use one another for benchmarking health services including the utilization and training of the health workforce (Connell, 2010; Latham, 2010).

Background

The development and form of professional doctorates across health disciplines in New Zealand and Australia is embedded in the unique context of these two countries, mainly their proximity to each other and their sociopolitical policies which are intentionally made to strengthen the relationship. The development and form of these professional doctorates is also embedded in the context of the political and the immigration-friendly relationship of these countries with the United Kingdom and, to some extent, with the United States and Canada, two other Western English-speaking countries (Kot & Hendel, 2012). In terms of close relationships, New Zealand and Australia have qualifications that are harmonized through bilateral policies such as the provisions of the Trans-Tasman Mutual Recognition Act 1997. This Act provides for the recognition in New Zealand of regulatory standards adopted in Australia regarding goods and occupations; Australia too has a reciprocal legislation with the same title (Cook, 2009). This legislation in the two countries has a great influence on the health sector, for example, in the medical field it has strengthened the sharing of accreditation systems.

However, different population sizes, health funding systems, and political priorities in these countries have led to different higher education policies, which in turn reflected in the development of discipline-specific professional doctorates. For example, while in Australia, discipline-specific professional doctorates in health such as psychology and medicine have proliferated since the late 1990s, in New Zealand most professional doctorates are still new, being more a phenomenon of the late 1990s and the 2000s. Currently, Australia has at least seven health disciplines offering professional doctorates: podiatry, medicine, dentistry, nursing, psychology, physiotherapy, and occupational therapy. On the other hand, in New Zealand there are only three disciplines in the health profession that offer professional doctorates: dental science, medicine, and clinical psychology. The most commonly offered doctorates are in psychology and medicine. Furthermore, while in New Zealand the two universities with medical schools offer professional doctorates in medicine, the scenario is different in the psychology discipline. Among the six universities that offer undergraduate psychology courses, professional doctorates in psychology are offered in only two universities that started these programs as recently as 2004 (I. M. Evans & Fitzgerald, 2007; University, 2004).

Rationale

Despite the fact that New Zealand and Australia have close geographical and sociopolitical ties that extend to professional practice in the health sector, studies that have specifically examined health-practitioner doctorates as case studies in the wider group of professional doctorates in these two countries are scarce. Studies that have contributed relevant literature to the New Zealand and Australian context have tended to focus on examining professional doctorates from a number of disciplines (Kot & Hendel, 2012). Some studies have focused on professional doctorates that are transdisciplinary, such as the doctor of education (EdD) (Maxwell & Shanahan, 1997; Poultney, 2010), and some on one specific discipline in one country (Helmes, 2001). Furthermore, some of these studies have tended to include courtesy doctoral-level qualifications at the master's level but with the title "Doctor" (Maxwell, 2011). Such a situation has resulted in conclusions based on doctorates that are either generic or outside the definition of professional doctorates. This study therefore has a particular focus on two disciplines, which are both in the field of health and are offered in the two selected countries. This will involve a cross-country case study of the main characteristics of professional doctorates in psychology and medicine in New Zealand and Australia.

This study is "instrumental" because the unique situation of these health practitioner doctorates in New Zealand and Australia is examined not only for understanding this context but also to provide insight into other professional doctorates in the world such as the continued "critical friendship" discourse about EdD (Storey, 2013; Storey, Carter-Tellison, & Boerger, 2011). In this way the Trans-Tasman scenario of professional doctorates in psychology and medicine is studied in order to provide insight into other programs by examining some characteristics that could be useful in the critical friendship discourses about other professional doctorates.

The following questions guided the study:

1. What are the characteristics of professional doctorates in psychology and medicine offered in New Zealand and Australia?
2. What factors within each selected country, across these two countries, and beyond, influenced their development?
3. How do these doctorates reflect the hybrid curriculum of the profession, practice, and research?

The second of the above questions is answered in the section below in the context of development in Australia and New Zealand. The rest of the questions are answered under the sections that follow the detailed discussion on the methodology used in this study.

Definitions

It is important to start by defining a doctor of philosophy (PhD) because while discussing characteristics of professional doctorates in this work, reference will be made to it consistently. A PhD has been defined as a qualification

> awarded to a candidate who, having critically investigated and evaluated an approved topic resulting in an independent and original contribution to knowledge and demonstrated an understanding of research methods appropriate to the chosen field, has presented and defended a thesis, by oral examination, to the satisfaction of the examiners (Biggs, 2000, p. 1).

In terms of process in the above definition, the most defining characteristic of a PhD is independence of the candidate in contributing original knowledge. In the above definition there is also no mention of the contribution of knowledge to a specific discipline of field of practice. There is also no mention of structured guidance and the only safeguard for structure mentioned is the scholarly rigor in the execution of research methods.

On the other hand, a professional doctorate is said to be

> a program of research and advanced study which enables the candidate to make a significant contribution to knowledge and practice in their professional context (Council of Australian Deans and Directors of Graduate Studies, 2007, p. 1).

It can be seen that in the case of professional doctorates, significant contribution of knowledge happens in a specific context and to a field of practice. According to the above definitions, these are the two features that distinguish a professional doctorate from a PhD. Another feature of a professional doctorate that is not emphasized in the above definition is that it usually has coursework and follows a more structured program than a PhD.

There are, however, some features that are shared by a PhD and a professional doctorate. In the context of New Zealand and Australia, what is shared by the two qualifications is, firstly, that the two are awarded at the highest level of these two countries' qualification frameworks (i.e., level 10). Secondly, candidates in these qualifications "make a significant and original contribution to knowledge," although in the case of a professional doctorate knowledge is generated and applied in the context of practice. In Australia there are further specifications about what constitutes a professional doctorate. These specifications are that research for a doctoral program will last at least two years and constitute two-thirds or more of the qualification. It is further specified that the program of learning may include advanced coursework to enhance the student's capacity to make a significant contribution to knowledge in the discipline. In this case the purpose of the advanced coursework will be to support, but not replace, the research outcomes (Council of Australian Deans and Directors of Graduate Studies, 2007).

Context of the Development of Professional Doctorates in New Zealand and Australia

It is important that the reader has an understanding of the development of professional doctorates in Australia before looking at the New Zealand scene, because it is argued here that the Australian context was in part an influence on the New Zealand one. For this reason, it will therefore be seen that the Australian issues are discussed before the New Zealand ones, only in this section.

The two sub-sections that follow argue that the proliferation of professional doctorates in both New Zealand and Australia came about as a result of government reforms in these two countries. The Dawkins reforms (National Board of Employment Education and Training, 1989) and the Kemp White Paper report are discussed in relation to Australia. John Dawkins was a Federal Minister for Employment, Education and Training in Australia from 1987 to 1991 while David Kemp was a Minister for Education, Training and Youth Affairs from 1997 to 2001 in the same country. The Tertiary Education Advisory Commission reports of the early 2000s are discussed in relation to the development of professional doctorates in New Zealand.

Australia

In Australia, most scholarship contended that the Dawkins report and the Kemp White Paper report were critical in the development of professional doctorates (Kot & Hendel, 2012; Maxwell & Shanahan, 2001). The Dawkins report, of the Higher Education Council of the Australian Federal Government, recommended the introduction of "doctoral programs more suited to professional settings in fields such as engineering, accounting, law, education, and nursing" (National Board of Employment Education and Training, 1989, p. 28). What followed after this report was a relationship between the university, government, and industry, with funding being used as a catalyst to drive the reforms (Maxwell, Shanahan, & Green, 2001). The funding system which gave autonomy to universities to drive their budgets by seeking specialized markets for students could also have either had a direct effect or provided a context for the development of professional doctorates.

Indeed, in almost a decade after the Dawkins report in 1998, scholars like Lee, Green and Brennan (2000) indicated that the number of doctoral programs jumped from 2 at the time of the recommendation to 63 in 1998. Although there is little literature available about the growth of medical professional doctorates, it is known that by 1998, psychology had the fourth largest number of discipline-specific doctorates after education (Lee et al., 2000).

Changes in the health workforce demand and supply which resulted in the new demands for health services also resulted in the proliferation of professional doctorates in Australia. For example, the aging population and the accompanying challenges of dealing with chronic diseases led to the need to develop nurse roles in areas such as diabetes care, aged care, and cardiology. Such a development led to the need to train these professionals at higher levels—doctoral qualification. For example, in Australia one university justifies the development of the nursing doctorate in the following statement:

> As the nurse practitioner role continues to emerge across Australia, so too has the need to further extend the scholarly opportunities for, and contribution from, this advanced practice nursing workforce . . . [this doctorate is] designed for experienced, registered nurses who are seeking to extend their professional development. (University of Canberra, 2015)

Furthermore, scholars such as Taylor & Maxwell (2004) have traced the development of professional doctorates to a significant shift in the view about the role of the university. This was a situation whereby universities were to be aligned with the industries in order to meet the economic agenda of the country—a recommendation articulated in the Dawkins report (Dawkins, 1988). This report was significant because it influenced the themes of further government reports. One such report was that by the National Board of Employment, Education and Training (NBEET) in 1989—an agency that advised the government on issues related to education, employment, and training.

The NBEET made a specific recommendation to universities about the need for education stakeholder collaboration. Through the report on higher education courses and graduate studies, the NBEET recommended that the universities should develop professional degrees that accommodated the needs of professional boards, students, and the industry (Taylor & Maxwell, 2004). Such a reform was said to mark a new era of growth and opportunity for higher education institutions. These reforms had potentially significant benefits for all Australians through economic growth and individual prosperity—a reform called the "knowledge economy." This meant that the generation and exploitation of knowledge played a predominant role in the creation of wealth.

In the recommendation for collaboration, the most relevant part of the report went as follows:

> For too long the implicit model of preparation for future employment has been one in which the roles of educational institutions and industry have been viewed as discrete and largely unrelated. In the past, institutions generally have not paid much attention to employers' views about course design and content. On the other hand, employers have complained of a lack of relevance of courses to their needs, while taking little action to address the problem. . . . Now, however, institutions and employers are recognising the need for a more positive and constructive relationship (Dawkins, 1988, p. 66).

Links with industries were achieved through collaboration in the design of qualifications and the teaching of those qualifications. It was therefore in the above statements that a context was created for the proliferation of professional doctorates, or rather doctoral qualifications that were judged by universities as being relevant to the economy and specifically to the industry (McWilliam et al., 2002).

Another development was the formation of the Council for Business and/ or Higher Education Co-operation, an influential arm in the area of education and industry links, consisting of representatives of the Business Council of Australia. The relevant aims of this body in the development of professional doctorates were to improve cooperation between industry and higher education in research and other areas of mutual interest (Dawkins, 1988).

As has been said earlier, the Dawkins report also provided a framework for other reports that followed (T. Evans, 2000). These included the West Report (1998), the Green Paper entitled "New Knowledge, New Opportunities: a discussion paper on higher education research and research training" (Kemp, 1999b), and the resultant White Paper entitled "Knowledge and innovation: a policy statement on research and research training" (T. Evans, 2000; Kemp, 1999a). The Kemp White Paper report criticized the former report for basing the funding of universities on student numbers rather than the completion of the qualifications. Other results of the reports that came after the Dawkins (1988) report were the introduction of a funding formula based on the number of research students completing their degrees, research income, and research output (Kot & Hendel, 2012), with completions being allocated 50%. This funding formula can provide a good context for professional doctorates as they are more structured than PhDs and as the didactic instruction may have a potential to improve chances of completion.

It was also observed (T. Evans, 2000) that, in particular, the Green and White papers put pressure on universities to commercialize their intellectual property through direct links with industry or through collaborative program developments, including professional doctorates (Kemp, 1999a). This further strengthened the implementation of the Dawkins recommendations on the link between industry and universities.

The implementation of the recommendations of these reports led to the growth in the number of professional doctorates in different disciplines, with psychology experiencing a growth increase of 267% between 1996 and 2000 (Maxwell & Shanahan, 1997). In this period, however, education was more popular in terms of the numbers of students enrolled. This could be because education enrolls students from a number of disciplines including health. Moreover, education was one of the pioneering professional doctorates to be offered not only in Australia, but the United Kingdom and the United States too.

Current Policies
Current policies that are still in place and serving to maintain a positive environment for research degrees include the Research Training Scheme (RTS), which exempts Australian students from paying student contributions and tuition fees. Some of the aims of the RTS, which were implemented from 2002 onward, were to ensure the relevance of research degree programs to labor market requirements and to improve the efficiency and effectiveness of research training (Department of Education Training and Youth Affairs, 2001). By 2002 it was once noted that 60% of Australian professional doctorates were RTS compliant and by 2011 the compliance

had grown to 70% (Maxwell, 2011). The RTS indeed bears an influence on professional doctorate program development, seen in how some of the Australian universities advertise their programs:

> This is a higher degree by research (HDR) and consequently the proportion of time and commitment is weighted much more heavily toward research than the other degrees in counselling psychology. The doctorates adhere to the Commonwealth Government definition of a research degree and may allow candidates to gain a funded research place [RTS] and to apply for Commonwealth scholarships (full-time).

The major influence of the RTS on the development of professional doctorates is that funding is not granted for qualifications that do not meet the higher degree research specifications. Some professional doctorate programs would logically put more weighting on research content to qualify their students for the RTS.

New Zealand

Three contexts for the development of discipline-specific professional doctorates are suggested here—developments in Australia, health workforce needs, and the Tertiary Education reports of the early 2000s. Firstly, the argument about developments in Australia is that the proliferation of professional doctorates in that country led to a mirroring effect in New Zealand, since the two countries have economic and social ties and the sharing of the labor force (Bedford, Ho, & Hugo, 2003). Similarly, development of professional doctorates in the United Kingdom, the Unites States, and Canada were also a factor. Indeed, scholars have argued that health discipline qualifications in New Zealand (and Australia) have tended to be influenced mainly by traditional sociopolitical links with the United Kingdom (Haig & Marie, 2011; Helmes, 2001). Other explanations are that, in addition to sharing the mobile health workforce, authorities in these countries use one another to benchmark health service delivery standards and health workforce training activities (Zurn & Dumont, 2008).

Kot and Hendel (2012) further argue that deliberate moves to allow graduates to be employable among these countries led to the development of similar standards in awarding qualifications. Indeed, health professionals have a long history of migrating for employment among these five countries. For example, estimates from the Medical Board of Australia, immigration data (Birrell, Rapson, Dobson, & Smith, 2004; Health Workforce Australia, 2013), and also the figures of Health Workforce Australia (2013) indicate that in 2013 there were 2,112 New Zealand medical practitioners in

Australia, making an average of 264 per state (Medical Deans of Australia and New Zealand, 2013). In North America, Canadian specialists in the United States in 2006 made up approximately 19.3% of the Canadian specialist workforce. Moreover, Canadian primary care physicians, who provided direct patient care in the United States, represented 8% of the Canadian primary care workforce. In contrast, in 2004 there were 408 US international medical graduates practicing in Canada (Jaakkimainen, Schultz, Glazier, Abrahams, & Verma, 2012; Phillips, Petterson, Fryer, & Rosser, 2007). Furthermore the United Kingdom is a major supplier of international medical graduates (IMGs) to both New Zealand and Australia. For example, from 2004 to 2012 the United Kingdom supplied an average of 500 medical practitioners to New Zealand every year and in Australia just under 50% of IMG specialists were from the United Kingdom in 2013 (Medical Deans of Australia and New Zealand, 2013). This dynamics concerning health professionals in these countries logically calls for similar standards in awarding qualifications that are transferable.

Secondly, and specific to health professional doctorates, the challenges of a mobile workforce, especially losses to Australia, created the need for innovations in the health workforce (Health Workforce New Zealand, 2013). These innovations were also driven by other health service demands such as the disease spectrum and the aging workforce. Such factors have created the need for role extension in terms of scope of practice and specialization. Current examples are the nurse practitioner role and prescribing pharmacists. Although the doctorates are not yet available, it is argued here that the need to train these professionals at a higher level will necessitate the development of professional doctorates in the next decade as has already happened in Australia.

Thirdly, the reports of the 2000s (Tertiary Education Advisory Commission Report Four, 2001; Tertiary Education Advisory Commission Report One, 2000; Tertiary Education Advisory Commission Report Three, 2001; Tertiary Education Advisory Commission Report Two, 2001) and reforms in the tertiary education sector provided a context for the development of professional doctorates. The Tertiary Education Advisory Commission in 2000 and 2001 produced a series of four reports about the future shape of the tertiary education system and its funding in New Zealand. The theme of these reports was the development of a more collaborative tertiary education sector that would help New Zealand become a leading knowledge economy and society in the world. The first one was "Shaping a Shared Vision" (Report One, July 2000) which proposed a strategy for New Zealand and how tertiary education should respond to changing economic and social needs (Tertiary Education Advisory Commission Report One, 2000). The second was "Shaping the System" (Report Two, February 2001), which presented a conclusion that there was a need to market institutions and steer funding to reflect national priorities and demands (Tertiary Education Advisory Commission Report Two, 2001). The key message in the third report "Shaping the Strategy," (Report Three, July 2001) was that the tertiary education system could no longer be isolated from the Government's wider goals and therefore needed to be more explicitly aligned with economic and social development objectives (Tertiary Education Advisory Commission Report Three, 2001). The direct relevance of these reports to the development of professional doctorates was that in the decade preceding the reports, health workforce needs were one of the top priorities of different New Zealand governments' social and political agendas (Gorman, Horsburgh, & Abbott, 2009).

"Shaping the Funding Framework" (Report Four, November 2001) (Tertiary Education Advisory Commission Report Four, 2001) resulted in the Performance Based Research Fund (PBRF), which was established in 2002. The funding formula meant that the research performance of tertiary education organizations (TEOs) was to be funded on the basis of their performance. However, in the early 2000s a mistake similar to that made in Australia still continued from the 1990s policies in New Zealand: allocating funds on the basis of student numbers enrolled rather than completions. This policy was reversed from the mid-2000s so that completions were the criterion instead of enrolments. The direct relevance of this funding to professional doctorates in the fields of health was that supervision of doctoral students and completions of doctorates counted toward the PBRF rating of individual tertiary education staff members and their institutions.

Current Policies
Current reforms such as the professional and applied research policy, which took effect from 2012, add to the context of sustaining the development of professional doctorates in New Zealand. Under this policy, the definition of research was extended to include original investigation of a professional and applied nature. The PBRF Quality Evaluation recognizes that high-quality research is not restricted to theoretical inquiry such as in traditional PhDs.

Summary of the Trans-Tasman Context of the Development of Professional Doctorates

It can be seen that in both Australia and New Zealand, government policy reforms, especially recommendations based on the growing need to support the knowledge economies of these countries, provided a context for the development of professional doctorates in psychology and medicine. The funding formulae based on completion rates and extension of scopes of practice also supported this context. The developments within the professions of psychology and medicine that led to the proliferations of discipline-specific doctorates still need further discussion from the angle of sociological literature on professionalization as follows.

The Professionalization Context

Profession and Context

There is a possible influence of self-regulation and professionalization in different health disciplines (Haig & Marie, 2011; Helmes, 2001). Professionalization is the process of becoming a profession—an autonomous group of practitioners with expertise and commitment to the generation of knowledge. The current rise of the need for professionals to advance and reorient practice for the good of the client has led to the drive to professionalization in different disciplines or niches within disciplines (Hunt, 2004). As professions seek dominance and extended scopes in practice, so is the demand to advance knowledge and to seek niches in disciplines (Rolfe & Davies, 2009). For example it has been argued that

> in professionalization . . . increasingly, clinicians seeking the highest levels of independent practice, parity with other . . . health professionals, and opportunities for career advancement within a specialization or niche will seek a professional doctorate (Southern, Cade, & Locke, 2012, p. 10).

In psychology this is witnessed by the growth of vocational scopes of practice such as the Australian Psychological Society (APS) College of Clinical Psychologists (Helmes, 2001). Currently there are a number of vocational psychology scopes and consequently professional doctorates in Australian universities. Examples are organizational psychology (Murdoch University), clinical neuropsychology (Monash University), and counseling psychology (Swinburne University of Technology). In this instance it can be seen that the need to seek niches or specialize is driving the development of professional doctorates.

The sociological literature also provides a rich account of the process used by disciplines to achieve professionalization by stating that the motivation is situations "where professions are defined in terms of attributes, such as formal education, . . . and associated skills etc" (James & Willis, 2001, p. 27). Indeed this argument is relevant even in the discipline of medicine where a number of subspecialties exist. The University of Western Australia is such an example where a doctor of surgery degree was introduced probably in a bid to target professional growth in this specialty.

Context and Profession

Lee et al. (2000) argue that professional doctorate learning takes place in the intersecting spheres of the profession, the workplace, and the university in the background of what they called "the context." Their scholarship drew on Gibbon et al.'s (1994) two forms of knowledge production—Mode 1 and Mode 2, and the later work by Scott et al. (1995). Lee et al. (2000) linked Mode 1 and Mode 2 with the university and the workplace, respectively.

According to Scott et al. (1995), Mode 1 knowledge is seen as linear, causal, and cumulative (synonymous with scientific knowledge). Mode 1 is also generated in the university and applied to practical problems usually outside the university (characteristic 1 of Mode 1). Another characteristic is that such knowledge is publicly funded, with the rationale for funding being that such scientific institutions guard the interests of the society (characteristic 4 of Mode 1). On the other hand, Mode 2 knowledge is produced in the market place as opposed to scientific establishments such as universities (characteristic 1 of Mode 2), and is socially accountable as it is defined in specific contexts (characteristic 4 of Mode 2) (Lee et al., 2000). Mode 2 knowledge is therefore synonymous with knowledge produced in the workplace sphere of the hybrid curriculum.

The context of development of professional doctorates in the Trans-Tasman region lays a foundation for the description of a research project focused on identifying characteristics of professional doctorates in the disciplines of psychology and medicine.

Methodology

This study focused on two countries offering professional doctorates, Australia and New Zealand, and was informed by the theory underpinning case study methodologies. Case studies are defined as in-depth studies of relatively bounded phenomenon where the scholar's aim is to elucidate features of a larger class of similar phenomena (Gerring, 2004; Yin, 1994). The term "case study" as used in this research is applied in two senses; firstly, "the case study of health discipline professional doctorates in New Zealand and Australia" and, secondly, "the case study of an issue or phenomenon," which, in this research, was the context of development of professional doctorates in New Zealand and Australia. This study investigated what Gerring (2004) refers to as a single phenomenon, which could be considered as a typical example of other similar phenomena: professional doctorates offered in other English-speaking countries in similar disciplines. According to Stake (1995), this type of case study seeks to study phenomena for its intrinsic value, as one is interested in a unique situation. This means that one has an intrinsic interest in the subject and is aware that the results have limited transferability. It is also important to mention that this case study method was employed for the purposes of description and exploration (Yin, 1994). It is at the level where the goal is to develop propositional ideas that could be used for further inquiry.

Methods

The method used in this research was website document analysis, previously utilized by Kot and Hendel (2012) in a similar work on professional doctorates across different countries. Ethical approval was not required, as the method entailed using information available to the public. The searches involved collecting data from published documents on the official websites of the universities offering psychology and medical professional doctorates. This data was triangulated with information that was publicly available from educational agencies, professional associations, and registration boards in each of the two countries. Websites analyzed included:

1. The New Zealand Psychological Society and the Australian Psychological Society, with information about qualifications that enable individuals to be admitted into membership.
2. Registration authorities such as the New Zealand Psychological Board and the Australian Psychological Board. These had details about qualifications with registration eligibility.
3. The Australian Psychology Accreditation Council (APAC), which is the accreditation authority responsible for accrediting education providers and programs of study for the psychology profession (Australian Psychology Accreditation Council, 2015).
4. The New Zealand Qualification Authority and the Australian Qualification Framework. These list qualifications and levels of award. They were important in determining the doctorates that met the criteria of a professional doctorate.

The searches were done in a systematic way in three phases. The first phase involved extensive searches of the webpages for program information or course outlines in universities offering doctoral qualifications. The content of interest in the program outlines included entry requirements, course content, and course structure in terms of the proportion of research, didactic content, and the practicum. Length of study, level of award, and detailed course descriptions of doctoral programs were also other items of interest. Website information on programs was also checked against entries in the postgraduate student handbook of each university.

The second phase of searches involved triangulating the information from the universities' websites using the information provided by registration and accreditation agencies and the qualification evaluation or framework authorities in the two countries. The third phase involved searching scholarly documents on these professional doctorates in academic databases mainly using Google Scholar and EBSCO health databases. All the search phases were carried out between July 20, 2014, and December 31, 2014. The data was further updated on January 10, 2015.

Sampling Strategy

The sampling strategy employed was purposive in the sense that the writer selected websites that were known to have the information sought. The criteria for selecting professional doctorates were firstly that the doctorate should be awarded at level 10 of the Australian Qualification Framework (AQF) and the New Zealand Qualification Authority (NZQA). The second criterion was that the professional doctorate must be offered in both New Zealand and Australia, and in at least two universities in each of the selected countries. The doctorates selected were to be discipline specific. The doctorates in psychology and medicine therefore met these criteria.

The specialist psychology doctorates such as neuropsychology, forensic psychology, and organizational psychology were excluded. Currently the Psychology Board of Australia has registered psychologists in the endorsement of community psychology, clinical neuropsychology, counseling psychology, forensic psychology, health psychology, organizational psychology, and sport and exercise psychology, and 71% of these have a clinical endorsement (Psychology Board of Australia, 2015). This study sampled the psychology doctorates in the clinical psychology endorsement. This allowed for a focused analysis of context; for example, issues that can lead to the development of a doctorate in clinical psychology endorsement may be different from those of the development of one in neuropsychology.

Among the medical doctorates, preservice medical doctorates (MD) were excluded because these courses were offered between the undergraduate and master's levels. For example, the Melbourne doctorate was advertised as follows: "The new Doctor of Medicine (MD) provides a fresh approach to medical training . . . as the only Australian professional entry Masters level degree" (University of Melbourne, 2015).

The websites of the universities selected in relation to psychology had more details about admission criteria, professional recognition, clinical requirements, course composition (such as units to be undertaken, the proportion of the research requirement, and course duration) than medicine ones. These fields were analyzed using the thematic analysis method as described by Braun and Clarke (2006). According to Braun and Clarke (2006), thematic analysis is a method for identifying, analyzing, and reporting patterns of themes within data by minimally organizing and describing the data set in rich detail. The guiding questions in the analysis were:

1. What are the characteristics of professional doctorates in psychology and medicine offered in New Zealand and Australia?
2. How do these doctorates reflect the hybrid curriculum of the profession, practice, and research?

Summary of Findings

Findings will be presented under the headings of entry requirements; content, structure, and university focus; research process, form, and output; practice focus; and professional focus. A discussion which links these with spheres of the hybrid curriculum will follow.

Professional Doctorates in Psychology

A total of nine professional doctorates in psychology met the sampling criteria and, of these, two were in New Zealand. The Australian universities offering these doctorates were located in the states of New South Wales (Charles Sturt University; University of Wollongong), Victoria (Swinburne University), and Western Australia (Murdoch University). The New Zealand universities offering these doctorates were located in North Island (Massey University and the University of Auckland).

Entry Requirements

All professional doctorates in psychology were very consistent in their entry requirement of a higher honors degree or equivalent, as shown in Table 2.1. There were other universities, such as Swinburne University of Technology, which extended emphasis to "appropriate research skills." The professional requirements were also of paramount importance in the entry criteria. For example, all the Australian universities required applicants to have completed a registration-eligible qualification before enrolling to the doctorate. On the other hand, the New Zealand ones did not add such statements on their websites. The following extracts from web documents are related to entry requirements:

> ... a four-year APAC-accredited qualification in psychology at Honours 2A level ... registration as a psychologist (Charles Sturt University, 2015).
> ... be eligible for registration with the psychologist Registration Board as a conditional/provisional psychologist. An exception to this may be made for

Table 2.1 Characteristics of Psychology Professional Doctorates

Institution	Admissions criteria	Credits allocation	Professional recognition	Clinical requirements	Didactic component	Research requirement	Duration
Charles Sturt University DPsych—Doctor of Psychology	Personal suitability 4-year APAC accredited qualification at Honors 2A Registration as a Psychologist	TOTAL = 192 points 64 points research Not specific about other points	Accredited by Australian Psychological Society (APS)	Information available lacked clarity	3 units	Two-thirds including research units	Full-time: 3 years
James Cook University DPsych(ClinPsych)— Doctor of Psychology (Clinical Psychology)	Honors 2A or above. One semester of supervised project work	36 credits coursework 18 credits practicum Credits research (?)	Accredited by APAC Membership of APS College of Clinical Psychologists	Total 1,000 hours practicum	12 units total	Thesis at least two-thirds	Full-time: 4 years
Massey University DClinPsych— Doctor of Clinical Psychology	Honors Good standing	TOTAL = 360 credits 30 credits coursework 90 credits practicum/ internship 240 credits research	Eligible for registration as a Clinical Psychologist	240–300 hours practicum per year in years 1 and 2 Full academic year-long internship in year 3	1 unit per year in years 1 and 2 only	Thesis two-thirds	Full-time: 3 years

(continued)

Table 2.1 (Continued)

Institution	Admissions criteria	Credits allocation	Professional recognition	Clinical requirements	Didactic component	Research requirement	Duration
Monash University DPsych(Clinical)—Doctor of Psychology in Clinical Psychology	APAC-accredited Honours 1 or Honours 2A	20% coursework 10% practicum 70% research	Accredited by APAC. Membership of APS College of Clinical Psychologists	1,500 hours practicum	8 units year 1, 2 units year 2, 1 unit year 3	60,000–70,000 word thesis 70%	Full-time: 4 years
Murdoch University DPsych—Doctor of Psychology in Clinical Psychology	4-year APAC accredited Honors (2A) Eligibility for registration Research proposal Name a supervisor	TOTAL = 84 points 18 points coursework 18 points practicum 48 points research	Accredited by APAC Approved by APS College of Clinical Psychologists	9 months at 2 days per week in year 1 Total of 157 days year 2 onward	6 units year 1 1 unit year 2 onward	57% thesis	Full-time: 3 years
Swinburne University of Technology DR-CLIPSY—Doctor of Psychology (Clinical Psychology)	APS-accredited qualification with Honors 1 or 2A Appropriate work experience Appropriate research knowledge	TOTAL = 400 credits 100 credits coursework 50 credits practicum 250 credits research	Membership of APS College of Clinical Psychologists	Practicum in years 1, 2, and 3 but length not specified	3 units per year in years 1 and 2, 2 units in year 3	40,000–60,000 word thesis	Full-time: 4 years

	Entry requirements	Credits	Accreditation	Practicum	Units	Thesis	Duration
The University of Auckland DClinPsy—Doctor of Clinical Psychology	Completion of Clinical Honors year Restricted to New Zealand/ Australian citizens or residents	TOTAL = 360 credits 60 credits coursework 150 credits practicum/ internship 150 credits research	New Zealand Psychologists Board Clinical Psychologist registration	200 hours practicum in year 1, 2 × 200 hour practicum in year 2 1,500 hour internship in year 3	1 unit per year in years 1 and 2 only	Thesis 42%	Full-time: 3 years
University of Wollongong DPsyc (Clin)—Doctor of Psychology (Clinical)	Superior Honors degree in psychology of at least four years duration of Class II, Division 1 standard or higher	TOTAL = 168 credits 44 credits coursework 12 credits practicum 112 credits research	APAC Accredited Approved by APS	Practicum in years 1, 2, and 3 but length not specified	4 units in year 1, 2 units in year 2, 1 unit in year 3	Thesis two-thirds	Full-time: 3.5 years

Note: (1) In all instances of a requirement of an honors degree, there was a statement giving an option for a master's degree. This was not repeated in the table for the sake of brevity.
(2) All universities had a different system allocating points to units and the total number of points required for each program differed. These were therefore written as they appeared in the website information.

currently registered psychologists who can demonstrate current compliance with Registration Board CPD requirements. (Murdoch University, 2015)

It can be seen above that entry into this qualification is restricted to those who are already registered and hence this is an in-service qualification. However, in New Zealand, universities seemed not to have registration as a requirement.

Another characteristic of eligibility for entry was personal suitability to be in a clinical environment by having a clean criminal record, the declaration of infectious diseases, and the requirement for interview to assess suitability. The application information related to personal suitability included the following extract:

> Applicants are assessed on personal and academic suitability. Applicants must possess:
> 1. personal suitability to undertake professional practice as a psychologist
> 2. registration as a psychologist (Charles Sturt University, 2015)
>
> Entry into the Clinical program is limited to 11 students per year and ... Entry is based on application, selection and interview (University of Auckland, 2015).

While the above statements emphasized personal qualities, statements from other universities had other requirements which were different in emphasis. For example, Massey University in New Zealand emphasized specific content in honors degrees. This content included requirements for specific research proportion of course and specific units that should have been covered by the candidate. For example, there is a requirement that the candidate should

> 1. have completed the requirements for a relevant Bachelor (Hons) ... 0.0 or the equivalent; ... research component constituting at least 25% of the qualification;
> 2. have passed the following papers, or their equivalents, in their qualifying degree: 175.738, and at least five papers from 175.701, 175.707 ... [Etc]. (Massey University, 2015)

In terms of the model of the hybrid curriculum it can be seen that the university still dictates entry in terms of an honors requirement as happens with the traditional PhD. The profession also dictates entry in terms of requirements for being accreditation eligible. The workplace is also of paramount importance in the entry requirement as it has been seen that candidates should possess attributes that make them suitable to work with patients.

Content, Structure, and University Focus

One item that seemed to vary among universities offering professional doctorates in psychology was the course content and structure. All universities seemed to offer different units and different patterns of study. Some universities, such as Charles Sturt University, seemed to emphasize both course content and the pattern of study in which the courses were to be taken. The University of Wollongong emphasized both research and content with no mention of practicum. Other universities, such as James Cook University, Murdoch University, and Swinburne University seemed to stress a balance between content, research, and practice. The Monash University professional doctorate emphasized research, as indicated in the fact that 70% of the content was research, 20% was course work, while 10% was devoted to clinical placements. In terms of advertisement, this university seemed to stress that it accommodates research, practice, and coursework—"This research degree integrates theory, practice and research to qualify you as a highly skilled clinical psychologist" (Monash University, 2015b). On the other hand, the University of Wollongong laid emphasis on clinical practice as was evident in the course structure having several course work units as can be seen in Table 2.1.

Course descriptions also provided an insight about the content-and-structure focus of programs. For example, in the course description of the University of Wollongong, the first two sentences emphasized content with no mention of research. There was one sentence in the course overview that mentioned research: "the course also includes advanced training, in the design, execution and writing up of a research project." Even the research component of this course was more structured, emphasizing "research training" being taught. On the other hand, Swinburne emphasized both research and clinical training in the first sentence of the course description, and this evidence was further highlighted in the aims and the graduate profile of the course information.

In summary, it can be seen that despite similar entry and accreditation requirements, all universities varied in course content and structure. It is here argued that the reason for variation could be because of the autonomy of the universities in determining course content and structure. This, however, does not seem to compromise standards as these courses are accredited by the same authorities.

Research Process, Form, and Output

Another item of interest was the process, form and output of research. In terms of process it was observed that some universities (University of Wollongong, Swinburne University of Technology) had the research thesis done throughout the year and as a standalone activity while others had a built-up structure in the form of preparatory units followed by an independent research project. One of the doctorates (Swinburne) seemed to immerse students in research from the beginning up to the end. The James Cook University professional doctorate was different from others because it specified three structured units that were to be conducted in preparation for research instead of clinical knowledge content. These were "Planning the Research for Doctoral Candidates" and "Situating the Research." The research item was clearly specified as being Clinical Psychology thesis research—"Professional Doctorate Research Thesis (Clinical Psychology)." The research component of Charles Sturt, James Cook, Monash, Murdoch, Massey, and Wollongong comprised two-thirds or more of the program. Most universities (Monash, Murdoch, Swinburne) had thesis sizes of between 57,000 and 60,000 words as shown in Table 2.1.

In the Australian context, the thesis components seemed to be tailored to meet the funding specifications, as some of the programs specified this as follows: "Candidates are eligible . . . to receive a Research Training Scheme (RTS) award" (Swinburne University of Technology, 2015). The forms which the theses took also varied. For example, some theses components took the form of portfolios while others were similar to traditional PhD theses. The publication of papers was not common among professional doctorates in psychology. This could have been because of the structured and restricted time in which the courses were supposed to be done. In the case of a thesis by publication it is noted that the peer review process of journal publications can delay up to periods beyond the required times specified for candidates to complete the course. The theses sizes of most professional doctorates in psychology seemed to be consistent. As has been said, this could have been due to funding specifications of the RTS scheme.

Practice Focus
The practice focus of professional doctorates in psychology was evident in the professional background of the teaching staff, the content of papers, and the general structure of the programs. In terms of the teaching staff, evidence of practice focus in professional doctorates in psychology was also shown in the fact that the teaching staff tended to be practicing psychologists. One university invited students to train at its "modern on-campus psychology clinic, established to give students practical experience dealing with real clients . . . [with] . . . teaching staff, who are all practising psychologists." Further emphasis on the profession was

seen in statements such as "Once accepted, you must be registered as a Provisional Psychologist or Psychologist upon commencement of the degree" (Murdoch University, 2015).

The universities in New Zealand seemed to put more emphasis on practicum and research. For example, Massey University had two 15-point units on practicum, a 60-point internship, and a research component. The thesis in Massey University was in three parts: a 90-point component, another 90-point component, and finally a 60-point component (Massey University, 2015).

Another evidence of a practice focus was in the naming of the content papers: the "skills in clinical assessment" and "skills in intervention." These names suggested that these papers were again leaned toward the practicum. This led to the conclusion that these papers are designed to support internship and hence the workplace focus.

Professional Focus
All clinical professional doctorates in psychology characteristics emphasized the role of the professional with a psychology degree. This was observed in the accreditation links with APS and also in terms of admission into membership such as the APS College of Clinical Psychologists. The Australian Psychology Accreditation Council also listed clinical psychology doctorates that were approved. Entries in the website information of the universities stressed accreditation as follows:

> This program is accredited by the Australian Psychology Accreditation Council (APAC) for Registration as a Psychologist, and as a qualifying degree for endorsement in Clinical Psychology. The program is also approved by the APS College of Clinical Psychologists as part of the requirements for full membership. (University of Wollongong, 2015)

Accreditation reports also had information suggesting the influence of professional boards on the curriculum. The following is an extract from one accreditation board prescribing the content for a university:

> Massey University's DClinPsych course of study has been granted accreditation . . . conditional . . . that the following requirements have been . . . addressed; More extensive coverage should be provided in . . . family practice . . . , and cultural competence. Furthermore, clinical skills training should be covered. (New Zealand Psychologists Board, 2014, p. 1)

From the above extract it can be seen that the accreditation board was even emphasizing how the structure of the program and the university activities should be tailored to meet practice needs of students. This demonstrates the intersecting spheres of the hybrid curriculum—the university, the workplace, and the profession.

Summary of Characteristics of Professional Doctorates in Psychology

All universities sampled tended to have similar entry requirements, duration (3–4 years), and accreditation requirements as can be seen in Table 2.1. There was a variation within each country and across countries mainly in terms of course structure, course content, points allocation to units/papers, and amount of time and patterns of placement for practicums. This scenario calls for further research on determining the criteria for evaluating standards of qualifications in such wide variations in course content. Moreover, there is a slight difference between the New Zealand and the Australian professional doctorates in psychology in that the New Zealand ones seemed to be designed for licensing while the Australian ones seemed to be designed to support academic and professional development.

Professional Doctorates in Medicine

The universities offering professional doctorates in medicine that were selected for the study were located in the following Australian states: Queensland (James Cook University, University of Queensland); New South Wales (Macquarie University); Victoria (Monash University); and Western Australia (University of Notre Dame, University of Western Australia). The New Zealand ones were located in both the North Island (University of Auckland) and the South Island (University of Otago).

Definitions and Categories

After analyzing the characteristics of the doctorates the writer came up with three groups of professional doctorates according to how they were named—higher doctorates, specialization doctorates, and professional doctorates. The higher doctorates were classified in the course outlines as belonging to a category separate from the other level 10 doctorates. In other cases there was a statement indicating that higher doctorates were of a higher standard than a PhD. For example, "This degree is of a higher standing than the degree of Doctor of Philosophy and is awarded for independent and original research which constitutes a substantial and distinguished contribution to the knowledge." As will be discussed later, the entry requirements for a higher doctorate in medicine are typically higher than those of other doctorates, including a traditional PhD.

The specialization doctorates that were selected appeared to be offered in collaboration with specialist colleges. One of them—the doctor of surgery—specifically indicated that it was linked with a specialist college of medicine. The other specialization professional doctorate—the doctor of advanced medicine—was open to different specialities. The ordinary professional doctorate was mainly defined in terms of being a level 10 for both the New Zealand and the Australian qualification frameworks.

See the institution and name of doctorate column in Table 2.2 for type of doctorate classification.

Entry Requirements

In terms of entry requirements, one characteristic feature of professional doctorates in medicine was that unlike the psychology ones, entry was by undergraduate medical degrees. The entry requirements were similar among all doctorates, that is, requiring an undergraduate medical qualification and requiring practice experience of five years and above. These requirements were also consistent across the two countries depending on the type of doctorate: variations were only across the three types of doctorates.

In the case of higher doctorates, entry requirements were higher as the candidates were expected to have published work of a substantial standard. For example, according to the University of Notre Dame (2015) applicants are expected to have published a body of work that:

1. represents a significant advance in knowledge in the given field; or
2. has given rise to significant debate amongst recognized scholars in the given field; or
3. has directly changed the direction of research or practice in a newer generation of scholars in the given field. (University of Notre Dame, p. 6)

Indeed the above requirements seem to emphasize highest standards of quality achievement before enrolling. The third item about presenting work that has "changed the direction of research or practice" is the most rigorous one. It can even be of interest for other researchers to find out the proportion of students graduating with doctorates who do not only contribute to knowledge by publication but achieve a step further and impact by changing the direction of research and practice.

In addition to quality, other universities emphasized quantity both in terms of years of publication and the number of journals published. The

Table 2.2 Characteristics of Professional Doctorates in Medicine

Institution and name of doctorate	Admissions criteria	Professional recognition	Clinical requirements	Didactic curriculum	Research requirements	Duration
James Cook University DMed—Doctor of Medicine	Division A Honors degree Research methods training Approved doctoral Learning Plan	N/A	Practicum an option		Thesis two-thirds	4 years
Macquarie University DAdvMed—Doctor of Advanced Medicine (Specialist doctorate)	MBBS Certificate of Good Standing Fellowship in specialist college Potential interview 4 years' recent experience	Accredited by the Australian School of Advanced Medicine	Reflective portfolio one-third	Units one-third	Thesis one-third	1.5–3 years depending on RPL granted
Monash University MD—Doctor of Medicine	MBBS Research training equivalent to honors	N/A	None	None	100,000 word thesis	4 years
Queensland University Doctor of Medicine (Research)	MBBS 7 years' standing	Indicated that professional recognition is not necessarily granted	None	None	Journal papers	Not specified
The University of Auckland MD—Doctor of Medicine	MBBS Research ability 5 years' experience	N/A	None	None	Wholly thesis	3–4 years
University of Western Australia MD—Doctor of Medicine (Higher doctorate)	MBBS Proven competence in medicine	N/A	None	None	Journal papers	Not specified

University of Western Australia Doctor of Surgery (Specialist doctorate)	MBBS of this University or equivalent Proven competence in surgery	N/A	None	None	Wholly thesis or journal papers	Not specified
University of Notre Dame MD—Doctor of Medicine (Higher doctorate)	MBBS 5 years' experience Substantial publications of three criteria: (1) niche, (2) triggered debate, (3) changed direction of practice	N/A	None	1 unit for administrative purposes	Thesis two-thirds	Not specified
University of Otago MD—Doctor of Medicine (Higher doctorate)	Medical degree. Substantial work of special quality. 5 years' experience	N/A	None	None	Journal papers (approximately 15)	Not specified

Note: In all instances of MBBS, it was indicated that an equivalent qualification is acceptable.

University of Otago required candidates to have published between 15 and 25 peer reviewed international journals. For example, their criteria for admission read:

> [I]t is expected that there will be several publications on work undertaken over a number of years. For example:
> 1. 15 to 25 or more publications in peer reviewed journals of significant international standard
> 2. on occasion the number of publications may be less than 15 but will still be in international journals of high standing. (University of Otago, 2014a)

It is argued here that the above entry requirements are rigorous given that the published work is supposed to have undergone peer review processes and be of international standards. In the same university, the writer found out what the requirements were for a traditional PhD by publication. In this university, some departments required approximately four to six journal publications (University of Otago, 2014b). This is indeed evidence that the requirements for professional doctorates are of a higher standard.

Although all professional doctorates in medicine did not require master's or honors degrees for entry, the robustness of qualifications cannot be questioned given that entry requirements tended to be stringent—more selective than those of ordinary PhDs. This was mainly evident in the higher doctorates in medicine.

Content, Structure, and University Focus

There were variations in professional doctorates in medicine with some higher doctorates having the content produced before enrolling in the university while other medicine doctorates were structured and had the content produced during the period of enrolment at a university. Other universities such as the University of Auckland gave options of both modes for all types of doctorates. Some seemed to be run along the lines of a traditional PhD in that there were no structured instructions or coursework—an example being the Monash University doctor of medicine degree course where the course outline states: "This program has no units and it has two supervisors like a PhD."

In general it was observed that professional doctorates in medicine did not have a prescribed content. The emphasis was only placed on duration of the programs, that is, completion was to be done in prescribed time frames (see Table 2.2). The emphasis was on demonstrating advanced skills in a research that contributed to medical practice.

The role of the university was highlighted by the fact that admission to these doctorates was at the discretion of the universities. The universities seemed to have autonomy in prescribing content. Such a scenario could explain the lack of prescribed structure in these programs.

Research Process, Form, and Output
The professional doctorates in medicine seemed to emphasize processes similar to a PhD in the sense of having research work done completely independently. For example, the higher doctorate seemed to bridge the gap between the traditional PhD and the professional doctorate while having the elements of a professional doctorate in terms of links to professional practice, it still emphasized independence.

The number of publications needed for presentation as a portfolio also varied, signifying the autonomous nature of the process. Examination processes seemed to vary according to the type of doctorate and from one university to another.

Other doctoral degrees seemed to have processes that were not very different from that of a traditional doctorate. For example, the Monash University doctor of medicine degree course overview states that

> completion of the program will signify that the candidate has successfully completed a course of postgraduate training in research under academic supervision, and has submitted a thesis that the examiners have declared to be a significant contribution to knowledge and which demonstrates the candidate's capacity to carry out independent research. (Monash University, 2015a)

It must be noted that with professional doctorates in medicine, even though the processes were similar to those of a PhD, evidence of impact on medical practice was emphasized. The most defining characteristic in terms of process, form and research output was autonomy of the candidate to determine their work. The university had limited input as it pertained to deciding on the physical form of the work to be examined and the examination processes.

Practice Focus
As has been said earlier, higher degree medicine doctorates emphasized practice in the sense that there was a requirement that the research produced should impact on practice. This is different from the case of professional doctorates in psychology which emphasized practice in terms of time spent in clinical placements. Statements in the medicine doctorates that emphasized practice included that "the Doctor of Medicine (MD) . . . provides the opportunity for experienced medical clinicians to undertake advanced study and research which can be directly applied toward clinical and practice issues" (University of Auckland, 2015).

In the above extract it can be argued that practice focus is also emphasized by the requirement that the doctorate is for experienced practitioners.

As has already been discussed, entry requirements of approximately five years of experience were one of the defining features of medicine doctorates. In a way, practice-focused professional doctorates in medicine were in retrospect rather than being something to be achieved during the period of enrolment. The enrolment period therefore appeared to be a university procedural route to conferment of a qualification. This was especially the case with higher doctorate by publication.

Among the doctorates in medicine, only situations of specialization seemed to require clinical placements or practice orientation of the program activities. This can be seen in the website entries that "students also undertake coursework and specialist attachments as part of completion of the doctorate" (James Cook University, 2015). This statement may be taken to imply that program attachments are only done as relevant. This adds to the view that professional doctorates in medicine do not seem to have a clear link with professional practice in the sense of clinical attachments.

Professional Focus
Credentialing is one way of judging the influence of professions on qualifications. Unlike some professional doctorates in psychology, the medicine ones except the specialist professional doctorates were not awarded for credentialing as seen in the following statement:

> While this degree may be accredited by an official industry accreditation body in Australia, completion of the degree may not result in graduates receiving automatic accreditation. Please contact the relevant registration body for details of any conditions for accreditation. (University of Queensland, 2015)

However, one argument that can be made is that even though credentialing was not a requirement for professional doctorates in medicine, the candidates already had basic medical qualifications that were recognized by professional boards. Since these qualifications are housed under the medicine disciplines it can also be argued that the acceptance to enroll and the examination processes are done by professionals within the field, and hence the evidence of professional influences.

Moreover, as has already been discussed, the professional focus of medicine doctorates is seen in the fact that all the higher doctorates emphasize that before enrolling the applicant must have contributed to research that has contributed significantly to medical practice or the profession of medicine. Further evidence of the links with the professions could be that other specialist doctorates have links with colleges of medicine, see Table 2.2.

In conclusion it can therefore be argued that what is emphasized in most professional doctorates in medicine is their impact on medical practice rather than the profession—there is less emphasis in their content being tailored to suit requirements of professional and registration boards or specialist colleges. This could be because educational progression in medicine has traditionally been unique from other health professions as postgraduate qualification is sometimes synonymous with specialist qualifications. These are usually awarded by colleges of medicine and take several years— usually four to seven. The specialist qualifications may lead to a further sub-specialization. Such qualifications are almost entirely controlled by professions, that is, colleges of medicine rather than universities. In this sense, the links between professional doctorates and professions or credentialing boards seem unclear. Moreover, not much scholarship is available on whether and how they may count toward continued professional development (CPD)—an involvement in clinical audit and peer review aimed at ensuring whether a doctor is competent to practice medicine.

Summary of Findings on Professional Doctorates in Psychology and Medicine

In summary, there are characteristics of psychology and medicine doctorates which make them both similar and different from one another. Both types of doctorates are awarded to candidates within the disciplines and they tend to be of three- to four-year duration. However, all professional doctorates in medicine are awarded to experienced practitioners while most psychology ones enable candidates to get a registration to practice or to be advanced practitioners. Moreover, most professional doctorates in psychology were accredited to professional boards while the medicine ones were not. Structure was also the defining feature of professional doctorates in psychology while the medicine ones tended to be unstructured. Variation in terms of content was also a key feature in professional doctorates in psychology while with medicine ones there was little variation.

Discussion: Characteristics in Relation to the Hybrid Curriculum

As has been seen earlier, the discussion of professional doctorates in both psychology and medicine can be framed under the hybrid curriculum described by Lee et al. (2000). In relation to this conceptualization, the results for the professional doctorates in psychology showed evidence of a balance between university ends, as well as research and practice. On the other hand, the professional doctorates in medicine emphasize research more than the workplace. The workplace in psychology doctorates was emphasized in so far as learning was concerned; for example, the requirements for practicum. In the professional doctorates in medicine, the workplace was emphasized by way of requiring that awards are recognition of work that has impacted on practice. It is in this context that an argument is made that more research is needed, to compare the two ways in which the workplace is impacted by professional doctorates in psychology and medicine.

In terms of Lee et al.'s (2000) sphere of the profession in the hybrid curriculum, it was noted that psychology professional doctorates seemed to be directly linked to accreditation and professional membership, while in the professional doctorates in medicine these links were not apparent. This might mean that the profession has a voice in the admission of candidates to psychology professional doctorates in the universities. Indeed, scholars have argued that in the professional doctorates in psychology, the profession plays a significant role in setting standards (Haig & Marie, 2011; Helmes & Pachana, 2005). In this instance, the professional requirements are dictating admission in the university which traditionally sets entry requirements. Registration, membership requirements, and personal suitability were emphasized in professional doctorates in psychology and these were all prescriptions for enrolment that emphasized the importance of both the workplace setting and the profession.

In terms of the sphere of the profession, location within a school discipline was one of the characteristics of the profession and practice focus of professional doctorates in both psychology and medicine. Some of the programs even emphasized that the supervisors were or should be within the discipline.

It is argued here that compared to professional doctorates in medicine, psychology doctoral education appears to be characterized by close links with the profession and the workplace. For example, these doctorates required an interview as part of the selection process. While this could also be due to limited places, another factor could be the need to consider personal characteristics as part of a recent movement in the patient-caring professions. None of the professional doctorates in medicine, except for specialist ones, required a selection interview or reference letters.

Professional organizational education agencies and qualification framework authorities influence entry into professional doctorates. Evidence of the influence of qualification framework authorities was seen in the fact that entry requirements for the professional doctorates in psychology seemed to be consistent within each country and across the two countries. The medicine doctorates too had consistent entry requirements, depending on the type. This might also be a result of standard-setting by the education agencies of these two countries. For example, in Australia it was required that for entry into doctoral qualifications applicants should normally hold a good Honours degree or Masters degree, with at least one third research methodology and research practice, relevant to their intended field of study. Evidence of recent professional expertise should be taken into account. (Council of Australian Deans and Directors of Graduate Studies, 2007, p. 2)

Although education agencies had an influence on entry into these doctorates, the bias toward doctoral entry requirements that emphasize practice and the profession still stood out in psychology doctorates. It is argued that such professional doctorates entail the explicit aims to be grounded in and to impact on the profession and practice settings.

Qualification authorities in these countries also stipulated the minimum requirements for content areas, for example, 67% of research work was required in Australia. However, this seemed to be interpreted in various ways by universities in these countries. The varied content and structure of professional doctorates in the same fields may indicate that universities still have the autonomy to decide the structure of their curricula. Moreover, the variation in the content and structures of professional doctorates can be interpreted as being a result of competing interest of the three spheres of the hybrid curriculum which have different effects in different universities. An illustrative scenario is that of the psychology doctorates in New Zealand which have limited entry every year, enrollment of between 11 and 14 students per university due to restriction in clinical placement requirements (University of Auckland, 2015).

On the issue of diversity of content areas, it is also argued that forms of diversity in professional doctorates in psychology and medicine are innovations that are not immune to wider government policy influences such as the regulatory and funding landscapes. Examples of funding landscapes include prescriptions about research-funding eligible qualifications such as the RTS policy, which has been previously discussed. Examples of regulatory prescriptive measures include the National Registration and Accreditation Scheme in Australia, which is a new development since 2010. Under this policy, 14 major health professions including psychology and medicine have been centralized for accreditation and registration. In New Zealand, 16 regulatory boards including psychology and medicine operate under one umbrella law—the Health Practitioners Competence Assurance Act (2003). These statutory requirements are there to safeguard patient safety through protecting the titles of health professionals and scopes of practice and therefore tend to impact preservice professional doctorates such as the psychology ones. In this case, it is also noted that in the field of psychology, in both Australia and New Zealand, a professional doctorate is a route to registration and professional membership of psychology specialist colleges as shown in Table 2.1.

Furthermore, in terms of diversity of content, all the professional doctorates examined required various pieces of research to be submitted. It was observed that the research requirements of professional doctorates in psychology varied, while the ones in medicine had a similar form and scale of research that needed to be completed. Variations in the psychology doctorates must be judged in the context of an environment of accreditation, which can be seen as standard-setting (Haig & Marie, 2011; Helmes, 2001). In this way such variations in requirements can therefore not be seen as compromising standards. As for medicine doctorates, the university and the workplace seem to have a big influence on the requirement for the production of published works for the award of the qualification. There is little evidence about the role of the profession in the context of producing the publications. It is assumed that while publishing, the candidates would have not been under the university but rather in a workplace. More research is needed to determine where people awarded higher doctorates tend to be located—whether in the research centers of hospitals or in teaching hospitals. If most of the publications are carried out in workplaces, this has implications for professional development opportunities given to medical doctors when they practice. This also has implications to whether and to what extent such publications and qualifications should count under medical doctors' continued professional development portfolios.

Finally, it is argued here that there was clear evidence about the standards and quality of higher professional doctorates in medicine in both New Zealand and Australia as measured by rigorous entry requirements and the emphasis on research outputs. Moreover, this research has highlighted that the processes of higher doctorates in medicine have impact on the research field which can be measured as higher than those of a PhD.

Conclusion

The robustness of New Zealand and Australian psychology and medicine professional doctorate qualifications is of special significance not only to the future practice contexts and the professions of these two fields but to the value accorded to other professional doctorates in general. The balance offered by these professional doctorates in meeting the university, profession, and workplace requirements is one way of measuring the robustness of these qualifications. Government policy priorities, within each of these countries, and the international context of the development of these programs in countries with similar health systems such as the United States, Canada, and the United Kingdom offer insight into the future directions that these programs might take. These do not act as prescriptions in program development but rather as broader contexts within which innovations in Australia and New Zealand may take place. Moreover, the challenge of professional doctorate programs remains as the need to balance requirements for those enrolled to contribute knowledge at the highest level without losing focus on their equally important role of contributing to professional practice.

The current situation of varied content and form within these doctorates should not be viewed as controversial, but would benefit from being viewed in the broader context of innovation in curriculum design. This situation of varied content and form calls for future studies that can measure how these varied forms compare, mainly in terms of impact on practice and profession. Future studies can compare how the impact on practice and the profession and the end results of these professional doctorates compare with those of the traditional PhD. The question of whether and how far students in professional doctorates do transform what they experience in practice through reflection in doctoral programs can provide a starting point for evidence aimed to link professional doctorates with practice settings. This work has implications for decisions regarding the extent and types of innovations that should be in place in order to prepare graduates who will have impact on professions, practice settings, and university ends.

Note

1. The author would like to acknowledge the enormous input from Louise Mara of Massey University, School of Management, New Zealand, who assisted in collecting data about the psychology degrees in Australia and provided feedback on the initial draft of this work.

References

Australian Psychology Accreditation Council. (2015). Currently accredited psychology courses in Australasia. Retrieved from https://www.psychologycouncil.org.au/course-search/

Bedford, R., Ho, E., & Hugo, G. (2003). Trans-Tasman migration in context: Recent flows of New Zealanders revisited. *People and Place, 11*(4), 53–62.

Biggs, M. (2000). Editorial: The foundations of practice-based research. *Working Papers in Art and Design, 1*, 1–4.

Birrell, B., Rapson, V., Dobson, I. R., & Smith, T. F. (2004). Skilled movement in the new century: Outcomes for Australia. Retrieved from http://www.immi.gov.au/media/publications/pdf/skilled_movement.pdf

Braun, V., & Clarke, V. (2006). Using thematic analysis in psychology. *Qualitative Research in Psychology, 3*(2), 77–101. doi:10.1191/1478088706qp063oa

Charles Sturt University. (2015). Doctor of Psychology. Retrieved from http://www.csu.edu.au/handbook/handbook14/postgraduate/DoctorPsychology.html

Connell, J. (2010). *Migration and the globalisation of health care: The health worker exodus?*. Cheltenham, UK: Edward Elgar Publishing.

Cook, L. (2009). *The future of the medical workforce: First annual report November 2007–December 2008*. Wellington, New Zealand: Medical Training Board.

Council of Australian Deans and Directors of Graduate Studies. (2007). Guidelines on professional doctorates. Retrieved from https://www.gs.unsw.edu.au/policy/findapolicy/abapproved/policydocuments/05_07_professional_doctorates_guidelines.pdf

Dawkins, J. S. (1988). *Higher education: A policy statement*. Canberra: Australian Government Printing Service.

Department of Education Training and Youth Affairs. (2001). *Research training scheme guidelines*. Canberra: AGPS.

Evans, I. M., & Fitzgerald, J. (2007). Integrating research and practice in professional psychology: Models and paradigms. In I. M. Evans, J. J. Rucklidge, & M. O'Driscoll (Eds.), *Professional practice of psychology in Aotearoa New Zealand* (pp. 283–300). Wellington, New Zealand: New Zealand Psychological Society.

Evans, T. (2000). Meeting what ends? Challenges to doctoral education in Australia. In M. Kiley & G. Mullins (Eds.), *Quality in postgraduate research: Making ends meet* (pp. 59–67). Adelaide: Advisory Centre for University Education.

Gerring, J. (2004). What is a case study and what is it good for? *American Political Science Review, 98*(2), 341–354. doi:10.1017/S0003055404001182

Gibbons, M., Limoges, C., Nowotny, H., Schwartzman, S., Scott, P., & Trow, M. (1994). *The new production of knowledge: The dynamics of science and research in contemporary societies*. London, UK: Sage.

Gorman, D., Horsburgh, M., & Abbott, M. (2009). *A review of how the training of the New Zealand health workforce is planned and funded: A proposal for a reconfiguration of the clinical training agency*. Wellington, New Zealand: Health Workforce New Zealand.

Haig, B. D., & Marie, D. (2011). New Zealand. In D. B. Baker (Ed.), *The Oxford handbook of the history of psychology: Global perspectives* (pp. 377–394). Oxford: Oxford University Press.

Health Workforce Australia. (2013). Health workforce by numbers. *Australia's Health Workforce Series(1)*. Retrieved from http://www.medicaldeans.org.au/wp-content/uploads/Health-Workforce-by-Numbers-FINAL.pdf

Health Workforce New Zealand. (2013). New roles and scopes. Retrieved January 23, 2013, from http://www.healthworkforce.govt.nz/new-roles-and-scopes

Helmes, E. (2001). Professional doctoral degrees in psychology in Australia: Prospects and constraints. In B. Green, T. Maxwell, & P. Shanahan (Eds.), *Doctoral education and professional practice: The next generation* (pp. 139–162). Armidale: Kardoorair Press.

Helmes, E., & Pachana, N. A. (2005). Professional doctoral training in psychology: International comparison and commentary. *Australian Psychologist, 40*(1), 45–53.

Hunt, G. (2004). A sense of life: The future of industrial-style health care. *Nursing Ethics, 11*(2), 189–202.

Jaakkimainen, R. L., Schultz, S. E., Glazier, R. H., Abrahams, C., & Verma, S. (2012). Tracking family medicine graduates: Where do they go, what services do they provide and whom do they see? *BMC Family Practice, 13*(1), 26. doi: http://dx.doi.org/10.1186/1471-2296-13-26

James, H. L., & Willis, E. (2001). The professionalisation of midwifery through education or politics? *The Australian Journal of Midwifery, 14*(4), 27–30.

James Cook University. (2015). Doctor of Psychology (clinical Psychology). Retrieved from http://www-public.jcu.edu.au/courses/course_info/index.htm?userText=102312-DPS-CLI#.VfE0q31qKAZ

Kemp, D. A. (1999a). *Knowledge and innovation: A policy statement on research and research training.* Canberra: Australian Government Department of Education, Employment and Workplace Relations.

Kemp, D. A. (1999b). *New knowledge, new opportunities: A discussion paper on higher education research and research training.* Canberra: Australian Government Department of Education, Employment and Workplace Relations.

Kot, F. C., & Hendel, D. D. (2012). Emergence and growth of professional doctorates in the United States, United Kingdom, Canada and Australia: A comparative analysis. *Studies in Higher Education, 37*(3), 345–364.

Latham, S. R. (2010). Too few physicians, or too many? *The Hastings Center Report, 40*(1), 11–12.

Lee, A., Green, B., & Brennan, M. (2000). Organisational knowledge, professional practice and the professional doctorate at work. In J. Garrick & C. Rhodes (Eds.), *Research and knowledge at work: Perspectives, case-studies and innovative strategies.* New York, NY: Routledge.

Massey University. (2004). Massey University Calendar 2004. Retrieved from http://tur-www1.massey.ac.nz/~wwcalend/2004/index.htm

Massey University. (2015). The degree of Doctor of Clinical Psychology – Course regulations. Retrieved from http://www.massey.ac.nz/massey/about-massey/calendar/2009-calendar/degree-diploma-and-certificate-regulations/bphil-mphil-doctoral-and-intermediate-programs/the-degree-of-doctor-of-clinical-psychology.cfm

Maxwell, T. W. (2011). Australian professional doctorates: Mapping, distinctiveness, stress and prospects. *Work Based Learning e-Journal, 2*(1), 24–43.

Maxwell, T. W., & Shanahan, P. (2001). Professional doctoral education in Australia and New Zealand: Reviewing the scene. In B. Green, T. W. Maxwell & P. Shanahan (Eds.), *Doctoral education and professional practice: The next generation* (pp. 17–38). Armidale: Kardoorair Press.

Maxwell, T. W., Shanahan, P., & Green, B. (2001). Introduction: New opportunities in doctoral education and professional practice. In B. Green, T. Maxwell, & P. Shanahan (Eds.), *Doctoral education and professional practice: The next generation* (pp. 1–14). Armidale: Kardoooorair Press.

Maxwell, T. W., & Shanahan, P. J. (1997). Towards a reconceptualisation of the doctorate: Issues arising from comparative data relating to the EdD degree in

Australia. *Studies in Higher Education, 22*(2), 133–150. doi: 10.1080/0307
5079712331381004

McWilliam, E. L., Taylor, P., Thomson, P., Green, B., Maxwell, T. W., Wildy, H., &
Simons, D. (2002). *Research training in doctoral programs: What can be learned
from professional doctorates?* Canberra, Commonwealth of Australia: Department
of Education & Sciences.

Medical Deans of Australia and New Zealand. (2013). Medical schools outcomes
database. *Projects and Activities.* Retrieved from http://www.medicaldeans.org.
au/projects-activities/msod

Monash University. (2015a). Doctor of Medicine. Retrieved from http://monash.
edu.au/pubs/handbooks/courses/3852.html

Monash University. (2015b). Doctor of Psychology in Clinical Psychology for 2015.
Retrieved from http://www.monash.edu.au/study/coursefinder/course/2116/

Murdoch University. (2015). Doctor of Psychology in Clinical Psychology.
Retrieved from http://www.murdoch.edu.au/Courses/Doctor-of-Psychology-
in-Clinical-Psychology/

National Board of Employment Education and Training. (1989). *Review of
Australian graduate studies and higher degrees.* Canberra: Higher Education
Council.

New Zealand Psychologists Board. (2014). *Accreditation report: Massey University's
Doctor of Clinical Psychology [DclinPsych].* Wellington, New Zealand:
Psychologists Board. Retrieved from http://www.psychologistsboard.org.nz/
cms_show_download.php?id=304

Phillips, R. L., Jr., Petterson, S., Fryer, G. E., Jr., & Rosser, W. (2007). The Canadian
contribution to the US physician workforce. *Canadian Medical Association
Journal, 176*(8), 1083–1087.

Poultney, V. (2010). Challenging the PhD: Managing the alignment of an EdD
program alongside a traditional PhD pathway. *Work-based Learning e-Journal,
1*(1), 71–84.

Psychology Board of Australia. (2015). Accreditation. Retrieved from http://www.
psychologyboard.gov.au/Accreditation.aspx

Rolfe, G., & Davies, R. (2009). Second generation professional doctorates in
nursing. *International Journal of Nursing Studies, 46*(9), 1265–1273.

Scardamalia, M., & Bereiter, C. (2006). Knowledge building: Theory, pedagogy, and
technology. In K. Sawyer (Ed.), *Cambridge handbook of the learning sciences*
(pp. 97–118). New York: Cambridge University Press.

Scott, D., Brown, A., Lunt, I., & Thorne, L. (2004). *Professional doctorates: Integrating
professional and academic knowledge.* Buckingham: Open University Press.

Southern, S., Cade, R., & Locke, D. W. (2012). Doctor of professional counseling:
The next step. *The Family Journal, 20*(1), 5–12.

Stake, R. (1995). *The art of case study research.* London: Sage.

Storey, V. A. (2013). *Redesigning professional education doctorates: Applications of
critical friendship theory to the EdD.* New York, NY: Palgrave Macmillan.

Storey, V. A., Carter-Tellison, K., & Boerger, P. (2011). Critical friends: Curricular
redesign and implementation of a small independent university's doctoral
and undergraduate programs. In M. Macintyre Latta & S. Wunder (Eds.),

Placing practitioner knowledge at the center of teacher education – Rethinking the policies and practices of the education doctorate. Charlotte, NC: Information Age Publishing.

Swinburne University of Technology. (2015). Doctor of Psychology (Clinical Psychology). Retrieved from http://www.swinburne.edu.au/study/courses/Doctor-of-Psychology-%28Clinical-Psychology%29-DR-CLIPSY/local

Taylor, N., & Maxwell, T. W. (2004). Enhancing the relevance of a professional doctorate: The case of the doctor of education degree at the University of New England. *Asia-Pacific Journal of Cooperative Education, 5*(1), 60–69.

Tertiary Education Advisory Commission Report One. (2000). *Shaping a vision: Report of the Tertiary Education Advisory Commission*. Wellington: Tertiary Education Advisory Commission.

Tertiary Education Advisory Commission Report Two. (2001). *Shaping the system: Report of the Tertiary Education Advisory Commission*. Wellington: Tertiary Education Advisory Commission.

Tertiary Education Advisory Commission Report Three. (2001). *Shaping the strategy: Report of the Tertiary Education Advisory Commission*. Wellington: Tertiary Education Advisory Commission.

Tertiary Education Advisory Commission Report Four. (2001). *Shaping the funding framework: Report of the Tertiary Education Advisory Commission*. Wellington: Tertiary Education Advisory Commission.

University of Auckland. (2015). Doctor of Clinical Psychology (DClinPsy). Retrieved from https://www.auckland.ac.nz/study-options/programs/postgraduate/7105/doctor-of-clinical-psychology-dclinpsy

University of Canberra. (2015). Professional Doctorate Nurse Practitioner. Retrieved from http://www.canberra.edu.au/faculties/health/courses/nursing/professional-doctorate-nurse-practitioner

University of Melbourne. (2015). Doctors/Masters Level – Doctor of Medicine. Retrieved from http://coursesearch.unimelb.edu.au/grad/1591-doctor-of-medicine

University of Notre Dame. (2015). Course regulations: Doctor of Medicine. Retrieved from http://www.nd.edu.au/__data/assets/pdf_file/0019/110638/Doctor-of-Medicine-14JAN.pdf

University of Otago. (2014a). Doctor of Medicine (MD). Retrieved from http://www.otago.ac.nz/courses/qualifications/md.html

University of Otago. (2014b). University of Otago handbook for PhD study. Retrieved from http://www.otago.ac.nz/study/phd/handbook/

University of Wollongong. (2015). Doctor of Psychology (clinical). Retrieved from http://www.uow.edu.au/handbook/yr2012/pg/hbs/H12006803.html

West, R. (1998). *Learning for life: Review of higher education financing and policy. Final report [West report]*. Canberra: Department of Employment, Education, Training and Youth Affairs.

Yin, R. K. (1994). *Case study research: Design and methods*. London, UK: Sage.

Zurn, P., & Dumont, J. C. (2008). Health workforce and international migration: Can New Zealand compete? *OECD Health Working Papers*. Geneva, Switzerland: Organisation for Economic Co-operation and Development.

3

Trends in Doctoral Education in Australia

Margaret Malloch

This chapter considers the trends and contributions of professional doctorates to the doctoral landscape in Australia. The emergence of the professional doctorate onto the Australian academic landscape began in the 1990s, and remains one of the forms of doctorates available today. This period of growth in professional doctorates has been followed by a retraction and a cutting back in the number of courses, particularly in education, that are offered.

Current trends for doctorates in Australia are reviewed and discussed against a backdrop of international developments. Research into a cross section of professional doctorate programs and participant observation, particularly the EdD, is drawn upon. As an "embedded" coordinator of a doctor of education, contributions have been made through the development, delivery, reflections from practice, and through the review of a specific course. Critical friends are integral to the course review and redevelopment, in addition to providing information pertaining to how we consider the varying forms, modes, and delivery of doctorates. It is argued that the Australian doctoral agenda has been minimized and functionalized due to a series of national policy shifts and through the assessment of institutional viability. As a result of the doctoral agenda being potentially compromised, suggestions for future directions are posed.

Introduction

Doctorates possibly began around the twelfth century in Paris, serving as a license to teach in the church, and then emerging as university degrees in medicine, theology, and law (www.worldwidelearn.com/

doctorate-degrees), which focused on professional preparation and entry. The research-focused doctor of philosophy (PhD) was an early nineteenth-century development introduced by Humbolt in Germany (Pearson, 2005) and by Yale, for example, in 1861. Internationally, the doctorate, with an emphasis on research, became the entry qualification for university academic appointments. Historically, the PhD was the first type of doctoral qualification offered in Australia. For the Australian academic context, links with England were integral for this level of research. Traditionally, the PhD was oriented toward full-time younger students undertaking scientific and technological research. Australia's first doctoral graduate was a PhD at the University of Melbourne in 1948, Joyce Stone with her thesis entitled "Virus Haemagglutination: a review of the literature" (Strugnall, 2010).

The first professional doctorate was awarded in the United States in 1921 in Education, in Australia in 1984 in the Creative Arts, and in the United Kingdom in 1989 in Clinical Psychology (Scott, Brown, Lunt, & Thorne, 2004). A doctor of business administration, doctor of psychology, and a doctor of education emphasizing applied research and professional relationships became more common. Thus, professional doctorates became prevalent in the twentieth century, attracting mature, professional, part-time students.

In Australia, the PhD continued as the sole doctoral qualification until the 1990s when a range of models of professional doctorates was introduced. Australian higher education took a prominent position in the 1980s and 1990s in the development and provision of a diverse range of over 100 professional doctorates, offered by 30 universities (Council of Deans and Directors of Graduate Studies, 1998) with the overall enrolments in doctoral programs doubling between 1996 and 2000 (Maxwell and Shanahan, 2001). Between 1989 and 1996, the number of doctoral students went from 7,000 to over 22,000 (Pearson & Ford, 1997), with two-thirds of the students aged over 30 and one-third being part-time students. The aforementioned represents the changing landscape of the doctorate.

This chapter explores the twenty-first century trends for professional doctorates in Australia, and the challenges they face for survival, with particular reference to the doctor of education.

The International Context

Changes in doctoral programs were also occurring in other continents and national education systems. In the United States, the Carnegie Foundation has conducted research into the doctoral agenda with specific emphasis on the development of new doctoral programs, via the Carnegie Initiative on the Doctorate. In a sense, the Foundation served as a critical friend encouraging new approaches to the doctorate. Shulman (2010) advocated that there should be PhD programs, for those wanting to pursue research and work in a university, and professional practice doctorate programs which would bring together study, practice, and study-embedded practice.

In the United States, the professional doctorate is closely linked to entry to professions. There has been considerable debate in recent times as to the development of a new practitioner-oriented degree comparing Shulman, Golde, Conklin Bueschel, and Garabedian's (2006) preference for the "actuality" of practice with a call for a more complex form of practice. Olsen and Clark (2009) at Arizona State University initiated a doctor of education which builds on the work of education professionals in the local schools community.

In England, doctoral awards include the following: (1) a "traditional" PhD, (2) a PhD by Publication, (3) the new route PhD with significant taught subjects, (4) the professional doctorate with taught elements and research, (5) and the practice-based doctorate, which includes a supervised research project, frequently a creative product accompanied by a written supporting piece (Park, 2007, p. 33) There is also the practice of a transition into a PhD or professional doctorate from a master's program. The United Kingdom Council for Graduate Education (UKCGE) defines the professional doctorate as

> a program of advanced study and research which, whilst satisfying the University criteria for the award of a doctorate, is designed to meet the specific needs of a professional group external to the University. (UKCGE, 2002, p. 62)

Professional doctorate programs have proliferated and grown quickly in the United Kingdom. Among an array of field-specific professional doctorates, in 1996/97 Middlesex University (MU) introduced the MU professional doctorate which focused on the individual learner's professional experience, practice, and interests delivered through the Centre for Work Based Learning. This doctorate program focuses on the candidate as a self-managed learner, building on their own professional experience (Stephenson, Malloch, & Cairns, 2006). Such models of doctoral programs have influenced some of the developments in Australia.

This "flowering" of professional doctorates in the 1990s and the first decade of the 2000s has been followed by a shift in focus, a shift in lexicon, and a shift in priorities with different agendas, which ultimately impacts the courses offered, their composition, and delivery.

The Australian doctoral agenda shares many aspects in common with international education, particularly with England and the United States. With massification of university education, along with the national goals for highly skilled workers, there has been more attention paid to enrolment, completion, and attrition rates (Neumann, 2003). Out of the Bologna Declaration of 1999 and the Lisbon Strategy, 2000, the European Union Research and Innovation strategy established goals to increase the number of doctoral researchers with a target of 3% of GDP from investment in doctoral research (Thomson & Walker, 2010). Australia similarly is concerned about outcomes from doctorates and workforce productivity (Australian Workforce and Productivity Agency, 2012). Usher (2002) argues that the knowledge economy has replaced an epistemological definition of knowledge with an economic one, with knowledge contributing to production. This has shifted what it means to be an academic and has made the focus of research to be more commercialized and marketed. There is an emphasis on innovation and performativity, with audits and risk assessments, whereas an example would include common activities to support strategic planning.

Greater attention to outcomes and the quality agendas is now more prominent in policy and funding of the Australian postgraduate research program, and is certainly evident in the United States (Council of Graduate Schools and Educational Testing Service, 2010), with concerns for more timely completions and goals for human capital replacement. The UKCGE in "Quality and Standards of Postgraduate Research Degrees," their 1996 discussion paper, identified quality assurance, monitoring, and mechanisms to support students concerns (Thomson & Walker, 2010). Along with the concerns for quality and outcomes, the achievement of doctoral skills and student competencies have also been emphasized and audited. The Research Training Scheme introduced in Australia in 2007 shifted the focus from load or enrolments, to an emphasis on completion rates (Barbara Evans in Powell and Green, 2007).

Another shift is in university funding. Funding for universities is decreasing with a shift in national budget priorities. With the Australian government's postgraduate research student funding based on completions, with reduced numbers of places and expectations of more timely completions of three years full-time with a possible one year extension, there is pressure on the institutions, the supervisors, and the students. Universities also have to provide research training plans with more structured programs, support for supervisors, and regular progress reviews. For professional doctorates with cohorts of part-time students, frequently full fee-paying economy of scale remains important. The rhetoric of the twenty-first century is that establishing financial viability through sufficient numbers is important;

universities are a business, a business that cannot afford to operate at a loss. The impact of this emphasis on a reduction of support for public institutions such as universities and education with increased production has led to the reconsideration of courses, their potential markets, their financial viability, and profitability.

Australian Professional Doctorates—A First Generation

The Australian Qualifications Framework (2013, p. 63) provides the following distinctions between the PhD and the professional doctorate:

> Research is the defining characteristic of all Doctoral Degree qualifications. The research Doctoral Degree (typically referred to as a doctor of philosophy or PhD) makes a significant and original contribution to knowledge; the professional Doctoral Degree (typically titled doctor of [field of study]) makes a significant and original contribution to knowledge in the context of professional practice. The emphasis in the learning outcomes and research may differ between the different forms of Doctoral Degree qualifications but all graduates will demonstrate knowledge, skills and the application of the knowledge and skills at AQF level 10.

In order to be classified as a research degree, a professional doctorate in Australia has to be formed to include one-third course work and two-thirds research. The degree generally consists of course work subjects and a thesis or portfolio. Part-time delivery is the most common form of delivery and/or study. This model of professional doctorate is generally referred to as first generation; such a structure and focus forms a model dominated by the constraints of the academy (Maxwell, 2003).

The courses frequently highlight the interaction, the importance of bringing together research, theory, and practice. Professional needs, professional practice, and the work of the candidate are focal points. The workplace learning and the work of the student or candidate form an important basis for the research in professional doctorates. Professional doctorates, which multiplied in the 1990s, were viewed as useful for busy professionals wanting to enhance their professional status through study at the doctoral level within a structural framework frequently delivered to cohorts of students. The professional doctorate offers a connection between work and study, research and practice.

Several Australian universities expanded their professional doctorate program into Asia. It became fashionable to provide a program for an overseas partner's cohorts. These programs provided opportunities for offshore delivery and for international students to study with an Australian

University from home. The courses provided models for partnership universities to utilize and establish similar courses. These doctoral programs presented many challenges and difficulties, for example, language, access to resources, and distance modes of delivery. Another potential challenge was related to enrolment numbers, which was key to financial viability in respect to partnership delivery.

The doctor of education has typically attracted mid-career professionals engaged in education and training from a range of fields, generally working full-time and seeking to enhance their skills. This description could also apply to candidates in the PhD in Education faculties. This raises the question of differentiation between the two types of doctorate, with the possibility of different target populations, differing entry requirements, and different fees structures, and students' and academics' concerns as to the status and international currency. In Australia, professional doctorates were full fee paying and when the federal government introduced student loans in 2003, the capacity to pay became an important distinguishing feature (Neumann, 2005). Thus challenges on the domestic and international fronts began to erode the earlier enthusiasm for professional doctorates.

Local Experience

The doctor of education in which I work is a professional doctorate characterized by a number of taught subjects and a substantial piece of independent enquiry presented in the writing of a thesis. There is an emphasis on professional practice and applied research. It may be classified as a first-generation style of professional doctorate with a focus on professional and applied knowledge.

The focus of this doctor of education is influenced by the professional identity of the students who bring their professional experience, expertise, and workplace learning into the taught subjects and assessment tasks. Theses focus on issues related to specific work challenges.

> The course aims to provide experienced professionals with opportunities to extend understandings about research and theory, as it relates to practice, to expert levels of scholarship; and enhance performance in roles in education and training to standards expected of leaders in the field. (www.vu.edu.au/courses/doctor-of-education-hzed)

The doctor of education was designed in the mid-1990s with a keen interest in delivery in Asia with a local partner university. The course initiator called a meeting for interested staff to join him in planning further development and delivery; there were three of us at the meeting. This did not provide a critical mass for constructive critique, but all were committed. This level of study was far from the core business of a School of Education, which focused mainly on providing preservice training for teachers. The majority of academics participating in the course were casual staff, as ongoing and/or tenured staff could not be spared from the undergraduate courses. The status of the course was also questioned at university level. Despite arguments of "different but equal," common in this doctoral landscape, there was criticism of what was viewed as not the same as a PhD, not a real doctorate.

The people enrolled in the course are professionals from the fields of nursing, school education, higher education, adult education and training, law, occupational health and safety, agriculture, and business. There have been more women than men taking the course, especially in the Thai cohorts, and candidates were generally in their forties or older (the oldest were in their late sixties). This is in keeping with the national numbers (Pearson, Cumming, Evans, Macauley, & Ryland, 2011) with increasing percentages of women and older candidates in the doctorate. The cohort delivery and the development of a community of support and encouragement have been important and a contributing factor for the selection of a doctor of education, for example, over undertaking a PhD.

Career goals of participants in the doctor of education are varied; for those working in universities, the doctorate has contributed to possibilities and hopes for career reinforcements and advancements. For the majority, achieving a doctorate was part of a rite of passage, an achievement of a goal, an enhancement of skills, and learning. There have been few interested in embarking on an academic career. Career goals are diverse (Pearson et al., 2011), again in common with national trends. Pearson et al. in their 2005 survey conducted with support from the Council of Postgraduate Student Association (2011, p. 530) found that 39% of respondents envisaged university work, with 23% not being sure (2011, p. 538).

Having a critical mass of doctoral students in cohorts increased pressures on the university procedures and processes of enrolment, candidature, ethics applications, and supervision. The examination of professional doctorate thesis has presented challenges with examiners more familiar with the PhD, and therefore with expectations in keeping with that degree. Given that in the field of education, candidates tend to research aspects of their own work and their professions, there can be a blurring and lack of distinction between a PhD and a professional doctorate thesis.

Within the university culture, there is still some uncertainty as to the value of the professional doctorate. The PhD is generally regarded as the gold standard, a model with academic familiarity, even if it can be argued that it may historically be a later entrant in the doctoral stakes than professional doctorates. Status is an issue, as Shulman et al. (2006, pp. 25, 26) noted that distinctions between the doctor of education and the PhD were not obvious, with theses having similar foci; however, the EdD was nevertheless considered a "PhD Lite." Such issues are experienced at local institutional levels and further afield.

Nearly two decades later, a series of minor course updates, two Thai cohorts, and a number of smaller local cohorts later, the course is being reviewed and revamped aiming for a stronger, more flexible course to attract both an international and local market. This iteration is drawing on an inner core course committee of invited personnel across the college and from the university research center. Monthly meetings are held with an executive officer to provide administrative support. Each core committee member nominated two members to form an expert reference group. The core group is drawing together internal and external data for an environmental scan, university course documentation, and benchmarking other courses, Australian and international. The expert reference group will provide additional input and critique and an external community group will also provide perspectives. These committee structures are intended to provide opportunities for critical conversations. Those unfamiliar with the doctoral landscape are able to contribute questions useful to the overall deliberations. It is also a challenge to bridge the gap between ideological positions held in education and the realities of financial viability and the need for senior management endorsement.

A positive outcome, such as the production of a new course, is not necessarily expected by some college members who see the existence of a selected core group as a limiting of critical conversation. Moore and Carter-Hicks's (2014) account of the use of a critical friends group approach for long-term and collaborative faculty development and the building of an intellectual community provides a positive example of how work for such a course development could be undertaken. This would be a goal for a project with a longer time frame and fewer organizational steps to go through. Handal (1999) points to the usefulness of having a critical mirror held by a friend on our work to help us improve the work. His recommendations for individual development are applicable for a group. This includes having several colleagues involved for meaningful discourse, with the competence to analyze, discuss, and provide critique. People who are not immediate colleagues but who are accepted as significant others can usefully contribute perspectives outside of the local context. This model resonates with the core and expert reference groups established to review and revitalize the course. It also has to be noted that with the usual organizational events such as leave and clashes of meetings, there are different faces at each meeting, which presents challenges for momentum. Another college is interested in collaboration and has joined in the deliberations. This course still follows the general structure common for the doctor of education in the 1990s, with coursework and a thesis with an orientation to research of professional practice (Maxwell & Shanahan, 1997). It is hoped that the critical conversations will eventually arrive at a model for an innovative and viable course, which will be attractive to potential students. There is a keen interest in keeping the doctor of education going, to expand it and to attract international students.

Second-Generation Initiatives

Drawing upon critical consultation processes, Maxwell (2003) has reported on shifts in the conceptualization, structures, and focus of professional doctorates. Maxwell (2003) writes of three case studies of second-generation professional doctorates. The first is a doctor of technology grappling with the challenges of addressing the rigor of the university, applied to workplace realities which include time, people, and financial constraints, while the second is a doctor of business administration who aimed for applied research, employing reflection on professional practice and development of the scholar executive. The third case study is of a doctor of education situated in the workplace with a partnership between the university and the employer integrating the degree experience with employer needs; employers can be co-supervisors. They have moved from Mode 1 knowledge focusing on disciplinary knowledge production to Mode 2 with an emphasis on knowledge arising from practitioner agency or reflection on practice.

Maxwell's (2003) university model of EdD, which was developed after meetings and a collegiate retreat, moved to a hybrid curriculum model with course work moving from Mode 1 to Mode 2 knowledge, which included more structured research methods and a portfolio rather than a dissertation to enable short workplace-relevant pieces of research.

Challenges of the Twenty-First Century

The discussion and debate on professional doctorates and their shape and place in the doctoral space in the academy and the economy continue. Maxwell's case studies raise issues of the modes of knowledge focused upon, the relationships between the academy, the student and the workplace, and the possibilities for doctorates within that discussion. They focus more on the learner, on applied research relevant to professional practice, and the workplace that includes employer needs.

The second generation of professional doctorates aims to move beyond the first generation of professional doctorates, which have been bounded by the concerns of universities to be different, but not too different, and understandable concerns to attract national research funding recognition and support. Some innovation and difference could be tolerated, but within procedural and financial limits.

Evans (1997, p. 178) had identified this effort to be different in the professional doctorates:

> One could argue that the professional doctorate has been embraced in Australia as a means to achieve a different, some would even say, better type of doctoral (usually research) degree.
>
> Its purpose is to produce useful or significant knowledge, where the usefulness or significance of the knowledge is determined by its application, relevance and pertinence to a professional or workplace context, rather than to a body of knowledge within an academic discipline (as in the case of the PhD).

This first generation of doctor of education professional doctorates has been moderately conservative rather than innovative. The product, the output, of a thesis, albeit shorter than that required for a PhD, could be criticized as too similar in focus, style, and examination to the PhD. Malfoy (2004) noted that professional doctorates have been framed as research degrees combining university rigor with workplace and professional engagement. Lunt (2002) identified challenges for the future of education professional doctorates questioning as to whether a thesis is the most appropriate way to examine for the doctor of education thesis, the qualification, parity with the PhD, assessment, suggesting exit qualifications for those unable to go onto the thesis, and asking what professional knowledge entails and its relationship to academic knowledge.

Evans (1997, p. 175) identified the increase in corporatization in universities, especially of management structures and procedures for greater efficiency and quality control; in tandem with this were shifts to flexible learning and flexible delivery. The broader range of students and different expectations of universities in relation to research, critique, and challenge have contributed in exploring different approaches to PhD research.

European and UK developments and vocational education and training agendas also were influenced by flexibility, that is, flexible learning and flexible delivery. He argued that the reshaping of the doctorate relates to this emphasis on flexibility, and indeed the shift to an expansion in this level of study required a shift to flexible learning.

The first-generation professional doctorates started out with vigor and enthusiasm, and were then challenged to survive by the shifts in national funding and research priorities. Overall, enrolments in doctorates have steadily increased in Australia, as have completions. However, McAlpine and Norton (2006) raise the important consideration of doctoral attrition rates at approximately 50%.

Interviews with doctor of education course coordinators (Malloch, 2010) identified five models in relation to the first generation of this course and its future. The first was *Elimination* in which the doctor of education was replaced by a PhD by project. Lack of financial viability and dwindling numbers sealed the fate of this EdD. This was a common response by several universities in relation to the doctor of education. They did utilize learning from the EdD in reframing their PhD programs, particularly with the inclusion of research subjects and modes of delivery.

The second, *Constant Reinvention*, entailed the regular revisions developed in consultation with staff, students, and the professional community. This provided a critical conversation that formed the basis for reviews and new ideas. The third was *Watchful Waiting*, a stance adopted by a prestigious university with a robust and marketable course. National and University policies were carefully considered along with monitoring of numbers and outcomes. There was as yet no need to make any changes. The fourth model, *Transdisciplinary*, entailed developing a pan university, across the professions course with an emphasis on electronic cohorts. Critical conversations within the academic community contributed to this development. The fifth model offered a guide for *future developments*. The interviewee felt that the days of the professional doctorate were gone, that use of pre-Internet resources and struggles with twenty-first century learning did not bode well. However, the interviewee advocated a model focused on the learner with consideration of what they bring to the course, and with five principles: respect rich, structure rich, conversation rich, information rich, and challenge rich. The interviewee advocated that commitment from the learner, industry, and the university is important. While each interviewee raised challenges for the doctor of education, there was a commitment to professional doctorates and their contribution to the doctoral landscape in Australia.

Other contributions to the further development of the doctor of education consisted of encouraging variations in the framework of subjects, research focus, and output or product.

McAlpine and Norton (2006) propose an integrative framework of nested discipline, department, and institutional contexts to guide research and action that would coexist with national goals for highly qualified people to contribute to research and development agendas. They stress the importance for student voices to be heard. Others raise the issue of the relationship of the workplace to doctorates. In the first-generation doctor of education programs, frequent reference was made to the workplace, the site for the student's professional experience and research, the relevance of the research, and the contribution to professional knowledge. However, meaningful interactions would be rare; students bring their professional and workplace experience and learning to the university and to their assessment tasks and theses, and take their learning back to their workplaces. Students link the workplace and the university.

The Doctor of Education and the Twenty-First Century

The professional doctorate for the twenty-first century in Australia is one that has managed to survive the vicissitudes of economic restrictions, academic conventions, prejudices, and uncertainties as to status, product, assessment, examination, and relevance. The growing political agenda to increase university fees, and to provide less funding for research, has impacted postgraduate research, and the numbers enrolling at the beginning of 2015 are considerably reduced. The challenge is to come up with a course, which is attractive to a sufficient number of students in order to be financially viable, and develop a curriculum that is respectful of the students and their professional expertise, which can be meaningfully incorporated into the workplace. Students in professional doctorates bring extensive and rich professional expertise and experiences to be built into the courses.

The current trend for the doctor of education in Australia has been to terminate the courses, and to utilize the units for the development of PhD students. The product, the thesis in some of these revamped PhDs, has also been modified, to emphasize more practice. Only a small number of the doctor of education courses which started out as first-generation professional doctorates continue.

As a participant-observer in my own workplace, I am seeing a strengthening of the PhD in changes to its composition and to the entry to the course. There is pressure to increase the numbers of students, the quality of their theses, and the timeliness of their completion. Supervisor training is integral to these targets. Efforts are being made to think of ways to attract students into the PhD. A working party is developing a pathway for an alternative entry to the PhD, thereby providing a bridge between course work master's programs and the research doctorate. This initiative is inspired by a similar course at another university that is attracting large numbers of international students. The PhD has been modified with the addition of two research units on the literature and methodology, and preparation of the research proposal. A set assessment result has to be reached in order to proceed to the thesis. The emphasis is very much on research per se, not bringing to the fore the professional experience of the students. This revamped PhD is similar to England's New Route PhD. It aims to develop the research skills and knowledge of the students to more successfully embark on their thesis. The length of candidature is not altered; there is more to fit in to the same number of years. Nevertheless, there are positive results to date: most of the students in the first groups to go through these modules are doing well and the students meet others from across the university and learn more of resources and support.

A university-wide framework for skill and research development to support the achievement of more timely completions of higher quality theses is now in place. Similar initiatives are seen in England with the VITAE Researcher Development Framework (2010). The university has other professional doctorates in Business and Psychology, a doctorate by Publication and the PhD. As Malfoy (2004) points out, professional doctorates have contributed to the thinking and approaches to doctoral study in general. The PhD is benefitting by applying learning from the professional doctorates and thereby possibly contributing to their demise. It does appear to be a competing environment rather than complementary provision of doctoral programs in the Australian context.

Where to from Here?

The model of a doctorate interlinking the university, the professional practice, and change (Malfoy, 2004) more accurately reflects the doctor of education at my workplace. This forms the basis for the current conversations for the course review. Challenges for the course review and revitalization are many. The debate on the role and relevance of the workplace in the doctorate is yet to be had. There are assumptions of relevance and commitment that are not borne out in practice. Workplaces can be antagonistic to doctoral research and to the student undertaking it. The inclusion of workplaces as more than sites for research may be able to be developed, especially with critical input from the external expert group. Letting the workplace into the academy in doctorates is difficult. Examples of involvement from other professional doctorates include employers as supervisors, contributions to curriculum, and support of the research projects. These are yet to be considered and built upon. There is a tension between involvement of the "outside world" in the university with its regulated structures and frameworks. There is also the tension between conceptions of knowledge; is the doctorate to contribute knowledge to a field, to a discipline, and/or to a profession? Should this be kept as a dichotomy? Shulman's (2010) work in conjunction with the Carnegie Foundation recommends that having clear distinctions between the PhD and a doctorate for professional practice offer a way of achieving similar but different doctoral programs. In Australia, local experience indicates a subsuming of the professional doctorate by a revised PhD.

The positioning of the student is also an issue. If the goal is to have the student as a self-directed learner managing their own doctorate, then ways to support and encourage this are required. The Five Pillars of Wisdom model (Malloch, 2010) provides a challenge to place the learner at the center of the doctorate with values of respect, trust, and challenge within a rich structure and context. To have a vibrant doctor of education program which will attract domestic and international professionals keen to develop their learning, skills, and expertise and aiming to contribute to change in their own professional work is the goal for the College Doctor of Education Committee. Whether this is realistic or wishful thinking in a climate of reduced national government support for higher education and research and declining enrolments is yet to be seen.

References

Australian Qualification Framework Council. (2013). *Australian qualifications framework*. South Australia: Australian Qualification Framework Council.

Australian Workforce and Productivity Agency. (2012). *Annual report 2012–2013*. Canberra: Australian Government. Retrieved from www.awpa.gov.au

Council of Deans and Directors of Graduate Studies (CDDGS). (1998). *Guidelines: Professional doctorates*. Brisbane, Australia. Unpublished Paper prepared by Terry Evans, Adrian Fisher and Wolfgang Gritchting.

Council of Graduate Schools and Educational Testing Service. (2010). The Path Forward: The Future of Graduate Education in the United States. Report from the Commission on the Future of Graduate Education in the United States. Princeton, NJ: Educational Testing Service.

Evans, B. (2007). Doctoral education in Australia. In S. Powell & H. Green (Eds.), *The doctorate worldwide* (pp. 105–119). Berkshire, UK, and New York: Society for Research into Higher Education & Open University Press.

Evans, T. (1997). Flexible doctoral research: Emerging issues in professional doctorate programs. *Studies in Continuing Education, 19*(2), 174–182.

Handal, G. (1999). Consultation using critical friends. *New Directions for Teaching and Learning, 79,* 59–70.

Lunt, I. (2002). *Professional doctorates in education*. Escalate. Retrieved from www.
escalate.ac.uk

Malfoy, J. (2004). Conceptualisation of a professional doctorate program:
Focusing on practice and change. *The Australian Educational Researcher,*
31(2) 63–79.

Malloch, M. (2010). Professional doctorates: An Australian perspective. *Work Based*
Learning e-Journal, 1(1), 35–56.

Maxwell, T. (2003). From first to second generation professional doctorate. *Studies*
in Higher Education, 28(3), 281–291.

Maxwell, T. W. (2011). Australian professional doctorates: Mapping, distinctiveness, stress and prospects. *Work Based Learning e-journal, 2*(1), 24–43.

Maxwell, T. W, & Shanahan, P. J. (1997). Towards a reconceptualising the doctorate:
Issues arising from comparative data on the EdD degree in Australia. *Studies in*
Higher Education, 22(2), 133–150.

Maxwell, T. W., & Shanahan, P. J. (2001). Professional Doctoral Education in
Australia and New Zealand: Reviewing the scene. In Green B., Maxwell T. W.,
and Shanahan P. (Eds.), *Doctoral Education and Professional Practice: The Next*
Generation? Armidale: Kardoorair Press, 16–38.

McAlpine, L., & Norton, J. (2006). Reframing our approach to doctoral programs:
An integrative framework for action and research. *Higher Education Research &*
Development, 25(1), 3–17.

Moore, J. A., & Carter-Hicks, J. (2014). Let's talk! Facilitating a faculty learning
community using a critical friends group approach. *International Journal for the*
Scholarship of Teaching and Learning, 8(2), 1–17.

Neumann, R. (2003). *The doctoral education experience: Diversity and complexity.*
Canberra: Department of Education, Science and Training, Commonwealth of
Australia.

Neumann, R. (2005). Doctoral differences: Professional doctorates and PhDs compared. *Journal of Higher Education Policy and Management, 27*(2), 173–188.

Olsen, R., & Clark, C. C. (2009). A signature pedagogy in doctoral education: The
leader scholar community. *Educational Researcher, 38*, 216–221.

Park, C. (2007). *Redefining the doctorate*. York, UK: The Higher Education
Academy.

Pearson, M. (2005). Framing research on doctoral education in Australia in a global
context. *Higher Education Research & Development, 24*(2), 119–134.

Pearson, M., Cumming, J., Evans, T., Macauley, P., & Ryland, K. (2011). How
shall we know them? Capturing the diversity of difference in Australian doctoral candidates and their experiences. *Studies in Higher Education, 36*(5),
527–542.

Pearson, M., & Ford, L. (1997). *Open and flexible PhD study and research*. Canberra:
Department of Employment, Education, Training and Youth and Affairs,
Australian Government Publishing Service.

Scott, D., Brown, A., Lunt, I., & Thorne, L. (2004). *Professional doctorates integrating*
professional and academic knowledge. Berkshire, UK: Open University Press,
McGraw Hill Education.

Shulman, L. S. (2010). Doctoral education shouldn't be a Marathon. *Chronicle of Higher Education, 56*(30), B9–12. Retrieved from chronicle.com/article/Doctoral-Education-isn't-a/64883/

Shulman, L. S., Golde, C. M., Conklin Bueschel, A., & Garabedian, K. (2006). Reclaiming education's doctorates: A critique and a proposal. *Educational Researcher, 5*(3), 25–32.

Stephenson, J., Malloch, M., & Cairns, L. (2006). Managing their own program: A case study of the first graduates of a new kind of doctorate in professional practice. *Studies in Continuing Education, 28*(1), 17–32.

Strugnall, D. (2010). The 21st century PhD. *University of Melbourne Voice, 6*(6), 8. Retrieved from voice.unimelb.edu.au/volume-6/number-6/21stcentury-phd

Thomson, P., & Walker, M. (2010). Doctoral education in context, the changing nature of the doctorate and doctoral students. In M. Walker & P. Thomson (Eds.), *The Routledge doctoral supervisor's companion* (pp. 9–26). Abingdon, Oxon, New York: Routledge.

UK Council for Graduate Education. (2002). *Report on professional doctorates.* Dudley: UKCGE.

Usher, R. (2002). A diversity of doctorates: Fitness for the knowledge economy? *Higher Education Research & Development, 21*(2), 143–152.

VITAE. (2010). *The researcher development framework.* UK: Careers Research and Advisory Centre. Retrieved from www.worldwidelearn.com/doctorate-degrees, accessed February 2015.

Victoria University. (2014). The Doctor of Education. Retrieved from http://www.vu.edu.au/courses/doctor-of-education-hzed, accessed March 2014.

4

Australian EdDs: At a Crossroad?

T. W. Maxwell

Introduction

Australia has been a leader in doctoral education over the last two decades. Proponents of the doctor of education (EdD), among others, in the early 1990s led the development of a range of awards termed "professional doctorates" (Maxwell & Shanahan, 1996), which were intended to contrast with the traditional PhD. The latter was then considered more academic, the former more professional, in orientation. A professional doctorate holder would not normally aspire for employment in a university though a good case can be made for professional doctorate holders to be hired by universities. A body of Australian professional doctoral literature has developed in Australia (see, e.g., Brennan, 1995; Ellis, 2006; Lee, Brennan, & Green, 2009; Malloch, 2010; Maxwell, 2011; Maxwell, Hickey, & Evans, 2005; Maxwell & Shanahan, 1996, 1998, 2001; McWilliam, 2003; Neumann, 2005; Pearson, 2006; Stock, 2013; Trigwell, Shannon, & Maurizi, 1997; Voudouris & Hunter, 2011). Some international comparative studies have been undertaken (e.g., Kot & Hendel, 2012; Servage, 2009; Whitechurch, 2009). A key doctoral education meeting place for 20 years has been the Quality in Postgraduate Research series of conferences held in Adelaide (see http://www.qpr.edu.au/).

In Australia we have previously made a distinction between in-service and preservice doctorates. A preservice doctorate is one that follows directly from undergraduate education leading to qualifications to act in a professional capacity. Preservice doctorates are also known as first degree doctorates in North America. In-service doctorates are awarded following some years of experience in the field. In Australia this distinction has become especially necessary because in recent times the University of Melbourne has followed the North American model and introduced what it terms the "Melbourne model" for certain prestigious master's (second cycle) awards. It includes in the award title the word "doctor," for example, doctor of medicine (MD) (see UMelb, 2011, p. 1). My concern here is with in-service professional doctorates. Additionally, I shall use the term "supervisor" of doctoral students. This term is equivalent to the North American term "advisor."

Theoretical Background

The early structural difference between the professional doctorates like the EdD and the PhD was relevant in the 1990s. The early rationale included (1) that busy professionals needed to become familiar with relevant literature, which was addressed through the course work. This familiarity was not always evident, perhaps understandably so, certainly among early EdD students at the University of New England (UNE) which started its EdD in the early 1990s (Taylor & Maxwell, 2004). UNE is a small, regional university with a strong distance education history and the early EdD courses were paper-based and had residential schools unlike now with most work completed online. (2) The PhD was seen as "too academic" especially by/ for busy professionals (Clark, 1996). This meant that the knowledge and skills learned were not useful in the workplace. This was a similar concern to that expressed by Chris Golde (2006) in her opening chapter of *Envisioning the Future of Doctoral Education* but different in that Golde's book appeared to privilege the disciplines and emphasized "scholars."

Our interest was in doctoral education for professionals. (3) Professional doctorates needed to be more practice-oriented and "equivalent to but different from" the PhD. Here "equivalent to" meant a research award of similar standing and "different from" meant not academic (see Seddon, 2001; Wellington, 2013). This contrasts with many professional practice doctorates in the United States as described by Zusman (2013). As a university award, the professional doctorate needed to contribute to the person becoming a better professional, even a researching professional, perhaps in North American terms, the scholar professional.

The theoretical breakthrough for the professional doctorate came about in the early 2000s for many of us. I argued (Maxwell, 2003), along with others, that the structural difference was not critical, not even important. The key to that argument was Mode 2 knowledge production (Gibbons et al., 1994, see below) and that professional doctorates were the logical site for that work. In fact, there is a long history of philosophical argument to support the position of knowledge creation through practice (Flood, 2011).

I further argued (Maxwell, 2003) that professional doctorates needed to address Mode 2 rather than Mode 1 knowledge production. Gibbons et al. (1994) distinguished between Mode 1 and Mode 2 knowledge production. Mode 1 knowledge production is essentially disciplinary based around the Newtonian model. Within Mode 1, cognitive and social norms of what counts as significant problems and the methodology for their legitimate solution are inherently intra-disciplinary (Gibbons et al., 1994, pp. 2–3). Moreover, Mode 1 knowledge production, they claimed, occurs in academic community contexts, specifically disciplinary subcontexts, validated by others from the relevant peer subcontext. In contrast, Mode 2 knowledge is produced in the context of application, or in practice. It is transdisciplinary, heterogeneous, heterarchical, and transient. It is also socially accountable and reflexive, including a wider and more temporary and heterogeneous set of practitioners than scholars, collaborating on problems defined in specific and localized contexts (Lee, Green, & Brennan, 2000, p. 124). Mode 2 knowledge production is congruent with research in the professions since its characteristics largely specify the work of the professional. Consequently my argument was that professional doctoral program designs ought to move from first- (essentially Mode 1) to second-generation professional doctorate design (Mode 2).

This is also broadly the stance of Lee et al. (2009). Professional doctoral education need be imbued, potentially at least, within "the generation of a different knowledge distinguished by an overall practice rationality" (Lee et al., 2009, p. 9). They argued that Mode 2 knowledge production was worthwhile and needed. Moreover, the complexities and nuances of practice and of the practice setting, and hence of Mode 2 knowledge production, demand experience. The experienced doctoral candidate has or needs to have deep knowledge of professional practices and of the context in its particularities and its generalities. The experienced person has the ability to make judgments in complex situations that are "good enough" (Flood, 2011) in the sense that they are the best that can be made in the act of doing. The consequences can be monitored and reflected upon preferably with the assistance of a critical friend. Such critical friends would have good experience of the professional practice and even the particular context. Specifically, they would ask provocative questions, and be in the position to fully understand the context of the work and the outcomes that the person was working toward (Costa & Kallick, 1993, p. 50). Such critical friends might make good supervisors. A university-based supervisor of an EdD candidate may know little of the specific context and little of the area of research. However, that person needs at least *some* knowledge of the relevant professional practice to know the general issues and language and certainly have relevant practice-based research experience. One implication here is that a critical friend may not be an academic in order to provide the practice-based support especially when this expertise does not reside with the intended academic supervisor. Preferably in the candidate's workplace, or within ready access, such a critical friend could be part of the supervisory team. Research is needed in this area.

From this discussion, substantive (not necessarily but preferably substantial) experience is essential to the professional doctorate candidate. This is because that person knows practice and what can, and needs to, be researched in practice. This has clear implications for professional doctoral entry requirements and the conception of knowledge creation in professional doctoral programs (see also Boud & Lee, 2005). A dissenting voice in this debate is represented by Deering (1998).

Doctoral Education in Australia

The Australian PhD, following the British model, was originally 100% thesis. This research-only model has slowly become more like the American PhD model in some institutions (see Neumann, 2005) over the last decade or so. The thesis is externally examined in contrast to some practice(s) elsewhere. We see this as a quality assurance issue. About 20 years ago, after the introduction of the PhD in Australia (1948), about 50% of PhDs had the potential to include coursework if the student need demanded it whereas almost 100% of professional doctorates had coursework (Neumann, 2005). Some universities expanded their PhD programs to (1) four years (full-time equivalent), often to incorporate English language learning by international students, or (2) broaden its focus to include practice-based research explicitly. Most universities now require a confirmation of candidature process prior to undertaking the research phase.

The PhD in Australia is essentially a post-WWII development (McWilliam et al., 2002). It was originally an award taken on campus mostly by males following a bachelor's honors degree usually in the sciences and arts. However, this stereotype no longer exists (Ryland, 2004). Moreover, many, perhaps as many as 50% of higher degree research students in Australia, study part-time and/or off campus (Evans, 2002). Science-based doctoral students were younger whereas those in the professions, notably education and management but also health, enabled by off-campus study, peak in numbers around 30 to 40 years of age (Ryland, 2004).

During the 1990s many professional doctorates were developed and the EdD led the way (Maxwell & Shanahan, 1996) amid government calls for research to address national economic interests. Funding was provided on doctoral *enrollment*. Universities found new markets in professionals wanting doctoral qualifications (May & Maxwell, 1996; Servage, 2009). This was especially the case in education. In the late 1990s, the Australian Government (Kemp, 1999) put pressure on universities to "increase throughput" of doctoral candidates via its funding mechanism, the Research Training Scheme (RTS). This was effective because the government provided critical funding at the *completion* of research programs.

The following is the accepted Australian definition of a professional doctorate:

> A program of research, scholarship and advanced study, which enables candidates to make a significant contribution to knowledge and practice in their professional context. In doing so, a candidate may also contribute more generally to scholarship within a discipline or field of study. Professional doctorate students should be required to apply their research and study to problems, issues or other matters of substance, which produce significant benefits in professional practice. (Council of Australian Deans and Directors of Graduate Studies [DDoGS], 1999, p. 1)

Not all professional doctorates under this definition were funded by the RTS. Those not funded by RTS had to pay tuition fees.

A series of conferences was held to stimulate interest in professional doctorates from 1996 to 2004. Maxwell et al. (2005) provide a summary of these events. Interest did grow and a government sponsored evaluation took place (McWilliam et al., 2002). The key findings were: (1) 61% of professional doctorate awards were research doctorates where "research doctorate" meant greater than 67% of the enrollment period was spent on research; (2) there was a proliferation of similar programs rather than growth in programs; (3) the throughput of student numbers was not impressive, which was accounted for by such issues as the older cohort and the work full-time/study part-time nature of the award; (4) professional doctorates were not "deeply" connected to industry/professions; (5) the dominant model remained university focused and driven; and (6) there were tensions around standards of professional doctorates.

Evans, Macauley, Pearson, and Tregenza (2005) showed that the number of graduates of professional doctorates remained relatively low. Implied in their argument was that the PhD award is, or should be, sufficiently robust to encompass the knowledge production of professional doctorates, or practice-based research. In contrast, Usher (2002, p. 150) had commented that the PhD was too restricted for knowledge production that "is produced in the context of application. . . It is perhaps for this reason that Mode 2 is seen as a more appropriate conception of knowledge for the knowledge economy" (p. 147). Such knowledge production does not necessarily lend itself to reporting by dissertation and the introduction of the portfolio more recently has extended the range of legitimate outputs for doctoral research (Clerke & Lee, 2008; Maxwell & Kupczyk-Romanczuk, 2009). My analysis of Australian university websites in 2011 found that three professional doctorate types could be identified: profession specific (e.g., the EdD), robust (e.g., the University of New England's professional doctorate (industry & professions)), and niche professional doctorates (e.g., the University of Queensland's doctor of biotechnology). Additionally, (1) the number of awards had approximately doubled in a decade and (2) the major growth had occurred in "niche" awards. However, the answers to the question put in 34 interviews of coordinators of whether professional doctorates in Australia are "distinctly professional" indicated that only a minority was clear about any such distinction. On the other hand, about 60% of coordinators thought their professional doctorate had a bright future but about 20% were more circumspect (Maxwell, 2011). A continuing issue has been the professional doctorates' connection with the profession itself (McWilliam et al., 2002) and, correspondingly, with those directly connected to the profession. Love (2003) pointed out the degree of connection appeared to depend upon the level of professional closure of professional bodies. For example, in Australia, professional educational bodies do not have legal authority to control employment and so the EdD, like so many other Australian professional doctorates, is not essential for a teacher's or principal's employment, or promotion.

Initial impetus for changes in doctoral education came from the Australian government in the late 1980s (the Dawkins Revolution). It wished to broaden doctoral education to better connect with the needs of the industry and the economy. There was a new market for students that universities were keen to tap. The initial enthusiasm for professional doctorates, including the EdD, waned in the 2000s following Australian government changes in funding (Malloch, 2010). It is likely that the Australian government's Excellence in Research for Australia (ERA, see http://www.arc.gov.au/era/) may have had a negative impact since funding is achieved through each university's ERA score, part of which is achieved through publication in scholarly journals. Publication in professional journals is generally not rated in the ERA. For some years the Australian government has funded research training to universities by a block grant known as the RTS. A concern about the skills of PhD graduates, and hence their employability, re-surfaced in the mid-2000s and at least two universities recently introduced explicit skills development in addition to research training (Cuthbert & Molla, 2015). The political environment of doctoral education has sharpened with the election of a conservative government in 2013. The Abbott government has proposed the introduction of student fees for research degrees and a corresponding reduction of 10% in block funding to universities (see http://www.ddogs.edu.au/#!resources/c1xgo). Scholarships are to be introduced for needy students. Thus, enrollments in research degrees will be subject to market forces. The government has had difficulty of getting these changes to higher education through the Senate (February 2015).

With this background, the focus of the remainder of this chapter is to map a particular professional doctoral award in Australia, the EdD. For example, what are its defining characteristics and what makes it distinctive compared to the PhD? Which universities offer the EdD? What are the issues surrounding the EdD?

Methodology

Bibliometric data were searched via the Australian Education Theses Research Database, a subset of A+ Education. Even though the list is probably not comprehensive, as reporting from the various schools/faculties of education from around Australia is relied upon, it provides the most comprehensive picture of doctoral outcomes in education in Australia. There is a lag time for inclusion in the database (perhaps 2–3 years). Nevertheless, the data can be indicative of the numbers and titles of EdDs and PhDs in education. In order to find the substantive content of EdD output, the same bibliographic data were analyzed using the DDoGS definition of the professional doctorate, particularly in the focus of research on practice. Specifically, one in five EdD titles were analyzed (random entry then every fifth title) and where a decision was unclear the abstract was used to clarify.

The websites of all 39 Australian universities were systematically searched for information about their EdD. For the website searches, a spreadsheet was developed which included such categories as admission requirements including professional experience and percentage of research in the award. Where necessary, clarifications on some awards were sought by email, for example, where the status of the award or the fee structure appeared uncertain. These data were compared to the Maxwell (2011) data.

Five coordinators (random entry then every fourth EdD program) were interviewed by telephone. Eight questions were asked (see Appendix). By way of illustration, the first question was, "If I was a doctoral candidate and I asked you 'what is the difference between your EdD and a PhD?' what would you say?" Additionally five universities that had discontinued their EdD were contacted. Interviews lasted from 20 to 35 minutes. Institutional Ethics Committee approval was granted and its procedures followed including requesting permission for voice recording. Main points were noted during the interview. These notes formed the basis of a thematic analysis while the recorded interviews were used to check the data.

Results

The data are divided into three sections: overview, EdD characteristics, and issues.

Overview
In 2015 there were 21 out of 39 Australian universities that offered the EdD. There were four other education-related professional doctorates, for example, the doctor of educational psychology at the University of Melbourne and James Cook University's doctor of medical education. Curtin University has a Science and Mathematics Education Centre (SMEC) established more than 25 years ago. "With over 400 students, including approximately 300 studying at the doctoral level, the Centre has the largest group of postgraduate students specifically in science, mathematics and technology education in the world" (SMEC, 2015).

Marginson (1997) clustered Australian universities according to a variety of characteristics. The "sandstone" universities are older and generally more prestigious. The "wannabe sandstones" are less prestigious but have aspirations. The "utecs" are historically technology-based, and, finally, the "new" universities have been more recently founded via amalgamations and so on. Table 4.1 shows the EdDs in these clusters. Whereas ten years ago all but one sandstone ($n = 8$) had an EdD, this contrasts with the present ($n = 4$) and a fifth has its EdD under review. Each of the utecs had a history of teacher education and the EdD is well represented in this group. All of the wannabes had EdDs ten years ago ($n = 10$) but now there are three less. Only four of the new universities have EdDs compared with twice that number ten years ago.

An analysis of EdD awards over time is also interesting especially when compared to the PhD in terms of education outputs. Table 4.2 shows collapsed annual data from the time of award of the first EdD in Australia (1994).

Table 4.1   EdDs at Different Clusters of Australian Universities, *n* (%)

Sandstones	Utecs	Wannabe sandstones	New
4 (44)	4 (80)	7 (70)	4 (31)

Table 4.2   EdDs and PhDs in Education Awarded in Australia, 1994–2014, *n* (%)

	1994–1996	1997–2001	2002–2006	2007–2011	2012–2014	Total
EdD	6 (1.5)	156 (11.8)	308 (17.6)	269 (17.9)	26 (8.4)	765 (14.4)
PhD	406 (98.5)	1,170 (88.2)	1,439 (82.4)	1,235 (82.1)	283 (91.6)	4,533 (85.6)
Total	412 (100)	1,326 (100)	1,747 (100)	1,504 (100)	309 (100)	5,298 (100)

Table 4.3   EdD Output—Focus on Practice or Not, *n* (%)

	1994–1996	1997–2001	2002–2006	2007–2011	2012–2014	Total
Practice	1 (100)	19 (59.4)	38 (62.3)	38 (70.4)	5 (71.4)	101 (65.2)
Not practice	0	13 (40.6)	23 (37.7)	16 (29.6)	2 (28.6)	54 (34.8)
Total	1 (100)	32 (100)	61 (100)	54 (100)	7 (100)	155 (100)

For the three middle periods, about one in seven doctorates in education were EdDs. There was a strong initial uptake with the pipeline effect evident in the middle two periods (2002–2011). The number of EdD awards may be diminishing relative to the PhD (2012–2014).

About two-thirds of EdD output (portfolios and theses) were practice-oriented (Table 4.3). There was a slight trend to greater proportion of practice studies over time. This is important given the DDoGS definition that intends to distinguish research in the professional doctorates from PhD research.

EdD Characteristics

What then were the kinds of programs that produced these EdDs? Firstly, the minimum entry requirement was a master's degree by coursework in 7 universities compared to 15 that required a research master's degree. Many would see the former as a quality issue or at least one that puts pressure upon supervisors to assist students to produce doctoral quality research. A small number of universities would accept evidence of other research background, for example, a research report or published research paper. All but two universities required relevant professional experience: greater than five years (*n* = 5), greater than three years (*n* = 6), greater than two years (*n* = 3). A further seven universities implied that professional experience was required.

Secondly, in terms of program structure, most programs could be completed in three years full-time or as a part-time equivalent (six years) though five programs were said to need four years full-time or part-time equivalent. One program allowed only part-time enrollment. Most EdDs had flexible delivery though six universities' EdDs were only available on campus. Two universities' EdDs were only available online. All but two universities had their research component comprising at least 67% of the award. This is not surprising since enrollments are covered by the RTS scheme. In terms of the coursework, 15 required some substantive units as well as research methods units whereas 6 universities tailored their course work as research-oriented only. In these cases, qualitative and quantitative methods units would sometimes be supplemented with units on the research proposal, ethics, and/or research paradigms.

Thirdly, supervisory arrangements were often not explicitly stated. Four universities allowed only one and seven required at least two supervisors. Most supervision would be carried out online. As a case in point, my first supervision of an EdD was a full-time candidate who finished in 1996, my ten other EdD completions were part-time, off campus one of whom I have never met face-to-face. Five universities allowed the possibility of an industry associate supervisor thus fostering industry/university links.

Fourthly, a formal examination of EdD outputs is required. However, examination information was hard to find. Only one university stated its criteria though all would have documentation available about this. Eight universities required examiners to be external to the university. This is common practice in Australian universities. One university allowed one internal examiner along with one external.

Fifthly, the nature of the EdD product was hard to find on the websites. Four explicitly stated a portfolio was required, three required a thesis and one EdD was awarded by three publications in refereed journals. "Refereed" is important here because many professional journals are not refereed in Australia. Four allowed some combination of thesis, or portfolio or publication or material product. One university provided detailed information about their EdD portfolio:

> The portfolio will comprise four components: three substantive components (comprising 17,000–25,000 words each) that reflect both the stature of the degree and scholarly and/or research engagement with professional practice; and an evidence-based Narrative of Personal, Professional and Scholarly Development (10,000–15,000 words). Each of the three substantive research components . . . will comprise two parts:
>
> a. Evidence of the development of professional work-place related practices or products that are based on research and/or scholarship, intellectually rigorous and provide evidence of critical thinking to identify the research niche; and
> b. A scholarly paper intended for public dissemination that contextualises the first component within the relevant literature, empirical research,

theory and policy as appropriate to the candidate's research. (7,000–10,000 words) (UWS, 2015)

Lack of data on the website would imply that the thesis is more likely. It is generally accepted that the EdD thesis word length requirement is somewhat less than that for a PhD although in practical terms this does not always apply. The course work requirement is the reason.

In summary, the typical EdD has a greater than 67% research component intended to be completed in three years full-time equivalent though most would be undertaken part-time. Several years of professional experience was required on entry. Two-thirds of the awards required previous research upon admission. The examinable work normally resulted in a thesis though other products such as the portfolio are becoming more evident. Respondents indicated that two external examiners were most commonly used.

Issues
There are a range of issues associated with the EdDs in Australia.
Distinctiveness. It is interesting to see how some universities portrayed their EdD on their websites. Many sites used terms associated with the DDoGS definition thus distinguishing it from the PhD in education. The theme of "research of practice" was most common. Another dominant portrayal concerned the audience—those who could benefit from undertaking the EdD. Typical of this approach was the following:

> The Doctor of Education is designed to meet the needs of practitioners who wish to research some aspect of their field of practice. Candidates embark on high-level, practice-based research into one of the areas of research strength ... The course caters not only for students committed to an academic path, but for senior practitioners from public and private sectors who wish to study and undertake research at the highest level. (UTS, 2015)

Another example was that the EdD was "designed specifically to meet the needs of the education industry and education professional group" (UTas, 2015). Several websites mentioned educational leaders as those that they wished to attract. Others pointed to the quality of their award and still others to the award aims or outcomes. The interviews confirmed these points with most interviewees making clear that the EdD was distinctive for other than structural reasons (cf. Maxwell, 2011, p. 32). They emphasized the "doctoralness" of the EdD and the importance of experience of EdD candidates (see below). In summary, university websites portrayed their EdD as practice-oriented and for active education professionals, if not leaders. The phrase "equal but different" appears appropriate.

Experience. The websites and all of the coordinators interviewed highlighted the importance of the candidates' professional experience. Coordinators indicated that most students did their research in their own workplace. Where this could create or was a problem, for example, in the case of some international students, the research was undertaken in a workplace similar to their own. In the words of coordinators, candidate professional experience provided

1. knowledge of the problems and what matters;
2. knowledge of the setting;
3. knowledge of the professional self;
4. knowledge that facilitates reflection;
5. background that allows the candidate to progress more quickly; and
6. access to the research site.

However, keeping "distance" in the workplace setting can be difficult. Additionally, despite the importance of this professional experience and the research being undertaken in the workplace, the linkage with the profession more generally was not evident. Coordinators indicated that the use of adjunct supervisors was minimal. Also, nonacademics examining EdD outputs were not common except at one university. Examiners had to fulfill university criteria. Few nonacademics possess a doctorate in Australia. However, academics with PhDs are not necessarily well qualified to examine an EdD (see below). Two coordinators indicated that it was difficult to find appropriate examiners.

EdD Status. All coordinators ($n = 5$) interviewed attested to the EdD's current high status among academics. This contrasts with earlier findings about professional doctorates, more generally (cf. McWilliam et al., 2002). Two coordinators thought the EdD was well received among the educational community but this is an issue that deserves further research.

Discontinuation. Five of the universities that had discontinued their EdD were contacted. Their reasons for discontinuing their EdD were practical and at the same time showed some lack of understanding of the nature of the EdD. Two sandstone universities that no longer had an EdD indicated their numbers were small and the structure of the EdD and the PhD had coalesced (coursework plus thesis) implying that the EdD no longer had a distinctive characteristic. One indicated that policy choice was key: numbers declined rapidly when the EdD became fee paying. Fees for this EdD were introduced because it was not 100% research. It would be interesting to know what this sandstone university does about fees when PhD students are required to do coursework. A third sandstone has its EdD under review. A new university had candidature quality control issues and hence its EdD was canceled. A wannabe sandstone university had small numbers and the flexibility of the PhD meant that the previous structural distinctiveness of its EdD was no longer evident. The largely structural reasons given might have been countered (Maxwell, 2003).

The Future and Other Issues. Coordinators were positive about their EdD, even "excited." Changes were taking place including a move to a cohort approach at two universities. One expressed concern about the present government's move to introduce fees for research awards. Three mentioned that completion rates continued to be a problem (cf. McWilliam et al., 2002).

Discussion

The fact that about one in seven doctorates in education were EdDs is a strong achievement (cf. Evans et al., 2005) especially if the students would not have otherwise completed a doctoral award. Additionally, if doctoral research can be thought of as a public as well as a private good (see Seddon, 1998) then the EdD outputs have been important. Only 21 out of 39 Australian universities offered the EdD, down from 28 in 2011 (Maxwell, 2011). These data and Table 4.1 certainly raise questions about why the number of EdDs has decreased. According to some universities whose EdD has recently been discontinued, this was due to practical realities and lack of structural distinctiveness. More research is needed on the apparent decline in award numbers and the numbers undertaking the EdD.

The high-practice orientation on research on EdD websites was supported by the EdD coordinators interviewed. The data from Table 4.3 provide considerable support for this focus in the EdD. In fact, the high-practice orientation in EdD research was really the only evidence of a strong connection with the profession. Need it be any more than this? However, one-third of EdD outputs were no-practice oriented. It may be that some PhD theses were practice-oriented as well and this is an empirical question that could be addressed. Maxwell and Vine (1998) showed that the focus could overlap in the EdD and PhD in education. Nevertheless, professional doctorates like the EdD are important alongside the PhD, since the former stimulate Mode 2 knowledge production.

Supervision is a complex task and it is no less complex when Mode 2 knowledge production is involved. In some ways the label "supervisor" does not sit well with EdD research. Perhaps "advisor" is more appropriate because the EdD candidate often has the experience to take the lead, to drive the research project, and to know what the decisions should be. While not all PhDs in education are Mode 1, Mode 1 knowledge production does not give a strong background for Mode 2 knowledge production. In relation to this issue, a useful study would be to see the proportion of academics who hold EdD qualifications and/or who undertake practice-based research. As mentioned above, an in situ critical friend, a respected professional might be a useful member of the supervisory/advisory team.

Examination of EdDs needs attention (cf. Kiley, 2013). More precisely, who can examine the issue at hand? Given that professional experience is critical to the award, highly regarded professionals in the field who have direct experience of the research outcomes could, logically, make ideal examiners. Arguments could be made on a case-by-case basis. Moreover, the introduction of the portfolio has put additional pressure on examiners and it has been reported that examiners are becoming hard to find. Research is needed into the examination of EdD and other professional doctorate portfolios.

Confirmation of candidature is common in doctoral awards in Australia. Confirmation of candidature does not rely on the coursework but rather the presentation of a research proposal to an internal committee and interested colleagues before data gathering can commence. Data on confirmation of candidature was not often forthcoming on websites. Similarly, research in Australia requires institutional ethics approval. This was not evident on websites but is understood by supervisors as a requirement prior to data gathering and usually is included as part of the confirmation process.

The nature of the course work in EdDs appears to be changing. In some universities the course work is explicitly tailored to research requirements. Specifically, the substantive component may be addressed through a literature task rather than a specific set unit of work that may or may not be relevant to the candidate's research area. Two city-based EdDs are moving to a cohort approach in the early stages, that is, before moving on to the research phase. At least one university has moved to combining the early tasks of EdD and PhD candidates. These may be seen as pedagogical moves rather than structural changes.

Finally, and importantly, the EdD may be at a crossroad. The decline in award numbers, perhaps decline in student numbers, and the potential for the introduction of fees for the EdD, along with other research awards, will challenge EdD awards and enrollments across the country. Where completion rates are a problem, this will provide added pressure. People in full-time employment gain the majority of EdDs, yet their employment and promotion are not dependent upon gaining higher qualifications. Imposing tuition fees in the context of a previous no-fee environment may make a difference. As far as I am aware, no university has canceled its PhD program and the increased flexibility of the PhD in many institutions means that students may be pressurized to undertake a PhD, especially where the substantive content can be molded to have research outputs that can add to the university's ERA score. These together provide an additional gloomy future. However, EdD coordinators were generally upbeat about their particular programs.

Conclusions

Some commentators have noted that the professional doctorates may decline in influence (Evans et al., 2005; Malloch, 2010) and the results indicated that there has been a decline in numbers of EdD awards over the last decade or so. About half of Australian universities have an active EdD program. Recent government moves to introduce fees for research degrees and a range of other potential impacts identified above mean that a serious challenge to the EdD may be on the horizon. More generally, these contextual features may challenge Mode 2 knowledge production and hence other professional doctorates. Even PhD enrollments might suffer.

The typical Australian EdD has greater than 67% research and is intended to be completed in three years full-time equivalent though most would be undertaken part-time. The majority requires previous research upon admission and the EdD work resulted in a thesis though other products such as the portfolio are becoming more evident. Two external examiners were required in the majority of cases. University websites portrayed their EdD to be practice-oriented and for active education professionals, if not leaders.

The status of EdDs appears to be strong among academics though this is likely to vary across universities. The distinctiveness of the Australian EdD appears to be well documented on websites and also in practice according to coordinators interviewed ($n = 5$). Also, two-thirds of completed EdDs were practice-oriented as indicated by analysis of the titles of EdDs in the Australian Education Theses database.

Finally, the experience that EdD candidates bring to the research task(s) is seen as a critical component of the program. This is indicated, for example, by their requirement for entry to most EdD programs. Professional experience gives knowledge of what matters, of the workplace setting of the research, and of the professional self. Such knowledge allows the candidate to move quickly into the research including providing access to the research site and facilitates reflection and hence professional development. Experience is essential to Mode 2 knowledge production.

Appendix: Interview Schedule

1. If I was a doctoral candidate and I asked you "what is the difference between your professional doctorate and a PhD, what would you say?"
   a) *What makes your professional doctorate distinctive? (profession; workplace; university; mix)*
2. Have there been any recent changes to your Professional Doctorate features?
   a) *Percentage is research*
   b) *Admission requirements*
      i. Professional
      ii. Academic
      iii. Experience
   c) *Full time/part time*
   d) *Reasons, for example, ERA*
3. What are typical places in which research is undertaken?
   a) *Workplace of researcher*
   b) *Workplace of others*
   c) *Other*
4. *How does the candidate's experience influence progress in the Professional Doctorate?
5. What relationship, if any, does your Professional Doctorate have with the profession/professionals outside the university?
   a) *Supervision*
   b) *Examination*
   c) *Consultative Committee*
   d) *Formal accreditation*
6. *What is the status of your Professional Doctorate?
   a) *Compared to the PhD*
   b) *Within the profession*
7. What issues does your Professional Doctorate currently face?
8. What future do you see for your Professional Doctorate?

Any other comments?

Note

* Additional items from the previously used schedule

References

Boud, D., & Lee, A. (2005). 'Peer learning' as pedagogic discourse for research education. *Studies in Higher Education, 30*(5), 501–516.

Brennan, M. (1995). Education doctorates: Reconstructing professional partnerships around research? *Australian Universities Review, 2,* 20–22.

Clark, J. (1996). Meeting the demands of R, D and E leadership in a rapidly changing social and business environment. In *Postgraduate skills: A view from industry.* F. H. Faulding.

Clerke, T., & Lee, A. (2008). Mainstreaming the doctoral research portfolio? In M. Kiley & G. Mullins (Eds.), *Quality in postgraduate research: Research education in the new global environment* (pp. 17–30). Canberra: CEDAM ANU. Downloaded from http://www.qpr.edu.au/2008/clerke2008.pdf

Costa, A. L., & Kallick, B. (1993). Through the lens of a critical friend. *Educational Leadership, 51*(2), 49–51.

Cuthbert, D., & Molla, T. (2015). PhD crisis discourse: A critical approach to the framing of the problem and some Australian 'solutions'. *Higher Education, 69,* 33–53. doi: 10.1007/s10734-014-9760-y

DDoGS (Council of Australian Deans and Directors of Graduate Studies). (1999). *Guidelines on professional doctorates.* Canberra: Commonwealth Government of Australia.

Deering, T. E. (1998). Eliminating the doctor of education degree: It's the right thing to do. *The Educational Forum, 62*(3), 243–248. doi: 10.1080/00131729808984350

Ellis, L. B. (2006). The professional doctorate for nurses in Australia: Findings of a scoping exercise. *Nurse Education Today, 26*(6), 484–493.

Evans, T. D. (2002). Part-time research students: Are they producing knowledge where it counts? *Higher Education Research & Development, 21*(2), 155–165.

Evans, T. D., Macauley, P., Pearson, M., & Tregenza, K. (2005). Why do a 'Prof Doc' when you can do a PhD? In T. W. Maxwell, C. Hickey, & T. D. Evans (Eds.), *Professional doctorates: Working towards impact* (pp. 24–34). *Proceedings of the 5th International Professional Doctorates Conference,* Deakin University, Geelong.

Flood, J. B. (2011). *Educating the wise practitioner.* Unpublished Paper, #5, EdD portfolio. University of New England, Armidale.

Gibbons, M., Limoges, C., Nowotny, H., Schwartzman, S., Scott, P., & Trow, M. (1994). *The new production of knowledge: The dynamics of science and research in contemporary societies.* London: Sage.

Golde, C. M. (2006). Preparing stewards of the discipline. In C. M. Golde & G. E. Walker (Eds.), *Envisioning the future of doctoral education: Preparing stewards of the discipline* (pp. 3–22). Stanford, CA: Carnegie Foundation for the Advancement of Teaching.

Kemp, D. A. (1999). *Knowledge and innovation: A policy statement on research and research training.* Australian Government Department of Education, Employment and Workplace Relations, Canberra. Retrieved from http://www.dest.gov.au/archive/Ministers/kemp/dec99/k15612_211299.htm

Kiley, M. (2013). Rethinking the Australian doctoral examination process. *TEXT special issue 22. Examination of doctoral degrees in creative arts: Process, practice and standards*, 1–12. Retrieved from http://www.textjournal.com.au/speciss/issue22/content.htm

Kot, F. C., & Hendel, D. (2012). Emergence and growth of professional doctorates in the United States, United Kingdom, Canada and Australia: A comparative analysis. *Studies in Higher Education, 37*(3), 345–364.

Lee, A., Brennan, M., & Green, B. (2009). Re-imagining doctoral education: Professional doctorates and beyond. *Higher Education Research and Development, 28*(3), 275–287.

Lee, A., Green, B., & Brennan, M. (2000). Organizational knowledge, professional practice and the professional doctorate at work. In J. Garrick & C. Rhodes (Eds.), *Research and knowledge at work: Perspectives, case-studies and innovative strategies* (pp. 117–136). London and New York: Routledge.

Love, T. (2003). *Implications for design-focused professional doctorates of Australian research into professional doctorates*. Third Doctoral Education in Design Symposium, Tsukuba, Japan (October). Downloaded from http://www.design-researchsociety.org/docs-procs/ded3/

Malloch, M. (2010). Professional doctorates: An Australian perspective. *Work Based Learning e-Journal, 1*(1), 35–58.

Marginson, S. (1997). Competition and contestability in Australian higher education. *Australian University Review, 40*(1), 5–14.

Maxwell, T. W. (2003). From first to second generation professional doctorate. *Studies in Higher Education, 2*(3), 279–292.

Maxwell, T. W. (2011). Australian professional doctorates: Mapping, distinctiveness, stress and prospects. *Work Based Learning e-Journal 2*(1), 24–43. Retrieved from http://wblearning-ejournal.com/currentIssue/E3011%20rtb.pdf

Maxwell, T. W., Hickey, C., & Evans, T. D. (Eds.). (2005). Professional doctorates: Working towards impact. In *Proceedings of the 5th Biennial International Conference on Professional Doctorates*, Deakin University, Geelong. Retrieved from http://www.deakin.edu.au/education/rads/conferences/publications/prodoc/index.php

Maxwell, T. W., & Kupczyk-Romanczuk, G. (2009). Producing the professional doctorate: The portfolio as a legitimate alternative to the dissertation. *Innovations in Education and Teaching International, 46*(2), 135–145.

Maxwell, T. W., & Shanahan, P. J. (Eds.). (1996). Which way for professional doctorates? Context and cases. In Proceedings of the conference entitled '*Which Way for Professional Doctorates?*', Coffs Harbour, 16–18 July. Faculty of Education, Health and Professional Studies, UNE, Armidale.

Maxwell, T. W., & Shanahan, P. J. (Eds.). (1998). Professional doctorates: Innovations in teaching & research. In Proceedings of the conference entitled '*Professional Doctorates: Innovations in Teaching & Research*', Coffs Harbour, 8–10 July. Faculty of Education, Health & professional Studies, UNE, Armidale.

Maxwell, T. W., & Shanahan, P. J. (2001). Professional doctoral education in Australia and New Zealand: Reviewing the scene. In B. Green, T. W. Maxwell, & P. J. Shanahan (Eds.), *Doctoral education and professional practice: The next generation?* (pp. 15–36). Armidale: Kardoorair Press.

Maxwell, T. W., & Vine, K. (1998). The EdD at UNE: The view through conceptual bifocals. In T. W. Maxwell & P. J. Shanahan (Eds.), *Professional doctorates: Innovations in teaching & research*. Proceedings of the conference at Coffs Harbour, 8–10 July. Faculty of Education, Health & professional Studies, UNE, Armidale, 75–84.

May, C., & Maxwell, T. W. (1996). Professionals' and professions' perceptions concerning professional doctorates. In T. W. Maxwell & P. J. Shanahan (Eds.), *Which way for professional doctorates: Context and cases*. Proceedings of the conference at Coffs Harbour, 16–18 October. Faculty of Education, Health & professional Studies, UNE, Armidale, 79–103.

McWilliam, E. (Ed.). (2003). *Research training for the knowledge economy. Professional doctorates 4th Biennial International Conference*. Brisbane: Queensland University of Technology.

McWilliam, E., Taylor, P., Thomson, P., Green, B., Maxwell, T. W., Wildy, H., & Simons, D. (2002). *Research training in doctoral programs: What can be learned from professional doctorates? Evaluations and investigations program*. Canberra: Commonwealth of Australia.

Neumann, R. (2005). Doctoral differences: Professional doctorates and PhDs compared. *Journal of Higher Education Policy and Management, 27*(2), 173–188.

Pearson, M. (2006). The changing environment for doctoral education in Australia: Implications for quality management, improvement and innovation. *Higher Education Research & Development, 18*(3), 269–284.

Ryland, K. (2004). Diversity of the doctorate by research student population. Paper presented at the *Australian Association for Research in Education Conference*, Melbourne.

Seddon, T. (1998). Contextualising the EdD research, recommendations and realpolitik. In T. W. Maxwell & P. J. Shanahan (Eds.), *Professional doctorates: Innovations in teaching & research*. Proceedings of the conference at Coffs Harbour, 8–10 July. Faculty of Education, Health & professional Studies, UNE, Armidale, 11–22.

Seddon, T. (2001). What is doctoral in doctoral education? In B. Green, T. W. Maxwell, & P. Shanahan (Eds.), *Doctoral education and professional practice: The next generation?* (pp. 303–336). Armidale: Kardoorair Press.

Servage, L. (2009). Alternative and professional doctoral programs: What is driving the demand? *Studies in Higher Education, 34*(7), 765–779. doi: 10.1080/0307507 0902818761

SMEC (Science & Mathematics Education Centre). (2015). Science and Mathematics Education Centre. Retrieved from http://smec.curtin.edu.au/, January 27, 2015.

Stock, C. F. (2013). Acquiring 'doctorateness' in the creative industries: An Australian perspective on professional research doctorates. *TEXT special issue 22. Examination of doctoral degrees in creative arts: Process, practice and standards*, 1–17. Retrieved from http://www.textjournal.com.au/speciss/issue22/content.htm

Taylor, N., & Maxwell, T. W. (2004). Enhancing the relevance of a professional doctorate: The case of the Doctor of Education degree at the University of New England. *Asia-Pacific Journal of Cooperative Education, 5*(1), 60–69. Retrieved from http://www.apjce.org

Trigwell, K., Shannon, T., & Maurizi, R. (1997). *Research-coursework doctoral programs in Australian Universities*. Canberra: Commonwealth of Australia. Retrieved from http://www.dest.gov.au/archive/highered/eippubs/eip9707/front.htm

UMelb (University of Melbourne). (2011). Guidelines – Professional degrees with the degree nomenclature of Doctor. Retrieved from http://www.unimelb.edu.au, May 12, 2011.

Usher, R. (2002). A diversity of doctorates: Fitness for the knowledge economy. *Higher Education Research & Development, 21*(2), 143–153.

UTas (University of Tasmania). (2015). Doctor of Education. Retrieved from http://www.utas.edu.au/courses/dvc-research/courses/e9d-doctor-of-education, January 12, 2015.

UTS (University of Technology Sydney). (2015). Doctor of Education. Retrieved from http://www.uts.edu.au/future-students/find-a-course/courses/c02050, January 12, 2015.

UWS (University of Western Sydney). (2015). Doctorate Policy. Retrieved from http://policies.uws.edu.au/view.current.php?id=00017, January 12, 2015.

Voudouris, N. J., & Hunter, M. (2011). Threats to the future of professional coursework Doctorates in Psychology. *InPsych, 3p*. Downloaded from http://www.psychology.org.au/Content.aspx?ID=3918, January 9, 2015.

Wellington, J. (2013). Searching for 'Doctorateness'. *Studies in Higher Education, 38*(10), 1490–1503. doi: 10.1080/03075079.2011.634901

Whitechurch, C. (2009). The rise of the blended professional in Higher Education: A comparison between the United Kingdom, Australia and the United States. *Higher Education, 58*, 407–418. doi: 10.1007/s10734-009-9202-4

Zusman, A. (2013). What's driving the new professional doctorates? *University World News*, July, Issue 279.

5

Learning to Think in the Corporate University: Developing a Doctorate for Practice

Elizabeth Smythe, Gary Rolfe, and Peter Larmer

From Process to Product (and Back Again)

Over the past few decades, health professional education in disciplines such as our own (midwifery, nursing, and physiotherapy) has shifted from an apprenticeship-based, learning-on-the-job experience to become fully integrated in the university. This has impacted not only on students who find themselves having to write theoretical assignments to rigorous academic standards, but also on those who teach them, for whom the measures of success (and in some cases, the criteria for remaining in employment) now focus largely on research outcomes rather than the quality of their educational practice. At the same time, universities have implemented the corporate business model in response to a variety of internal and external pressures to make money and to meet the demands of students who attend universities primarily as an investment in a future career. Indeed, it could be argued that university education is becoming a financial transaction in which money (course fees) is exchanged for a degree certificate, which is then redeemed in the workplace for a graduate-level salary (Rolfe, 2013).

Arguably, health professional education has therefore moved from being largely process-based to being product-driven and outcome-oriented. Furthermore, those products and outcomes are increasingly concerned with research and theory rather than practice per se. This is particularly noticeable at postregistration and/or postgraduate level. The highest academic qualification, the PhD, is often referred to as a "research training," and traditionally results in a large research thesis which is seldom read other than by the examiners and one or two academic specialists. PhDs are increasingly being undertaken by health care practitioners as a means of advancing their careers, but there is typically little space within the program for them to think about how practice could be made better for patients, let alone to explore the means by which such changes could be achieved. Not only are we witnessing an ever-widening schism between those who research and those who practice, but we suggest that there is a danger of neglecting the importance of "thought" at all levels within the business model of education. As Readings (1996) points out, in the economy of the corporate university, "Thought is non-productive labor, and hence does not show up on the balance sheets except as waste" (p. 175). Thinking (by which we mean a critical reflective engagement with ideas) is fast becoming an expensive and unnecessary luxury in the corporate university and, we would suggest, is less and less necessary in order to pass examinations.

As educators and health care professionals with a particular interest in doctoral education, we (Liz, Gary, and Peter) are therefore faced with a double challenge. On the one hand, we find ourselves in an institution where product increasingly takes precedent over process and where thinking (as defined above) is no longer necessary for success for either students or academics. On the other hand, the products which are valued most by the university are of little use to aspiring health care students who are hoping and expecting that a doctoral education will help them to think about and develop their practice.

This chapter is the result of an ongoing dialog between critical friends (Taylor & Storey, 2013). It began when Liz, Peter, and colleagues read Gary's paper on professional doctorates (Rolfe & Davies, 2009) at a time when they were re-thinking a doctor of health science curriculum at Auckland University of Technology (AUT) in New Zealand. The dialog found synergies when Gary came as a visiting scholar to AUT to review its professional doctorate program. We sought to ask each other provocative questions toward enhancing our programs. Rather than despairing about the impact of the business model on the university, we came to see how that impetus could be employed to refocus our understandings of what can be offered in the name of doctoral education. In acknowledging that the main customer or stakeholder or both are the health care providers who employ our prospective students, we recognize that the currency of the transaction is no longer simply academic qualifications. Rather, we must ask ourselves: How can the university work with a student in a way that gives a tangible return back to health care provider organizations? This corporate, business-oriented question begs a series of professional- and practice-based questions: How can patient care be improved? How can change be managed more effectively? How do health care providers know if what they are doing works? And what is going on in a practice situation that needs to be better understood? Unless universities can convince funders (usually the students' employers, who are likely to either pay the fees or give time release) that they will get value for money, doctoral qualifications are likely to become restricted to employees of the university itself. The schism between practitioners and academics will grow wider and research projects will simply build on what has already been published rather than responding to issues arising from practice. And even in cases where research projects do address practice-related issues, it is widely recognized that there is a substantial time lag between new evidence being produced and any related change in practice (Balas, 2001; Balas & Boren, 2000; Buchan, 2007; Teasell, 2012). We should therefore acknowledge that academic research has, at best, a delayed and tangential impact on practice and begin to rethink the idea of doctoral education for health care practitioners.

In thinking about how to design a doctoral curriculum which focuses on developing and improving practice and practitioners rather than merely adding to the existing body of theoretical research, we draw, in this chapter, on the American school of pragmatism and on German hermeneutics. Although at first sight these two philosophical traditions might appear somewhat disparate, several writers have remarked on their similarities. For example, the neopragmatist Richard Rorty identifies John Dewey and Martin Heidegger as two of the most important philosophers of the twentieth century (Rorty, 1979, 1982), and while he offers no synthesis which combines and/or transcends their positions, he notes that both pragmatism and hermeneutics reject the usual epistemological accounts of "truth" in favor of something more practical and action-oriented. For both traditions, knowledge is not something to be acquired or possessed, but a relationship with the world, and both therefore accord with our aim of developing a scholarship grounded in practical rather than theoretical knowledge.

In thinking about what education in the health professions is for and how it might be done better, we begin by examining Dewey's writing on the nature of "means and ends," and consider how our habitual ways of engaging with doctoral students might change. We then ponder the nature of "thinking" as it relates to the issues of practice, drawing on the pragmatist philosophy of Dewey [1859–1952] and the hermeneutics of Heidegger [1889–1976] and Gadamer [1900–2002]. This raises the challenge of how we might reconcile the demands of the university with those of practice.

Finally we give examples of how our insights are being enacted in our own experiences with doctoral students.

Means, Ends, and Habits of Thinking

We have suggested above that the corporate business model adopted by many universities has led to the commoditization of education, whereby writing an essay becomes for the student little more than a means to the end of gaining a qualification. If the desired end is a degree certificate and if the means to acquiring it is to pass assignments, then the content and subject matter of the student's academic studies need have little relevance to their work as healthcare practitioners.

Dewey (1988) argues against this simple means-ends dichotomy, stating that "means and ends are two names for the same reality" (p. 28) and that each end in turn becomes the means to further ends. Ends are therefore merely temporary "ends-in-view" (Dewey, 1958) rather than final endpoints or outcomes. He gives the example of building a house, where the completed house is regarded as a temporary end-in-view and the various activities and materials employed in building it are the means to that end-in-view. However, once the house is built it becomes the means for the next end-in-view, for example, that of raising a family in it. For Dewey, the ongoing process of means and ends is encompassed by the idea of an aim, which is "an orderly and ordered activity, one in which the order consists in the progressive completing of a process" (Dewey, 2007, p. 79). As educationalists, we tend to think in terms of outcomes rather than ends, but whereas educational ends and/or outcomes are generally expressed in terms of the acquisition of skills and knowledge, aims are mental activities or ways of thinking. In any case, Dewey argues that knowledge is not a product which can be acquired from books and owned by academics, but a *process* of engagement and experimentation with the world. Knowledge is therefore better thought of as a verb rather than a noun; it is made through *action* rather than acquired through a *transaction*. Furthermore, educational aims are always intrinsic: "the aim of education is to enable individuals to continue their education" (p. 78). Our concern is that when students and lecturers alike are focused on meeting extrinsic ends or outcomes such as passing assignments or acquiring skills and knowledge, the means by which these ends are met are therefore no longer truly educational.

In order to become engaged in the process of making knowledge, the student must develop what Dewey (1910) refers to as "a disciplined mind." He points out that the word "discipline" usually refers to the mechanical activity of "drill" or training which results in "uniform *external modes of action"* (p. 63). However, this form of discipline is not appropriate for education, which is concerned with "habits of thinking" rather than with *physical* activities and outcomes. Moreover, while the mechanical habits instilled through training or drill are restrictive and constraining, habits of thinking are "identified with freedom in its true sense" (ibid., p. 64). Dewey refers to this as reflective thinking, which includes the ability

> to "turn things over," to look at matters deliberately, to judge whether the amount and kind of evidence requisite for decision is at hand, and if not, to tell where and how to seek such evidence. (Ibid., pp. 66–67)

While healthcare education aspires to Dewey's description of reflective thinking, our concern is that reflection is often taught as a "drill" and as a means to passing assignments rather than as an intrinsic aim to further the educational process. Moreover, we are increasingly worried that mechanistic, means-ends training is pervading all levels of healthcare education up to and including the doctorate by research. Thus, while the aim of education is to instill the habit of reflective thinking for its own sake, doctoral students are increasingly being drilled to produce narrow and closely specified outputs in order to satisfy external "quality control" standards. Our intention here is to demonstrate that education undertaken for its own sake, that is, without any extrinsic aims in mind, is more likely to result in worthwhile and meaningful practice-oriented outcomes than goal-driven "academic" courses.

The "Standard Doctorate"

Many doctoral programs are built around Dewey's "uniform external modes of action" such as doing a comprehensive literature review (deemed to be rigorous if it follows predefined habits in the manner and process of critique), identifying a research question within a named methodological paradigm (which introduces its own drills), and writing a research proposal under prelabeled headings within a prescribed word limit, appropriately referenced, time-lined, and budgeted. The research phase of the program typically also involves a variety of uniform drills and disciplines in order to ensure rigor and satisfy agreed-upon academic standards. On completion, the thesis is sent to external examiners who share habitual expectations of what counts as doctoral research, and who judge the research accordingly. All of this has to happen within a set time frame in accordance with a corporate fee-for-service arrangement between the university and the student. The teacher and/or supervisor adopts the role of guide, safeguarding the student who might veer from the habitual path, encouraging them to keep to schedule, and ensuring that the nature of the work fits within customary standards and expectations.

Our concern is that by conforming to these drills and habits, we might well succeed in developing a standardized product whose "quality" can be objectively measured and verified, but that the process of knowledge-making (i.e., of reflective thinking in Dewey's sense) is devalued and neglected. The resulting "standard doctorate" might be *academic* (in the literal sense of the word), but it would not be *educational*; it might be *practical* (in the sense of being relatively quick, simple, and cost-effective to complete) but it would not be relevant to *practice*. Furthermore, when product is valued more than process, the means to achieving a successful completion tends to take second place to the end of gaining the qualification. The question for prospective students then becomes "Which research project will most quickly and simply allow me to complete my doctorate?" rather than "Which research project will make the biggest difference to my practice?"

There is neither the time nor the inclination in the rapid and cost-effective process of the "standard doctorate" to stop and consider the possible impact of the research on practice. The freedom simply to *think* is rare. Rather, our students follow predetermined means which lead inextricably to predictable and often meaningless ends, where the habits of others about the way things get done have been laid down in advance. And yet, as academics, we are the very people who are writing learning outcomes, assessing student work, guiding students toward research choices and supervising their theses. Not only have our students become habituated into standard and standardized ways of working, but so have we as academics. We suggest that it is our responsibility to reclaim and reassert a mode of doctoral education for health care professionals that privileges thinking and asserts the primary function of research as making a real and substantive difference in the local context of practice. We believe that it is time to examine the internal dispositions and external pressures that are driving the means by which we support and guide students. We suggest that the first priority is to set aside space that allows and protects "thinking."

Calculative and Meditative Thinking

How then can doctoral students become more actively involved in the process of contextually specific reflective thinking which draws their own practice experience into the heart of their educative encounters? Doctoral students come to us with a vast understanding of practice grown though experience. They bring their questions, their confusions, and their quest to develop practice that is more fitting to the task. Yet, as experienced practitioners, they know the enormity of the quest before them; they recognize that there are no easy fixes and off-the-shelf solutions:

> In quality, the good is never twice alike. It never copies itself. It is new every morning, fresh every evening. It is unique in its every presentation. For it marks the resolution of a distinctive complication of competing habits and impulses which can never repeat itself. (Dewey, 2008, p. 140)

As Dewey tells us, each new encounter with the world (and with practice) is different from any previous encounter; the challenges of practice are "new every morning." Our prior experience is of limited help, and in order to "know" each new situation it is necessary to engage with it in a reflective and reflexive relationship, what Dewey (2007, p. 107) describes as "an experiment with the world to find out what it is like."

Gadamer advocates a very similar process when he points out that the hermeneutic attempt at understanding is, in fact, the act of *coming to an understanding*; arriving at an agreement on meaning through dialog with another person, with a text or with a situation. For both the pragmatists and the hermeneutic philosophers, the knowledge and understanding necessary to respond to the *new* requires engagement, dialog, and creative thinking. The challenge for teachers, then, is to work with practitioners to develop their skills of discerning what constitutes quality practice and to help shape their dispositions to seek to find, in Dewey's words, the *new* which is *good*. It is to awaken them to both the interpretive nature of practice and the practicalities of getting the work of practice done, but in a manner which is deemed *good*. It is to recognize that what is *good* in one situation may not be *good* in another. It is to nurture the habits of reflective thinking rather than to rely on the ingrained and repetitive habits of drill.

But this is only one side of the story. The thinking required to interpret and understand a clinical problem on the spot, in the midst of practice has to be focused, goal-directed, and incisive; yet to be effective, it must also draw on thinking of a very different kind. As Heidegger (1966, p. 46) points out, there are "two kinds of thinking, each justified and needed in its own way: calculative thinking and meditative thinking." Calculative thinking plans and investigates, it is always *about* something. It seeks the right answer and then rushes ahead to the next thing. Heidegger's somewhat prescient fear, expressed more than 50 years ago, was that "calculative thinking may someday come to be accepted and practiced *as the only* way of thinking" (ibid., p. 56, italics in original). Heidegger therefore calls us to meditative thinking, to the open space where we stop thinking "about" and simply let the thoughts emerge:

> Meditative thinking demands of us not to cling one-sidedly to a single idea, nor to run down a one-track course of ideas. Meditative thinking demands of us that we engage ourselves with what at first sight does not go together at all. (Ibid., p. 53)

Meditative thinking is about being "waitful"; it is incongruent with learning outcomes that demand and expect predefined structures of thinking within tight time frames. The literature review sends the student to find out what has already been written and to organize those insights in a way that is more likely to shut down thought than to set it free to wander and wonder (Smythe & Spence, 2012). The student essay also constrains thinking in a particular way, and never without the links (correctly referenced) back to the thinking of others (Gardner & Rolfe, 2013). The research proposal assumes that the way ahead can be prethought. Calculative thinking dominates the academy where, as Heidegger (1966, p. 45) notes, "we take in everything in the quickest and cheapest way, only to forget it just as quickly, instantly," usually immediately after the assignment has been written and submitted. Where and how, then, are students exposed to "new openness to new experiences" (Gadamer, 1982, p. 320), and how does any of this necessarily improve practice?

Learning as Thinking

Bold approaches to reclaim the thoughts that emerge from the on-the-ground experience (rather than the theoretical and research-based literature of the discipline) need to start with first creating an open space where thoughts are free to come. Reflective or meditative thinking is not directed by a given topic, set of rules, or manner of presentation. Rather, it is for the university to provide a space at a distance from the busy world of practice where the practitioner is free simply to stop and think. Michael Oakeshott (2001, pp. 113–114), writing in 1950, referred to studying at a university as "the gift of an interval," but too often the modern-day university presents students with such a busy, predetermined list of learning objectives that they have no time to do their own thinking. Thinking and learning are closely related. Shallow, surface thinking leads to rote learning which is quickly forgotten. For deep and lasting learning to occur, deep meditative thinking is required. With this in mind, Heidegger (1968, p. 380) points out that the role of the teacher should simply be "to let learn. The real teacher, in fact, lets nothing else be learned than - learning." He adds that,

"The teacher is ahead of his apprentices in this alone, that he has still far more to learn than they—he has to learn to let them learn" (ibid., p. 380). We can therefore substitute "think" for "learn" in the above passage without altering Heidegger's meaning or intent: the real teacher is concerned simply with allowing her or his students to think.

Doctoral level learning and thinking is expected to be deep and has long been termed "independent," and yet we argue that it still has not opened the space and set aside the interval that allows learning and/or thinking to find its own way, thus free of predetermined expectation that dictates and dominates. As soon as we privilege standard academic expectations we begin to shut down thinking. That might be acceptable if the ends-in-view of the journey remain within the world of the university. Our point, however, is that everything in the doctoral journey for the clinician should point back to practice, where questions of how to structure a paragraph or what referencing system to use are largely irrelevant to patient care. That is not to say that the skills and techniques of good academic writing are unimportant or irrelevant, and there are rules of the academic game that must be followed if the student is to meet the requirements for a doctorate. Indeed, we would further suggest that good thinking and good writing go hand in hand. Yet, we argue, the essence of doctoral scholarship for the clinician is how thought informs and illuminates practice. Without such a connection to practice, the work is akin to a chef cooking a meal without diners to eat the food; an engineer designing a bridge that will never be built, never put to the test, never able to make a difference to people trapped on the other side of the ravine. There can be no scholarship of practice without practice itself, without there already being patients in need of care. It is from the thing in itself that scholarship must find its grounding. As Heidegger (2002, pp. 31–32) points out:

> A university cannot truly profess to have its beginning in theory. Its beginning originates in mood [*Stimmung*], springing from the *thaumazein* or astonishment of which Aristotle spoke as the concrete bond between life and thought.

This, then, should be the aim of all university education; to bind together life and thought through the experience of astonishment.

Our starting point for the project of binding together life and thought, doing and thinking, is Heidegger's concept of "dwelling." Heidegger (1993, p. 349) contrasts dwelling with building. Dwelling has the sense of preserving and nurturing rather than making: "it tends the growth that ripens into fruit of its own accord." To build is to construct, to fabricate, to work toward a particular end, whereas to dwell is to linger, to settle, and to cultivate. Contrary to the common understanding of the term, dwelling precedes building: first we settle and cultivate, and only then do we build. Dwelling invites, encourages, gives time to ponder, and reveals what really matters. When we dwell on a thought we take our time over it, we turn it over in our mind, we examine it from all angles, and we allow meaning to gradually emerge. Such meditative thinking does not stay single-mindedly fixed on one thing in order to build an argument. Rather it is open to thoughts that come, new possibilities of exploration, unexpected synergies, ideas that are born amidst chaos. It is meditative thinking that allows health professionals to reflect on the tensions and possibilities of practice in order to ponder and reveal what matters; it is "dwelling on a thought" that will allow new ideas to come. It is only when excused from the pressure of being expected to know everything that we are free to dwell, able to throw ourselves into that which calls. It is then, Heidegger (1993) says, that a light is ignited that will not be extinguished. Such a light becomes a guide to our own practice and that of those around us; it leads the way forward like no written word can ever hope to do.

Beyond Means and Ends

We have seen that meditative thinking is fundamentally different from calculative thinking and requires a very different disposition on the part of the teacher, the student, and the university. For example, the question of what outcomes need to be met in order to pass an assignment would be supplanted by questions such as "What was the thinking that came as a result of taking the course?" and "What difference did that thinking make to practice?" Moreover, questions such as these beg larger and more fundamental questions such as "How can we as educationalists working within the 21st century university system encourage and nurture meditative thinking in the face of an ends-driven curriculum?" and "How can we subvert the system so that it privileges practice over theory, patient outcomes over academic ones?"

Further, how can we as educationalists separate out and disconnect the process of taking the course from the outcome of passing the assignment? That is, how can we interest the students in the course (literally, the path or the flow) and in thinking *for its own sake* rather than merely as the means to the end of getting a qualification? Clearly, one way would be to abolish the assignment, so that the students would not feel compelled to give all their attention to the assessment requirements instead of the educational process. But this is simply not practical or even possible in the twenty-first century. Indeed, the idea was already considered archaic in the mid-nineteenth century when Newman wistfully longed for "a University which had no professors or examinations at all, but merely brought a number of young men together for three or four years, and then sent them away as the University of Oxford is said to have done some sixty years since" (Newman, 1982, p. 145).

Rather than separating the means (education, scholarship, and practice development) from the ends (the assessment task), an alternative strategy would be to allow the students to set their own means and ends, in which each student identifies and negotiates her or his own individual outcomes and her or his own process for achieving them. As Dewey (1958, p. 374) points out, the *means* only become *meaningful* in relation to the end-in-view:

> The end-in-view is present as the meaning of the materials used and acts done; without its informing presence, the latter are in no sense "means"; they are merely extrinsic causal conditions.

If the end is to pass an assignment, the meaning of the course is simply to gain a high mark. However, if the students are free to set their own ends-in-view, ends which have meaning to each individual student, then the means to those ends-in-view will also be meaningful to the students.

A third and more radical approach would be to integrate ends and means, so that the assignment is not regarded as the ends (a demonstration that means have been achieved) but as part of the means of the educational process. That is, we need to regard academic writing as part of the process of knowledge creation rather than as evidence that knowledge has been acquired. As we have seen, Dewey argues that knowledge is not a "thing" but an interactive process; thus, rather than setting writing against practice, we should try to integrate the two. In other words, writing is seen as part of the *process* of discovery rather than a *record* of the discovery; a dialog with ourselves as a way of coming to an understanding. Rather than "writing up" the thesis, the practice of writing *is* the thesis. We therefore need to design courses in which writing is integral to the process of learning, scholarship, and practice development, so that by the time the student has reached the end of the course, the assignment has (so to speak) written itself. This approach to some extent inverts ends and means, such that writing the thesis becomes the means to the end-in-view of improving practice rather than an end in itself or a demonstration that the ends have been achieved.

Such a radical approach to integrating means and ends entails trusting our students to find a meaningful and worthwhile way that leads to insight, and that finding their own way is integral to coming to know. It would mean that every student would submit work that was uniquely their own, which might include mind maps, art, poetry, journal writing, photography, video clips of practice situations, or any other means that draws forth thinking. Formal writing in the early phase of the thesis might be sacrificed for free writing that simply thought-as-it-wrote, or verbal accounts, or a video tour of issues and initiatives. Lectures might be replaced with readings of poetry, taking students back to the experience of being human. Lecturers might be replaced with patients recounting their experiences of care. Practitioners would find themselves sitting alongside colleagues from a wide range of other health care disciplines, being provoked to think new questions arising from different viewpoints, unified by the singular patient sitting at the center of it all. Literature reviews would likely be overshadowed by reports of conversations, visits, and any other encounter that would provoke insight and astonishment. Stakeholders from practice, whether managers, colleagues, or clients, might well become key to deciding what matters most. The supervisor would take the role of dialogic partner rather than expert scholar. The key question in relation to "ends" would likely be, "How might this impact practice?" recognizing that the ends-in-view are concerned with a new understanding of go-forward means. The outcomes might, for example, be something as simple (and astonishing) as health care managers, patients, and colleagues delighting in the impact that came from the change initiative. It is somewhat ironic and deeply subversive that all of this still fits the corporate business model. By putting the key stakeholders of health care at the center of what matters, everything else falls into place. However, the first requirement is a commitment to challenge the status of the university as the sole controller, regulator, and validator of knowledge (Rolfe & Davies, 2009) and to recognize that unless we work "with" our practice partners, all we will achieve is a growing pile of dust-collecting outputs.

The Brave New World

At AUT our interprofessional doctor of health science degree aspires to create the open space where students can recognize the challenges and opportunities within their own practice world and call them into question. We hold the tension of being practical (recognizing that these students continue their clinical roles and must meet tight university time frames) while setting thinking free to roam. We begin with a series of three papers (assignments), one per semester. The first paper gives students time to play with both their research interest and their methodological approach. We expose them to the philosophical assumptions that underpin the different approaches both to get them thinking and to help them to discern the best fit. The students themselves decide how they will meet the very broad learning outcomes. The first four outcomes allow and facilitate a creative submission; we simply ask that they show us their thinking. The fifth outcome asks them to write a draft paper for publication, thereby schooling them in the currency of the university. The second paper is very similar in approach to the first, with its focus on the context in which the issue sits. Work from each of these papers leads to the third: writing the research proposal. Our pragmatic disposition says "everything you do can count towards your thesis."

A key thread across these three papers is leadership. Our students are already leaders; we do not teach them the theory of leadership. Rather we ask them to reflect on how they go about leading. We encourage them to tell their stories, to recognize the unique style of their leading, to ponder the constraints and possibilities within their practice context. The seminar which introduces the leadership thread is run by Andrew Norton (Smythe & Norton, 2007, 2011), who uses poetry as a catalyst for thinking. Students report that while in the past they have done many leadership courses, they have never before felt personally engaged with what it means for them to be a leader. We are committed to developing stronger connections with practice, drawing practice leaders into supervisory teams. Students are working on proposals that integrate projects from their own work areas. Change is already happening long before thesis submission. It seems to be more manageable for the students; they are not taking on something different but rather strengthening existing work projects with the support of university staff. A disposition of working together, of expecting practice to be at the focus of everything, and of celebrating the impact of change that comes is alive and well. A new enthusiasm has been born that attracts us all.

Conclusion

Developing and improving practice and practitioners requires the courage and confidence to breach the strongholds of university academe in order to create a fresh sense of what matters most, thus the cultural values of academe. We argue that our students (practitioners of health care) deserve to find a sanctuary where they are free to dwell with the thinking that arises from their real world practice ideas and concerns. To think, to question, to come to new insights, empowers change. Enabling the university to work more closely with stakeholders from practice is to ensure that such change directly impacts health care. Education therefore becomes the means to improving health outcomes because each student embarks on his or her own quest toward making a change that impacts on real people by improving their experience; people the student will come face-to-face with in their future practice. When the university takes its eyes off research for its own sake and academic writing per se, and instead glimpses the possible contribution that can be made to a known person, a specific community, with potential ripples around the globe, then education truly counts.

References

Balas, E. A. (2001). Information systems can prevent errors and improve quality. *Journal of the American Medical Informatics Association, 8*, 398–399.

Balas, E. A., & Boren, S. A. (2000). *Managing clinical knowledge for health care improvement.* Stuttgart, Germany: Schattauer.

Buchan, H. (2007). Turning knowledge into action. *Australian Prescriber, 30*(5), 114–115.

Dewey, J. (1910). *How we think.* Boston, MA: D.C. Heath & Co.

Dewey, J. (1958/1929). *Experience and nature.* New York, NY: Dover Publications.

Dewey, J. (1988/1939). *Later works, Vol. 14.* Carbondale, IL: Southern Illinois University Press.

Dewey, J. (2007/1916). *Democracy and education.* Teddington, UK: Echo Library.

Dewey, J. (2008/1922). *Human nature and conduct.* New York, NY: Barnes & Noble.

Gadamer, H. G. (1982/1960). *Truth and method* (G. Barden & J. Cumming, Trans.). New York, NY: Crossroad.

Gardner, L., & Rolfe, G. (2013). Essaying the essay: Nursing scholarship and the hegemony of the laboratory. *Nurse Education Today, 33*, 31–35. doi:10.1016/j.nedt.2011.10.009

Heidegger, M. (1966/1959). *Discourse on thinking* (J. Anderson & E. H. Freund, Trans.). New York, NY: Harper Row.

Heidegger, M. (1968/1954). *What is called thinking?* (J. G. Gray, Trans.). New York, NY: Harper Row.

Heidegger, M. (1993/1954). Building dwelling thinking. In D. F. Krell (Ed./Trans.) *Basic writings* (pp. 243–255). London: Routledge.

Heidegger, M. (2002/1945). Transcript of the deposition of Professor Dr Martin Heidegger. In M. A. Peters (Ed.), *Heidegger, education and modernity* (pp. 27–45). Lanham, MD: Rowman & Littlefield.

Newman, J. H. (1982/1858). *The idea of a university.* South Bend, IN: University of Notre-Dame Press.

Oakeshott, M. (2001). The idea of a university. In T. Fuller (Ed.), *The voice of liberal learning* (pp. 105–117). Indianapolis, IN: Liberty Press.

Readings, B. (1996). *The university in ruins.* Cambridge, MA: Harvard University Press.

Rolfe, G. (2013). Thinking as a subversive activity: Doing philosophy in the corporate university. *Nursing Philosophy, 14*(1), 28–37. doi:10.1111/j.1466-769X.2012.00551.x

Rolfe, G., & Davies, R. (2009). Second generation professional doctorates in nursing. *International Journal of Nursing Studies, 46,* 1265–1273. doi:10.1016/j.ijnurstu.2009.04.002

Rorty, R. (1979). *Philosophy and the mirror of nature.* Oxford: Blackwell.

Rorty, R. (1982/1974). *Consequences of pragmatism (Essays: 1972–1980)* (pp. 37–59). Brighton, UK: The Harvester Press.

Smythe, E., & Norton, A. (2007). Thinking as leadership/leadership as thinking. *Leadership, 3*(1), 65–90. doi:10.1177/1742715007073067

Smythe, E., & Norton, A. (2011). Leadership: Wisdom in action. *The Indo-Pacific Journal of Phenomenology, 11*(1), 1–11. doi:10.2989/IPJP.2011.11.1.6.1105

Smythe, E., & Spence, D. (2012). Re-viewing literature in hermeneutic research. *International Journal of Qualitative Methods, 11*(1), 12–25.

Taylor, R. T., & Storey, V. A. (2013). Leaders, critical friends, and the education community. *Journal of Applied Research in Higher Education, 5*(1), 84–94. doi:10.1108/17581181311310298

Teasell, R. (2012). Challenges in the implementation of evidence in stroke rehabilitation. *Top Stroke Rehabilitation, March–April,* 93–94.

6

Redesigning the EdD at UCL Institute of Education: Thoughts of the Incoming EdD Program Leaders

Denise Hawkes and Sue Taylor

Introduction

UK Context for Doctor in Education

Professional doctorates were introduced to the United Kingdom in the 1990s. The UK Council for Graduate Education report found that the number of professional doctorate programs in the United Kingdom grew from 109 in 1998 to 308 in 2009. For the doctor of education (EdD) alone there were 38 programs in 2009, with some 2,228 students.

Growing numbers of professional doctorates in the United Kingdom lead to their inclusion on the Quality Assurance Agency's (QAA) qualifications framework. Within this framework they were described as follows: "Professional doctorates aim to develop an individual's professional practice and to support them in producing a contribution to (professional) knowledge" (QAA, 2008, p. 25). This contribution to professional knowledge has enabled professional doctorate programs, such as the EdD, to recruit a body of students not usually attracted to traditional PhD programs. EdD students often come into the program with a wealth of professional knowledge and looking for ways to develop research skills and attain an advanced qualification, often without the desire to make the transition into academia (QAA, 2011). The professional doctorate was therefore able to respond to criticism from employers that PhD students lacked the wider applied subject knowledge, practical experience, and generic skills necessary in the workplace (Owen, 2011; Taylor, 2008).

EdD Programs at UCL Institute of Education

The EdD program at UCL Institute of Education was established in 1996. Since then the program has undertaken several redesigns and developments such that in 2013, there are three variants of the program: EdD (Home), EdD (International), and EdD (Dual Award with NIE Singapore). The EdD (Home) recruited largely a London-/England-based cohort and the EdD (International/Dual) recruited almost exclusively an international group of students. The programs were treated as separate programs and the students of each did not meet those on the other EdD programs (Table 6.1).

All students had a supervisor to guide them through from the start of the EdD program to their thesis. Each variant had its own range of taught courses based on intensive face-to-face delivery and work by e-mail with a tutor for assessed coursework. During the research phase the students also had access to a program of workshops designed to help support their journey through independent research. The offer was a well-respected program that drew students from around the world with

Table 6.1 UCL Institute of Education, EdD Structure

	Pre 2014			Post 2014
Year of study	EdD (International)	EdD (Home)	Year of study	EdD
Year 1	Foundations of Professionalism Methods of Enquiry 1 Methods of Enquiry 2		Year 1	Foundations of Professionalism Methods of Enquiry 1 Methods of Enquiry 2
Year 2	International Education Portfolio IFS proposal	Optional course	Year 2	Selection of courses from PhD program (RTP) Portfolio IFS proposal
Year 3	IFS Thesis proposal		Year 3	Selection of courses from PhD program (RTP) IFS Thesis proposal
Year 4–7	Thesis		Year 4–7	Thesis

the EdD alumni recommendations being the main source of recruitment for the program.

In September 2013 the primary author of this chapter became the program leader for all three variants of the EdD programs at UCL Institute of Education with the secondary author becoming the deputy EdD program leader (and then Institution Focused Study [IFS] course leader in September 2014). This merger of leadership was an innovation in itself as previously the programs were operated separately with different program leaders, although the EdD (International) and EdD (Dual) were initially spin-offs of the EdD (Home). This chapter provides an account of how, as the incoming program leaders for the EdD, we were able to cast a fresh pair of eyes over this much respected program and enhance it through four main innovative ideas:

1. Providing greater flexibility for students and access to a wider group of critical friends through program merger.
2. Enabling more engagement with critical friends through innovative use of the Virtual Learning Environment (VLE, Moodle).
3. Allowing the EdD students to find critical friends in the PhD student body through the use of PhD courses.
4. Complete overhaul of the IFS workshops to focus on the process of research rather than more research methods.

More details on the reasons for these developments can be found in Hawkes and Taylor (2015). This chapter will outline the developments and their link to critical friend theory.

Greater Flexibility through Program Merger

In September 2013 EdD programs followed two distinct routes with no discourse between the student bodies. The EdD (Home) program was delivered on three Fridays and Saturdays a term and recruited largely London and the Southeast education practitioners. The EdD (International) and EdD (Dual), called EdD International henceforth, were delivered in block delivery of six days (Monday to Saturday) and recruited globally. This separation between the two programs was largely due to the separation of program leadership.

Looking at the content delivered, it was clear that the only differences between the programs were the mode of delivery (week or weekends) and the optional courses offered—three options were available for the EdD (Home) and all EdD (International) students took international education. Later in the chapter we will return to these options and see how this was addressed. The three taught courses —Foundations of Professionalism (FoP), Methods of Enquiry 1 (MoE1) and Methods of Enquiry 2 (MoE2)— were in essence the same courses run twice as were the workshops for the IFS and thesis. This provided the option to be able to merge the programs under the umbrella of one EdD program and give students a choice at each term as to which delivery mode they would like to select.

The merger of these two programs provided students with a degree of flexibility that had previously been lacking with regard to the face-to-face delivery and also provided a starting point for the development of online versions of each course. The new program started in September 2014. Students were asked at interview which delivery they preferred for term one. Between interview and induction, 2 of the 35 students starting the program changed modes for term one; this increased to 4 students changing modes in term two and 5 in term three. While most London-based students remain on the Friday/Saturday delivery and most internationals remain on the weeklong delivery, there has been movement in both directions between delivery modes. As a result of these changes we have avoided the handful of student interruptions to study required each year previously, which has meant in previous years students waiting for a year to rejoin the program. This has enabled students who have built up connections with others on the program not to lose touch with these valuable critical friends.

In order to establish and maintain connections between the two groups of students a single induction event was held on the Saturday before the first week of teaching. All but one of the 35 students attended, and although some may not meet again in person there is evidence of their engagement with each other on the discussion forums and other tools on the VLE. Cohort development is a critical part of any EdD program, as it is often this cohort that helps the student through, especially at difficult times. The shared induction and shared online resources provide the tools for the students to engage with each other. There is evidence of this continued relationship online especially with those who migrate between groups. To promote this development of a wider cohort to develop more options for establishing critical friends, from 2015 each course will share the first two days together, with weeklong delivery changing from Monday to Saturday to Friday to Thursday, which will enable all students to meet on Friday and Saturday.

Enabling More Engagement with Critical Friends through Moodle

Moving to a single EdD program has enabled the program team to invest time in developing our use of the VLE (Moodle) in supporting our students. The development of good quality resources to support the face-to-face provision and the creation of virtual alternatives to face-to-face sessions, which maybe missed due to life events, has formed the basis of a more blended delivery mode from 2014–2015. In addition the development of these enhanced Moodle sites will form the basis of an online version of our EdD program, which could be offered from 2015–2016.

The second core course, MoE1, has extended the development of the enhanced Moodle sites further to include online activities that could be shared between students on the two face-to-face modes as well as the use of peer feedback on draft assignments using the Moodle forums. This development has been very well received by the students, especially for those on the weeklong delivery who have felt more engaged with the program when not with us in person. Clearly there is a cost in terms of staff time especially for setting up tasks and moderating them, but it is hoped that a reduction in the need for staff input in assignments and the need for resits will help to mitigate this. Largely the development has been well received by staff and students.

The use of combined Moodle sites has also enabled the students to develop their own independent critical friends groups. Students with similar research interests, regardless of mode of face-to-face delivery, are seen on the Moodle site initiating chat and discussion between sessions. While in the first year of the program it is too early to tell if this will continue into the research phase, it is encouraging to see that development of the VLE resources has been fruitful in many directions.

Critical Friends: Blurring the EdD and PhD

In the merger of the two EdD programs the issue of optional courses was especially tricky. As noted above, in the first term of the second year, the EdD students completed an optional course. The EdD (Home) students had a choice of three courses (Leadership and Learning in Educational Organizations, Post-Compulsory Education and Lifelong Learning, and Rethinking Education: Psychoanalytic Perspectives on Learning and Teaching) while the EdD (International) students all completed the International Education course. It was clear that these options needed revising but there was little will to do so as the courses were not formally assessed, although they contributed to the portfolio of practice.

Rather than revisit the options the team decided to remove them completely and replace them with a selection of courses from those offered to the PhD students within the Institute. Given that these courses would be more helpful during the research phase, it was decided that 30 hours of these courses would be selected from the PhD student's Research Training Program (RTP) and could be taken at any time in the second and third years of the program.

This innovation has been taken in light of the agenda within the Institute of Education to blur the line between PhD and EdD students in an attempt to enhance recognition of the EdD as a valid route to a doctorate. Access to the RTP would provide EdD students with insights into doctoral-level work and also provide those on a more traditional PhD route to see the excellent work undertaken by our EdD students.

For those who wished to select the previous options, comparable courses could be found in the RTP. For those wishing to explore other areas available, this development helped to broaden the curriculum offered without developing new EdD options. In addition, students would be able to develop critical friends in the wider research student body. While the PhD students may bring a larger academic understanding of the field, the EdD students would contribute to these discussions their professional practice and experience, which many PhD students lack. We will need to wait until 2015–2017 to see the impact of these innovations but the idea was warmly welcomed when proposed by the EdD student representatives and EdD current students/alumni.

Developments in Research Phases—The IFS

Context

Sue Taylor (an author of this chapter) has been involved with the EdD since 2001: as a student; a tutor across all taught courses; a supervisor; and a course leader for MoE1 (Home) taught course. Consequently, she has seen many changes but nothing as radical and potentially transformational as that proposed in 2014. She shares the vision of the new program leader to support widening participation in professional doctorates being mindful that student characteristics have changed over the years. The replacement of the optional courses with access to the RTP for the PhD students has enabled a radical rethink of the IFS workshops with the intent of developing a holistic approach to student transition from taught-course to research phase. This transition might be seen as fundamental to the future success of students completing their EdD.

What Is the IFS?

The IFS is an interim piece of research following the taught-course phase and must be successfully completed prior to moving into the thesis phase. It might be considered akin to the upgrade from MPhil to PhD.

The purpose of the IFS paradoxically is explicit yet vague: perhaps due to the way it is conceptualized and articulated to both students and supervisors. The student handbooks state:

> The purpose of the IFS is to enable you to carry out a small-scale research study normally based upon your own "institution"...You should also show how the proposed study will contribute to your professional understanding and development and to the "institution" on which your research has focused. (EdD Handbook, 2013/14, p. 76)

The supervisor handbook does not explicitly discuss the IFS whereas MPhil/PhD upgrade is mentioned. EdD supervisors' access to IFS information is via student handbooks.

At the end of the taught-course phase supervisors "approve" a portfolio of assignments and feedback together with a 2,000-word reflective statement. This is usually the first time supervisors engage with students' research since agreeing to supervise at the point of application (for some, 18 months beforehand).

Students are advised but not compelled to build on their taught-course phase and develop their proposal (MoE1) and their pilot of a method (MoE2) and submit an IFS proposal. The purpose as articulated to students (and supervisors through the EdD handbook) states:

> The IFS will build on concepts, understanding and skills that you have developed during the taught courses, and may build on work you have carried out for these courses. Although it is not necessarily tied tightly to the thesis, it may inform the thesis and permit the evolution of ideas and understanding for the thesis, or provide the foundation from which the thesis will develop ... reflecting on the taught elements of the course in relation to your own institution; identifying a problem for investigation and locating the research in its context; reviewing relevant literature and investigating how far it has informed an institution's policy documents; conducting a pilot investigation prior to the thesis; investigating a range of institutions similar to the one to be investigated in depth in the thesis; acquiring specific knowledge of the institutions required for the thesis; conducting an investigation complementary to that for the thesis. (EdD Home Handbook, 2011/12, p. 78; EdD International Handbook, 2011/12, p. 72)

The IFS then can but does not necessarily serve as an interim piece of research to establish potential to write and work at doctoral level (paralleling the MPhil/PhD upgrade). The above extract illustrates the vagueness of purpose.

IFS workshops therefore, were and are designed to supplement individual supervisions.

Why Change?

Previous IFS workshop structure extended MoE2 focusing on more *methods* training:

> The Research Weeks include practical workshops on planning and doing research, collecting and analyzing data and helping you in the particular challenges of researching an institution. (EdD Home Handbook, 2011/12, p. 79; EdD International Handbook, 2011/12, p. 73)

Having reviewed IFS proposals it was evident that students are not wholly aware of the purpose of the IFS many failing to propose research of suitable scale and scope. Perhaps something was being "lost in translation" about the purpose. It therefore seemed appropriate to redevelop the IFS taking into account the redesign of the EdD. Redevelopment of the IFS is designed to support students' understanding of the general principles of the IFS and of individual independent research and being able to make the transition from taught-course to research phase seamlessly.

The quality of previous IFS proposals suggests too much emphasis on *methods* training rather than focusing on transition from the taught-course phase to the independent-research phase.

Aligning the Institution Focused Study within the EdD Redevelopment Framework

The proposed structure of the IFS from 2014 can be divided into three main themes:

1. A focus on project management and big conceptual ideas.
2. An andragogical approach to adult learning (Brookfield, 1986; Knowles, 1990) to develop independence in the research process.
3. A reflective discussion on how to work with your supervisor.

Table 6.2 provides an overview. The proposed changes are designed to ensure student equity and alignment with the principles of EdD redesign. The seven sessions are the same irrespective of mode of attendance and are designed to support students make links between taught-course, IFS, and thesis phases.

A further common element has been a sharing opportunity at each session. Face-to-face sharing is supported with online activity in between IFS workshops. Students' understanding of andragogy will facilitate their

Table 6.2   Proposed IFS Structure

Session	Theme
1	1. From portfolio toward IFS 2. Working with your supervisor (1) 3. Sharing opportunities
2	1. What makes a good proposal—project management 2. Sharing opportunities
3	1. Peer review of proposals 2. Working with your supervisor (2) 3. What is an IFS? 4. Sharing opportunities
4	1. Proposal for IFS 2. Argument and structure 3. Sharing opportunities
5	1. Review of previous IFS 2. Working with supervisors (3) 3. Sharing opportunities
6	1. Writing up the IFS a. Getting down to details b. Contribution to professional practice 2. Sharing opportunities
7	1. Final thoughts a. Submitting the IFS b. Link between IFS and thesis 2. Thesis proposal and formal review

willingness and ability to engage in and develop self-support networks. This has a proven track record on the PGDip Social Science Research Methods course of the Institute of Education (IOE). These workshops and the online sessions provide an opportunity for students to obtain thoughts from their critical friends.

Students are currently encouraged during MoE1 to keep a research journal but this is not a requirement. Within the redeveloped IFS, students will keep an online research journal via the IOE's VLE (Moodle). This requirement supports students' reflections on their methodological decision-making as well as on their transition from taught-course to research phase.

The developments on the IFS workshops will help to inform the development of the thesis workshops in 2015, which we hope to move toward a flipped classroom strategy. The students who have engaged with the online resources and/or attended the workshops have found these to be helpful. In the evaluation of the IFS proposals this year more students were proposing ideas that were more achievable within a 12-month research time frame and being more mindful of the research process.

Conclusion

We are often fearful of making large-scale changes to established and successful programs like UCL Institute of Education's EdD programs. It is therefore our privilege to have been given the opportunity and support to undertake such an extensive redesign of this well-loved program. The developments outlined above were informed by student requests (to have more engagement with other research students and more online resources), program team insights (listening to the issues faced on the coal face and the experience of colleagues), and administrative staff concerns (around frequent interruptions due to inflexible program structures). In taking bold steps in program development these must be supported by the department and based on the collection of evidence. They also need to be evaluated, and this chapter is one of those publications that results from this evaluation of our EdD redesign.

The strength of any EdD program is the quality of the cohort it has. Much of the learning on the EdD is from the sharing of experience between the EdD students. By its nature the EdD program is well suited to critical friends group and with the start of developing these in our first year as part of the redesign we hope that these groups can help support the students throughout the program. There is much scope to do more as the program develops.

Finally, we would like to urge program teams and program leaders to be willing to think creatively at time of program revalidation and institutional change. Such processes will be much better used as opportunities rather than as administrative burdens to create truly innovative programs for our EdD students.

References

Brookfield, S. D. (1986). *Understanding and facilitating adult learning.* Milton Keynes, UK: Open University Press.

EdD Program Handbooks. (2011/12). London, UK: Institute of Education, University of London.

Hawkes, D., & Taylor, S. (2014). So who wants to do an EdD anyway? Evidence from the Institute of Education EdD Completions 1996–2013. *Work Based Learning e-journal International, 4*(1), 1–10.

Knowles, M. S. (1990). *The adult learner: A neglected species* (4th ed.). Houston, TX: Gulf Publishing.

Owen, C. (2011). The international EdD at the Institute of Education, University of London. Paper presented at *Scottish Researcher Career Coordination Forum & QAA Scotland Joint Conference*, Glasgow, UK, June 9–10, 2011.

QAA. (2008). *Framework for higher education qualifications in England, Wales and Northern Ireland*. London, UK: QAA.

QAA. (2011). *Doctoral degree characteristics*. London, UK: QAA.

Taylor, J. (2008). Quality and standards: The challenge of the professional doctorate. *Higher Education in Europe, 33*(1), 65–87.

7

A Different Practice? Professional Identity and Doctoral Education in Art & Design

Jacqueline Taylor and Sian Vaughan

The doctoral study of Art & Design has significantly evolved over the past 20 years; while in the United Kingdom in particular, the increase in practice-led research and practitioners undertaking PhDs has contributed to the expansion of Art & Design doctoral study. Despite the growth of Professional Doctorates, only a small number of Universities in the United Kingdom offer one in Art & Design. Based on our research into doctoral study at Birmingham City University we argue that through the entwining of professional practice and practice-led research, the ethos underpinning the Professional Doctorate is encapsulated in the very nature of the Art & Design PhD. Our students have revealed aspirations and motivations in which academic, practitioner, industry and other creative roles are complexly entwined, blurring the traditional binary of academic and nonacademic professional roles both inside and outside the academe, nuanced aspirations which we locate as "para-academic." Moving on from the PhD and Professional Doctorate viewed dualistically as either aligned with the philosophical and theoretical or the professional, doctoral study in Art & Design occupies a more fluid space in which the para-academic is a positive position in relation to professional identity. We contend that doctoral study in Art & Design and the Professional Doctorate in other disciplines can play the role of critical friends to one another, whereby both parties can be enhanced by not just seeing but recognizing reflections of the self within the other.

The UK Context

In the United Kingdom, the number of Professional Doctorates has been increasing, however in Art & Design it remains less common than in other disciplines (McCay, 2010). A UK Council of Graduate Education (UKCGE) report in 2010 revealed a distinct upward trend with the number of awards at UK Higher Education Institutions (HEIs) almost tripling between 1998 and 2009 (Brown & Cooke, 2010). Engineering, Business and Education remain the most dominant subject areas for UK Professional Doctorates alongside rises in the Social Sciences and Clinical Psychology. For example, 38 institutions offered Professional Doctorates in Education (under various nomenclatures) with a total of 2,228 students in 2009. However, in comparison there were only 59 students at 9 institutions studying for Professional Doctorates in "Arts/Architecture and the Built Environment"; thus 59 out of 7,882 students across all disciplines in 2009. Within the subject grouping of "Arts/Architecture and the Built Environment," 31 of the 59 students were registered for the DBEnv (Professional Doctorate in the Built Environment/ Doctor of Built Environment), and another 5 were registered for the DMA (Doctor of Musical Arts). This leaves only 23 students registered in what we might consider Art & Design, all registered for the DFA (Doctor of Fine Art) at the same institution (Brown & Cooke, 2010).

In contrast, the United Kingdom has seen significant growth in Art & Design in the traditional PhD, and in particular an increase in practice-led and practice-based PhDs (Mottram, Rust, & Till, 2007, p. 26). Metcalfe (2006) notes that a common aspect of Professional Doctorate programs is that they are often undertaken by practitioners researching within their own practice. They are for students working in a professional environment to further develop their skills and the development of practice within a profession in order to find novel approaches for integrating academic and professional knowledge. According to the UK Economic & Social Research Council (2005) students undertaking a Professional Doctorate are expected to make a contribution to both theory and practice in their field, and in particular to develop professional practice by making a contribution to professional knowledge. The growth in PhDs in Art & Design is in part due to increasing numbers of creative practitioners undertaking doctoral research. This relationship between creative practice and the professional is pertinent to the expansion of Professional Doctorates in Art & Design. Indeed, according to the UK Arts & Humanities Research Council (AHRC) Review, between 1996 and 2005 there were 406 PhDs awarded in Art, Design & Architecture, with approximately 20% investigating practice in some way (Mottram et al., 2007, p. 21). This growth is highlighted by Wilson and van Ruiten who assert that through the expansion of doctoral platforms available in different disciplines and domains, there has been a massification of doctoral education in the arts in the past decade (2014, p. 8).

The PhD in Art & Design

The ecology of Art & Design doctoral study has significantly evolved over the last 20 years. The emergence of the terms "practice-based" and "practice-led" research has successfully highlighted practice as being as important as theoretically-based methods in generating knowledge, ostensibly acknowledging creative practice in its various forms as a central part of the research process (Gray & Malins, 2004; Mottram et al., 2007). It is now widely accepted in Art & Design research, that theory and practice form a complementary relationship in which they "mutually participate in each other's endeavours" (Davey, 2006, p. 20).

To begin to unpick these terms, practice-based research has been most notably defined by Candy (2007) as referring to creative artifact(s) as the basis of a contribution to knowledge, by means of practice and the outcomes of that practice. She asserts that it is demonstrated in a doctoral thesis through creative outcomes (designs, performances, exhibitions) and textually with direct reference to those outcomes. By comparison, Candy identifies practice-led research as research that leads primarily to new understandings about practice in which it "includes practice as an integral part of its method" (2007, p. 3). For Candy, in the doctoral thesis the results of practice-led research do not necessarily include the submission of creative work(s). It is important to note that Candy represents an Antipodean school of thought and that in the United Kingdom the term "practice-led" research is most widely used and is defined more broadly, as "research in which the professional and/or creative processes of art, design and architecture play an instrumental part in an enquiry" (Mottram et al., 2007, p. 11).

In this context, the distinction made in 1997 by the UKCGE between creative practice as part of PhD research that reflects a research focus on the creative product within an academic context, and the professional creative practice in a Professional Doctorate such as a DMus or DArt which focuses on the quality of the creative product, (UKCGE, 1997, p. 12) seems too dichotomous and simplistic. The reality is that the practice-led PhD in Art & Design is not isolated within an academic context, nor necessarily results in the examination of creative products. More recently the UKCGE has attempted again to delineate between the practice-led PhD in Art & Design and the growth in Professional Doctorates:

> Practice-Led Doctorates . . . were not developed in response to any specific needs of the professional Arts, Design and Architecture domains, for

the ultimate award of a PhD. In fact, the very concept of practice-based/ practice-led research in AD&A refers more generally to a specific approach to academic research in these subject areas – this is the key characteristic, by contrast with many professional doctorates. (UKCGE, 2011, p. 63)

Here, the distinction appears to center on the origin of research, and purpose of the doctoral award, rather than for the benefits of the professional practice and sector more widely. However, even this distinction is not unambiguous when considered in relation to the nature of Art & Design doctoral study and research students. In this emergent field, there is not one accepted definition of Art & Design research. There is panoply of related terminology such as "art-practice-as-research," practice as research and following on from Frayling, research through practice (1993, p. 5) in which research may or may not center on practitioner roles and professional practice. Practice can be methodology, location of and/or subject of the research. Within Art & Design research, definitions vary by discipline and are thus fluid terms, difficult to fully articulate.

As a UK Higher Education Academy report on practice-based doctorates reveals, many research students as practitioners are not simply in dialog with the professional community, but part of that community (Boyce-Tillman et al., 2012). There is an element of linguistic ambiguity and fluidity here. In Art & Design, to have and engage in a creative practice, particularly at the advanced level recognized in Postgraduate study, is to have a professional practice. Thus in Art & Design, students often come into the PhD experience with an already established creative and/or professional identity and aspire to enhance or transform this identity through undertaking academic study. Wilson (2014) outlines the complexities that this involves:

> The identity "researcher" cannot simply be collapsed into the identity "artist" . . . here is a willful orientation towards becoming something other than that which one already is, a willed change in the postionality of the subject who wishes to know something not yet known. This is a tremendous challenge for any professional practitioner. (2014, p. 204)

Through the process of undertaking the PhD, the challenge for students is navigating the development of an academic identity while still maintaining a sense of self as a creative practitioner. Hockey's research demonstrated what he termed the "shock" experienced by practice-based research degree students in Art & Design in this process of negotiating a new sense of self:

> Students encounter a number of problems which collectively generate a shock and challenge to their artistic identity, for they have to engage with

unfamiliar research processes and procedures, which have a disturbing impact upon that identity . . . Engagement in academic research involved some degree of risk, either in terms of failure to pass and consequent denouement, or in terms of the negative impact of critical analysis on their creative capacity. (Hockey, 2008, p. 117)

Many PhD students in Art & Design have to make the transition to being a student, often while still maintaining their professional status, inhabiting simultaneous identities as expert, professional, student, and beginner. This complexity is one that can be troublesome to navigate, and comes in addition to the isolation and trepidations that are axiomatic of the doctoral experience regardless of discipline.

There are also external challenges encountered through the necessity to shapeshift in this respect; labels and expectations are imposed upon Art & Design research students by those for whom academia and creative and/or professional practice are still conceived of as dichotomous. So not only must doctoral students in Art & Design be comfortable inhabiting and enfolding multiple identities, they must continually project, communicate, and defend them in different contexts. This is exacerbated by the implicit assumption that because Art & Design PhD students are often highly regarded creative professionals, and the majority are perceived as experienced students as they have a Master's degree, providing more general support for the student experience that takes into account such complexity and its associated anxieties is not a priority. It both raises questions of the potential misapplication of andragogy when dealing with Art & Design doctoral study and the need to employ emotional intelligence in holistically considering student experiences (Knowles, 1984; Mortiboys, 2005).

Learning from Our Doctoral Students' Experience

The Art & Design PhD cohort at our institution reflects this complexity and diversity in relation to identity, practice and the professional. Birmingham City University has one of the largest Art & Design PhD cohorts in the United Kingdom and it is growing fast from 48 students enrolled in 2012–2013, to over 70 at the start of the 2014–2015 academic year, approximately a 50% increase in 2 years. Our students are working across a range of disciplines from Fine Art to Typography, Ideas Management to Antiquarian Horology, Landscape Architecture to Art Education, rooted in a diverse range of cultural, sociopolitical, philosophical, artistic, professional, practical and theoretical contexts. They are drawing from the Humanities, Social Sciences, Philosophy, Linguistics, as well as developing a variety of creative design and artistic practice methodologies often alongside more traditional historical as well as sociological, ethnographic, quantitative, and qualitative methods. In 2012–2013 we undertook a research project entitled "Investigating and increasing the employability of research students in Art & Design: understanding the student experience," based on the Art & Design doctoral experience at Birmingham City University. This research project built on Dr Vaughan's previous Destination Tracking Study into the career destinations of the 71 former research students who had completed an Art & Design research degree at our University since 2000. Somewhat counterintuitively given assumptions about the general growth in PhDs in Art & Design, it revealed that over 70% of these former students whose current employment could be identified were working in Higher Education (HE). However, we anticipated that with the changing nature of Art & Design doctoral study and the emergence of practice-led and practitioner-researchers, traditional assumptions about the motivations and aspirations for doctoral study (as either pure subject interest or an academic "licence to practice") would also need to change.

Following on from this, our research study aimed to: improve our understanding of demographic shifts identified in Art & Design doctoral study including the growth of practice-based research and practitioner-researchers; uncover what careers our students aspire to in relation to this shifting landscape; and consider the doctoral experience in Art & Design in terms of employability and developing provision. We carried out qualitative research using two in-depth questionnaires, one for current students in the 2012–2013 cohort and one for former students who had completed their research degree since the year 2000. The survey results were triangulated with data from informal exploratory interviews and cohort data already held within the institution. We were able to gain substantial qualitative and narrative responses, providing rich and detailed new insights into students' perspectives and the wider landscape of Art & Design doctoral study.

Our results demonstrate that it is difficult to generalize student aspirations based on age, mode of study or discipline as both current and former students identify a highly individualized mix of personal, financial, strategic and opportunistic motivations for study. For example, somewhat paradoxically, the youth, older age, existence and lack of children are all cited as deciding factors in the timing of undertaking a PhD. A personal sense of enjoyment of and interest in their research subject or discipline was a strong motivation. However, overall, the majority of reasons provided by both current and former students for undertaking Art & Design doctoral study were strongly career-driven and focused on academic work. We initially anticipated that the growth in practice-related PhDs in Art & Design would be accompanied by an intuitive move to "alt-academic" aspirations (Nowviskie, 2011, p. 7); alternative or nontraditional career paths by those who have undertaken PhD research either in the academy (specifically not in teaching or researcher roles) or beyond it altogether (e.g., those who have set up their own business or work as a school teacher). In what can perhaps be perceived as a counter-intuitive move, we discovered that in fact—as with former students—there is a strong ambition by our current Art & Design PhD students to work in academia. However, the growing numbers of practitioners and "practice-led" students seem to correlate with increasing numbers of current students' aspirations to have "para-academic" rather than academic or alt-academic careers.

The term para-academia is drawn from Whitchurch's notion of "third space professionals" who inhabit an emergent territory between traditional academic and nonacademic roles (Whitchurch, 2008, p. 377). She notes that traditionally, activity in Higher Education has been in binary terms such as these; however new hybrid institutional spaces are developing. MacFarlane first used the term "para-academia" to refer to what he calls the "unbundling" of the traditional academic (MacFarlane, 2010). He refers to para-academia as the disaggregation of traditional academic roles in which senior academics are de-skilling and nonacademics are up-skilling to create a new para-academic role. He also notes that this accounts for increasing numbers of part-time and casual positions in academia and doctoral students taking on some roles traditionally associated with the academic. Para-academia in this sense can be interpreted as having negative connotations through what MacFarlane (2010) calls a "hollowing out" of academic roles. The prefix para is here perceived as an auxiliary or subsidiary term to a more qualified term (e.g., as in "paralegal" or "paramedic"), with etymological roots also meaning "irregular," denoting subordinate modification (Oxford Dictionary, 2014). While MacFarlane focuses on the para-academic as existing within the University context, we contend that para-academia can also be interpreted using other readings of the prefix para- as implying beside and beyond (e.g., as in paranormal and paradox) or even guard against (as in paratrooper). This instead offers a vision of empowerment where the para-academic can coexist with the academe; working both independently and with the University, but on their own terms. Para-academia has not yet been discussed in the context of Art & Design. We identify it as a potentially useful term if appropriated to reflect current doctoral student's engagement and aspirations to combine practitioner, industry and other professional roles with those traditionally perceived as being firmly situated within the domain of academia such as teaching and research. This blurs previous distinctions of working inside or outside academia, especially within and beyond the University context.

These more nuanced career aspirations have meant that our student's expectations of how doctoral study relates to and effects their professional development are changing. While nearly all of our current students identified aspirations to undertake academic work, these were alongside aspirations to "increase practitioner status" and due to "artistic vision." Individuals seemed to more explicitly aspire to careers combining teaching, research and working as a professional practitioner, for example, as a consultant, artist, arts educator or head designer. Indeed, the PhD was seen by many as a framework for both artistic and professional practice whereby the subject of their PhD was directly concerned with their practitioner roles. For example, one student located their research as based on "school-based research in combination with my art-practice" and in relation aspired to teach, engage in research, as well as maintain their art practice. Another current student self-identified as a "designer-maker" located their practice as a basis for their research. They stated that they actively resisted the definition of career and saw themselves on the peripheries of academia with "one foot in and one foot out." They continued:

> I quite like being an outsider and combining roles as a practitioner and researcher . . . I need to maintain my practice in order to use it as a location and basis for research.

For many of our doctoral students, these roles are not separate but complexly entwined whereby one informs the other through a reflexive relation; research impacts upon one's professional role outside academia and vice versa. This entwining is bound up in the very nature of many Art & Design doctorates through their contribution to both theory and practice. It also reflects the concept of the portfolio career recognized as distinctive in the career trajectories of Art & Design graduates (Ball, Pollard, & Stanley, 2010) and the practitioner-lecturer as a common model in Art & Design HE (increasingly employed through fractional posts). Therefore, in many ways, it is only natural for doctoral students in Art & Design to also aspire to portfolio careers. However we do not believe there has been sufficient attention to, or recognition of this to date in terms of provision and support.

A Different Practice Shared with Critical Friends

We contend that by playing the role of critical friends to one another, the Art & Design PhD and Professional Doctorate are able to learn from one another. The critical friend offers a way to ask provocative questions and provides another lens with which to critique one another by understanding both the contexts and the outcomes they are working toward (Costa & Kallick, 1993, p. 49). While there does indeed seem to be a resistance in the United Kingdom to adopting the Professional Doctorate in Art & Design, the Art & Design PhD is also very different to the traditional PhD with its theoretical and academic focus. As the 2007 AHRC review notes in relation to practice-led research, the professional disciplines of Art, Design and Architecture have many differences; however, they all situate learning and scholarship in a professional practice setting (Mottram et al., 2007, p. 10). Therefore, it seems that the Professional Doctorate is not so dissimilar to these definitions of practice-related research in Art & Design.

Indeed, the increasing entwining of professional and academic knowledge with creative practice as the basis of study and textual and nontextual outputs submitted as part of the thesis means the ethos that underpins the Professional Doctorate is also intrinsically embedded in many of the PhDs undertaken by our Art & Design doctoral researchers and encapsulated in the very nature of the Art & Design PhD. In relation to the distinction between the Professional Doctorate and the traditional PhD, the Art & Design PhD conforms entirely to neither one nor the other model, but draws on both to occupy a more fluid space, one which we believe can be considered as a different practice. In reflecting upon this different practice, designers of both Professional Doctorate and Art & Design PhD programs can learn from one another and in doing so also reframe their own activities and pedagogies.

The notion of collaboration and cohort identity is pertinent here with the emphasis in Art & Design doctoral pedagogy on fostering independent enquiry through a minimal taught structure. As Blaj-Ward points out:

> Doctoral education in the Arts and Humanities (A&H) is traditionally linked with the image of the lone scholar, pursuing independent research with (minimal) support from an experienced discipline scholar. (2011, p. 697)

In comparison, most Professional Doctorates include a large taught or directed study element to provide researchers with transferrable skills in their field in relation to their professional roles and thus an awareness of employability. The use of the cohort model in many Professional Doctorates in particular provides academic, social, emotional and also professional support through enhancing interpersonal development, personal attributes, and management and communication skills (Bista & Cox, 2014).

The establishment of a similar cohort identity that accommodates the complex developing identities of our Art & Design PhD students beyond the initial PhD stages could have many benefits. It can potentially facilitate interdisciplinary learning, innovative thinking, and provide a way to enhance awareness of and enfold employability into provision through shared learning communities. Following on from McAlpine who highlights academic community as a crucial component of identity development in doctoral study (2009), it can also provide more general support for the student experience that accounts for and builds confidence in navigating the multilayered and often ambiguous nature of creative professional identity. The increasing provision of studentship funding by UK Research Councils through Doctoral Training Partnership (DTP) consortium mechanisms is influencing moves toward cohort-designed provision. This is particularly in relation to enhanced training that draws on the consortium's broader expertise and professional practice(s) to offer opportunities to the DTP-funded cohorts. However, there is a danger of hierarchies here in terms of funded students being able to benefit from these broader opportunities compared to those within the same institutions who are not funded through the DTP. A more holistic consideration of cohort-identity and cohort pedagogies is perhaps one way that the Art & Design PhD can learn from the Professional Doctorate, which appears to be more democratic and supportive in enabling cohort formation and peer support among doctoral students (e.g., Bista & Cox, 2014; Lei et al., 2011).

The recognition of the complexity, multiplicity, and fluidity of professional identities is one example where perhaps those designing Professional Doctorates can draw on the Art & Design PhD. An acknowledgment of research as reflectively and reflexively responding to practitioner and professional roles as also academic, moves beyond a distinction between theory and practice but enfolds the two. The challenge for us is in enabling individualized provision within a supportive cohort identity and "community of research practice" (Wilson, 2014, p. 204). As Blaj-Ward points out, "a clearer pedagogic grounding" can reconcile lone scholar models of scholarship with more practical concerns about researcher development and employability (2011, p. 698).

Beyond the specificity of Art and Design research practice, the nature of PhD study in the United Kingdom is also changing more generally as there are external drivers to embed professional skills training and the employability agenda into all doctoral provision. The Roberts's (2002) review of doctoral education in the United Kingdom concluded that the training a PhD provided was inadequate, particularly in the more transferable skills. Funding was initially made available to HEIs to address perceived research training needs and such training is now expected as part of all UK HEIs' doctoral provision (Crossouard, 2013). It has been enshrined by various UK funding and research bodies such as the RCUK's Concordat to Support the Career Development of Researchers (2011); the AHRC's Research Training

Framework (2011); the QAA's UK Quality Code for HE (2014), which sets and maintains subject benchmarks, and Vitae's Researcher Development Framework (RDF) (2010). In particular, this requirement is demonstrated in Vitae's development of an explicit Employability Lens (2012) as part of the RDF covering skills under categories such as Personal Effectiveness and Knowledge and Intellectual Abilities.

This has resulted in a more overt, and to a limited extent cohort-based, provision of research training programs alongside the supervisory relationship. For example, our own Art & Design PhD students are now required to successfully complete an initial Postgraduate Certificate in Research Practice over three months in the first year of their studies, comprising a formal taught element of their PhD. As Wilson and van Ruiten have noted:

> The increase in structured programs, which include substantial taught elements and measures to develop generic and transferable skills, are arguably, bringing PhDs more into line with core features of the professional doctorate. (2014, p. 43)

There are still distinctions, however. Traditionally PhD provision has focused primarily on the role of the supervisory team to strategically support academic progression and additional research skills training by researcher developers which may or may not include professional development and career management depending on the subject discipline and institutional practice. Thus cohort-based and professional development activities tend to be seen as separate from the research project, as additional and optional.

Our research into our Art & Design PhD students' career aspirations has shown that employability is not an additional consideration and that professional development should not be assumed as targeted either within or external to the academe. As Fenby-Hulse asserts, careers and professional development orientated training should not be perceived of as appendage (2014). Indeed, our research has shown that our students do not perceive that different skill sets are used within and outside the academe. This is significant and needs to be recognized in developing and communicating training provision that embeds transferrable skills within and throughout the doctoral research process that at the same time acknowledges "para-academic" career aspirations in which working inside the academe or outside of it in industry and practice is not presented in binary terms.

As our research into our Art & Design PhD students' aspirations has demonstrated, they do not see the two arenas of professional creative practice and academia in such oppositional terms, aspiring instead to engage and contribute to both as "para-academics." Unfortunately in relation to the PhD, binaries and hierarchies still persist in traditional conceptions of career development and aspirations. "Alternative" careers located outside the academe are often seen as a consolation, or failure. Admittedly in the slightly different context of history doctorates in the United States, Grafton and Grossman (2011) very vividly describe the embedded hierarchies involved:

> We tell students that there are "alternatives" to academic careers. We warn them to develop a "plan B" in case they do not find a teaching post. And the very words in which we couch this useful advice makes clear how much we hope they will not have to follow it—and suggest, to many of them, that if they do have to settle for employment outside the academy, they should crawl off home and gnaw their arms off.

Arguably, both the traditional PhD and the Professional Doctorate perpetuate this distinction. In its explicit framing as informing and enhancing students' professional practice and not academic employment, the Professional Doctorate positions alternatives to academic employment firmly and avoids confronting either the implied hierarchy or the possibility for more fluid professional roles. The emergence of the Art & Design PhD has forced, at least within the disciplines of Art & Design, the "recognition of a more complicated world of multiple and co-existing professional identities and contexts" (Wilson & van Ruiten, 2014, p. 20). Although this is something that still needs to be addressed more coherently in pedagogical terms, at least in our own institution.

Conclusions

We hope that an insight into the Art & Design PhD is beneficial to those designing and running Professional Doctorates in Education. The Art & Design PhD is a different practice in which the complexities of multiple identities and the relationships between the academic, professional and practice are being actively considered, challenged and repositioned. Through our research project, our students have revealed aspirations and motivations in which academic, practitioner, industry and other creative roles are complexly entwined, blurring the traditional binary of academic and nonacademic professional roles both inside and outside the academe, nuanced aspirations which we locate as "para-academic." This has prompted a wider consideration of doctoral pedagogies in Art & Design as well as the vocabularies used, institutional (and personal) attitudes, and value systems.

We do not wish to present the Art & Design PhD here uncritically as a model for redesigning Professional Doctorates. Indeed, in conceptual, policy, and pedagogic frameworks, there are clear distinctions between the two (McCay, 2010). However, as critical friends, the Art & Design PhD and Professional Doctorate can be advocates for one another's success and stimulate reflections of the self within the other in relation to concepts of professionalism, practice, identity, and cohorts. This has the potential to enable a dynamic and positive relation between the two that avoids resistances, hierarchies, and dualisms and opens up new perspectives that critically inform holistic doctoral provision. We would argue that this is a necessity given the expansion of doctoral provision, and the changing landscapes of tertiary education.

References

Arts and Humanities Research Council. (2011). *Research training framework*. Retrieved from: http://www.ahrc.ac.uk

Ball, L., Pollard, E., & Stanley, N. (2010). *Creative graduates creative futures*. London, UK: The Creative Graduates Creative Futures Higher Education Partnership and the Institute for Employment Studies.

Blaj-Ward, L. (2011). Skills versus pedagogy? Doctoral research training in the UK arts and humanities. *Higher Education Research & Development, 30*(6), 697–708.

Boyce-Tillman, J., Bonenfant, Y., Bryden, I., Taiwo, O., de Faria, T., & Brown, R. (2012). *PaR of the course: Issues involved in the development of practice-based doctorates in the performing arts*. Higher Education Academy Development Report. Retrieved from http://www.heacademy.ac.uk

Brown, K., & Cooke, C. (2010). *Professional doctorate awards in the UK*. Lichfield: UKCGE.

Candy, L. (2007). *Practice-based research: Aguide*. Sydney: The University of Technology.

Costa, A., & Kallick, B. (1993). Through the lens of a critical friend. *Educational Leadership, 51*(2), 49–51.

Crossouard, B. (2013). Conceptualising doctoral researcher training through Bernstein's theoretical frameworks. *International Journal for Researcher Development, 4*(2), 72–85.

Davey, N. (2006). Art and theoria. In Holdridge, L., and Macleod, K. (Eds.), *Thinking through art: Reflections on art as research* (pp.20–39). Oxon: Routledge.

Economic & Social Research Council. (2005). Recognition of professional doctorates. In ESRC. *Postgraduate training guidelines*, Appendix 2. Retrieved from: http://www.esrc.ac.uk

Fenby-Hulse, K. (2014). Is an arts-based PhD a professional qualification? [blog post]. Retrieved from: http://thecreativeresearcher.wordpress.com/2014/07/30/is-an-arts-based-phd-a-professional-qualification/

Frayling, C. (1993). Research in art & design. *Royal College of Art research papers, 1*(1), 1–5.

Grafton, A. T., & Grossman, J. (2011). No more Plan B: A very modest proposal for graduate programs in history. *Perspectives on History.* Retrieved from: http://www.historians.org/publications-and-directories/perspectives-on-history

Gray, C., & Malins, J. (2004). *Visualising research: A guide to the research process in art & design.* Aldershot: Ashgate Publishing Ltd.

Hockey, J. (2008). Practice based research degree students in Art & Design: Identity and adaption. In Hickman, R. (Ed.), *Research in Art and Design Education: Issues and exemplars,* (pp. 109–120). Bristol: Intellect.

Knowles, M. S. (1984). *Andragogy in action.* San Francisco, CA: Jossey-Bass.

Lei, S., Gorelick, D., Short, K., Smallwood, L., & Wright-Porter, K. (2011). Academic cohorts: Benefits and drawbacks of being a member of a community of learners. *Education, 131*(3), 497–504.

MacFarlane, B. (2011). The morphing of academic practice: Unbundling and the rise of the para-academic. *Higher Education Quarterly, 65*(1), 59–73.

McAlpine, L., Jazvac-Martek, M., & Hopwood, N. (2009). Doctoral student experience in education: Activities and difficulties influencing identity development. *International Journal for Researcher Development, 1*(1), 97–109.

McCay, G. (2010). *Taught professional doctorates: An overview of structure, content and their role within the professional community.* Edinburgh: University of Edinburgh.

Metcalfe, F. (2006). *The changing nature of doctoral programs.* Cambridge: Portland Press.

Mortiboys, A. (2005). *Teaching with emotional intelligence.* London: Routledge.

Mottram, J., Rust, C., & Till, J. (2007). *AHRC Research review: Practice-led research in art, design and architecture.* London: AHRC.

Nowviskie, B. (Ed.), (2011). *Alternative academic careers for humanities scholars.* MediaCommons, Retrieved from: http://mediacommons.futureofthebook.org/alt-ac/e-book

Oxford Dictionary. (2014). Online edition, Oxford University Press. Retrieved from: http://www.oxforddictionaries.com/definition/english/para

Quality Assurance Agency for Higher Education (QAA). (2012). Research degrees. In: *QAA code for higher education.* Gloucester: The quality assurance agency for higher education. Retrieved from: http//www.qaa.ac.uk

Research Councils UK. (2011). *The concordat to support the career development of researchers.* Retrieved from: https://www.vitae.ac.uk/policy/vitae-concordat-vitae-2011.pdf

Roberts, G. (2002). *SET for success: The report of Sir Gareth Roberts' review.* London: HMSO.

UK Council for Graduate Education. (1997). *Practice-based doctorates in the creative and performing arts and design.* Lichfield: UKCGE.

UK Council for Graduate Education. (2011). *Professional doctorates in the UK.* Lichfield: UKCGE.

Vitae. (2010). *Researcher development framework.* Retrieved from: https://www.vitae.ac.uk

Vitae. (2012). *Researcher development framework: Employability lens.* Retrieved from: https://www.vitae.ac.uk/images/news/employerslens_image_web.jpg/view

Whitchurch, C. (2008). Shifting identities and blurring boundaries: The emergence of Third Space professionals in UK Higher Education. *Higher Education Quarterly, 62*(4), 377–396.

Wilson, M. (2014). Discipline problems and the ethos of research. In Wilson, M. and van Ruiten, S. (Eds.), *Handbook for artistic research education* (pp. 203–17). Amsterdam: ELIA.

Wilson, M., & van Ruiten, S. (Eds.). (2014). *Handbook for artistic research education.* Amsterdam: ELIA.

8

Pedagogical Strategy, Design Strategy, and Positioning of Practitioner Doctorate: Grounding Business Practice in Subjectivism and First-Person Research in an Irish Institution

Eleanor Doyle[1]

Introduction

For the practitioner doctorate program offered at the School of Economics, University College Cork, Ireland, the focus is on enhancing effectiveness of participants' professional and organizational practice. For this to happen consideration of "personal elements of knowledge" (Polanyi, 1966, p. 11) is required, that is, knowledge as experienced, accumulated, and transformed in both practice and in reflection on practice. Such knowledge is based on "tacit thought . . . an indispensable part of all knowledge" (Polanyi, 1966, p. 11). While economics as a discipline has over recent decades displayed increasing formalization and mathematization, alternative lines of thought outlined here provide foundations for our program within business economics and business.

One such theme is "subjectivism" which facilitates expression of practitioners' meanings as these are what govern practice (Boulding, 1956). Penrose (1959) offers conceptual depth for practitioners, both in new business practice and in reflecting on practice, from the underpinnings of growing firms she identified, which relate to the meaning-making capabilities of managers. More recent research into economics-related first-person research (Arnsperger, 2010) identifies both contexts and methods appropriate for self-reflection and new practice generation. Thus the three areas of subjectivism, foundations of business growth, and first-person research are identified as essential elements in our program pedagogy.

Complementing these themes, and fundamental to their unfolding in our cohort-based program, is the approach of Critical Friend Groups (CFGs). Although unaware of the approach when the program was launched in 2008, CFG offers a comprehensive scaffolding of the process through which engagement and transformation with the program members and the program teaching team unfolds. In terms of each of the above themes, connection to CFG and its centrality for the enactment or execution of the pedagogy of the program are presented in the sections that follow.

Subjectivism or an economics of meaning is explored to consider the role of meaning-making in business decisions and action, where the subjective perspective of the individual is central. Penrose's (1959) theoretical work has (belatedly) been read from a subjectivist perspective and offers a means of bridging the gap to empirical investigation. Her concept of "subjective productive opportunity" provides coherence across several strands of her theory, which pertains to the growth of the firm as well as points to questions and issues worthy of exploration thereby bridging business practice with what is going on in the minds of practitioners, suggesting routes to transformation of business practice.

Approaches are then outlined for conducting empirical research grounded in the meaningful experience of the individual under the term "first-person research." This requires substantial reframing of the goal, purpose, and outcomes of research relative to prevailing methods in economics. Reflexivity becomes a central feature since the researcher is explicitly under the spotlight of the research.

The discussion and conclusions are presented in the final section and point to the novel orientation of the program and its outputs and outcomes for participants, and the CFG pedagogy.

Subjectivism as a Conceptual Bridge to Practice

Hayek (1942, p. 283) explained that subjectivism in social science starts from "what men think and mean to do." Subjectivism denotes a specific approach to social theory and is not limited to particular technical problems within economics (Mises, 1957). The subjectivist interest in economics focuses on purposes, intentions, and the meanings people make (Kirzner, 1992, 2000; Lachmann, 1971; Lavoie, 1991a; Weber, 1922). Subjectivism has been referred to as an "economics of meaning" where subjective perspectives of individuals studied has been identified as central for understanding how the economy works (Boettke, Lavoie, & Storr, 2001). As Knight (1956, p. 177) indicated, economics requires "interpretive study *(verstehende Wissenschaft)*" and so subjectivism is identified with a nonpositivist orientation.

As with its accounts in other fields, for example, psychology, subjectivism has been accused of attempting to access the inaccessible—the contents of individual human minds. Hayek (1945) recommends we interpret the actions of others on an analogy of our own mind, that is, that we group their actions, and the objects of their actions, into classes or categories which we know solely from the knowledge of our own mind (Hayek, 1945, p. 63).

Echoing the point Lavoie (1991, p. 482) explains that "meaning" is not in anyone's head but in the world:

> [I]t is not [to be found in] an isolated, individual mind, but [in] a communicative process, a discourse.

Boettke et al. (2001) explain that one means of conducting meaningful research from the subjectivist perspective is by focusing on meaningful human experience, prompted by John Dewey's view that inquiry must begin and end in meaningful human experience and action. Such inquiry into the meanings made by individuals is clearly accessible once communicated with others.

In circumstances where CFGs provide structure and scope to support articulation of meanings, they operate within the subjectivist realm and can generate reflections which, once shared, can allow for collaboration in surfacing and exploring assumptions around practice. As outlined by Breidenstein, Fahey, Glickman, and Hensley (2012) structured conversations or protocols are useful to support such conversations, which are generally novel in educational environments; yet, for purposes of adult development, they are not only appropriate but necessary so that practitioners are required to slow down, share practice, and address the standard discomforts that emerge when subjective meanings are the center of attention.

Hence, analysis or exploration based on such inquiries grounded in meaningful human experience *can* be conducted in a scholarly fashion following accepted methods in social science research. In a cohort-based program with a broad spectrum of content interests across diverse business backgrounds there are generative rather than practice-specific similarities across participants. This implies some limited relevance for "communities of practice" (Mindich & Liebermann, 2012) approaches. A CFG that both shares and applies the commonality of subjectivism takes an important initial step in the understanding of practitioners interested in developing their practice.

Linking Business Growth and Meaning-Making

Penrose (1959) examined firm growth in her approach. Although it was conceptual, it was also based on extensive hands-on business analysis. Her theory focuses on the conditions conducive to growth, and she is identified as a foundational researcher in the field of the Resource-Based-View of the firm. Her work has also, more recently, been associated with subjectivism (e.g., Chen, Doyle, & Fanning, 2012; Foss, Klein, Kor, & Mahoney, 2008). Penrose makes a fundamental assumption that "subjective productive opportunity" (Penrose, 1995, p. 41) lays the foundation for the growth of the firm. Subjective productive opportunity relates to what a firm considers it can accomplish, what it intends to accomplish, or what it sees as its purpose. While productive opportunities are identified in the context of a firm's environment, the environment is considered in a subjectivist sense as an "image" (Penrose, 1995, p. 5) in the *mind* of its managers.

As a required reading for all program participants, Penrose's work points to the capacities of managers as central for identifying and selecting resources to be used. The culmination of this dynamic is observed in the activities of the business practitioner. This dynamic fit between resources, services, and productive opportunity is inherently subjective and involves ideas generated in the minds of managers, as well as the ideas communicated and discussed between them. Such an opportunity "will be restricted to the extent to which a firm does not see opportunities for expansion, is unwilling to act upon them, or is unable to respond to them" (Penrose, 1995, p. 32).

Penrose's distinction between resources and services indicates how the process through which managers make meaning of external opportunity in the context of available resources and the services they can generate is the essence of knowledge generation in business, grounded in the thinking processes of managers. The distinction indicates that the source of heterogeneity across firms that may have access to the same resources is in terms of what they *mean* to those who imagine appropriate uses for them. This knowledge-generation process governs the functions or services that can be released from resources in organizations. Through the distinction the

CFG is prompted by processes of facilitation and coaching. An example would be the extent to which CFG members' own practice has tended to focus on the resources element of the business, rather than on the services generated from resources. Such conversations invariably provide linkages to broader business literatures discussing topics, such as the relative strengths of strategy versus execution and planning versus emergent strategy (encompassing comparisons of Porter, 1985 and Mintzberg & Waters, 1985). Reflective discourse underpinning CFG, structured and provoked by Penrose's ideas, facilitates identification of change agendas around business practice. These agendas are a required output and outcome of the first year of the program—and so demand of participants "publicly" shared developmental goals.

All participants and the facilitators are challenged by the CFG approach to generate thorough descriptions and engage in thoughtful listening and provide detailed feedback (National School Reform Faculty, 2012) requiring a nontraditional teaching experience where knowledge and expertise are not presumed to lie in the hands of the facilitators (usually two or three in each session), but are generated by the interactions of CFG members.

Knowledge from Experience

In Penrose's theory two types of knowledge are identified as analytically separate, namely, objective knowledge and experience, where experience stands for subjective knowledge (1995, p. 53). While objective knowledge is independent of any particular individual or group of individuals, can be accessed from outside of the firm, and is potentially transmissible to anyone on equal terms, experience is possessed by individuals and is impossible to transmit. The relation between experience and productive services released from the firm's resources was explained by Penrose:

> [E]xperience . . . produces a change—frequently a subtle change—in individuals and cannot be separated from them . . . increasing experience shows itself in two ways—change in knowledge acquired and changes in the ability to use knowledge . . . with experience a man may gain in wisdom, in sureness of movement, in confidence—all of these become part of his very nature, and they are all qualities that are relevant to the kind and amount of services he can give his firm. (1995, p. 53)

A number of points in terms of education arise, particularly when working with practitioners. Educational programs have a tendency to shy away from accessing, exploiting, or developing subjective knowledge, which

Penrose argues governs the very identification of productive services. In the context of the developmental orientation of our doctorate, changes in participants' *subjective* knowledge are an explicit goal. And as Swaffield (2003, p. 1) contends, CFGs are appropriately applied in such a process as "critical friends . . . work with people who are open to fundamental change rather than simply seeking the solution to a specific problem." The doctoral program itself, therefore, is a process supporting transformation where both knowledge acquisition and the separate transformed capacity to apply that knowledge are worthwhile goals and imply that new constructions and understandings based on viewing experience through new lenses is one valid output of the program for practitioners.

On a broader level, the role of subjective knowledge in the knowledge-generation process of businesses indicates that to support growth requires neither "objective" information nor specific management techniques or skills, but refers to the manner in which meaning is constructed in people's minds. So as long as the image updating process continues, the evolutionary growth of a business can proceed along with its changing productive opportunity.

> A theory of the growth of firms is essentially an examination of *changing productive opportunity* of firms. (Penrose, 1995, p. 31, emphasis added)

Firm growth consequently depends on a *transformational* knowledge-generation process in the firm, which is predicated on transformations of the subjective knowledge of its members.

Research by Kegan (1994) and Kegan and Lahey (2009) coupled with Penrosean theory supports explorations by program participants designed to challenge and develop their meaning-making complexity (i.e., transformations of their understandings and subjective knowledge). The means through which it is supported are through CFG challenges and supports to expanding participants' portfolio of business theories and their reports on using these in new practice.

First-Person Research

Reports of lived experience are the focus of first-person research and can be linked to the generation of outputs supported by the CFG process (i.e., developmental agendas and the experience of their execution). In social science first-person research offers one research avenue to generate empirical data in circumstances where lived experience, meaning-making, and inferences based on interpretation or perception are of interest.

First-person research questions are oriented to the sense being made of a situation by an individual, as they live it, articulate and communicate it, and as it may develop over time or through reflection. Such sense is not fixed but can be represented contingently and the object of first-person research is shedding light on such contingent representations, and their transformation over time. To some extent this can be captured by recordings of the CFG-structured sessions, shared among the participants after the sessions, to facilitate participants' tracking of changes in their own views, their reflections on experience, and their perceptions of changes in others.

Varela and Shear (1999) outline how "subjective" has a different connotation to "private" and subjective accounts of experience can be open to intersubjective validation and scrutiny. The role of the first-person and its research questions are qualitatively different and often unrelated (but not necessarily so) to those of third-person research where individual experience or meanings made lie outside the (direct) field of inquiry. Cognitive science, for example, where the focus of investigation directly implies and implicates the social agents is one field where first-person research can be appropriate, depending on the issue.

Since lived experience is at the heart of first-person research the concept of reflexivity is central as the researcher's own actions and decisions impact on the meaning and context of the experience being investigated. Inquiry by a researcher into their action and its basis in terms of theory, assumptions, and beliefs can support developmental adaptation if researchers so wish *and* if they can engage in appropriate activities. The search for greater effectiveness in practice by a student of the program requires such ongoing reflexivity and would be evident in a change in the researcher's relationship to others—including clients, organizations, and colleagues, as well as their own assumptions, prior knowledge, and actions. Fook (2002, p. 43) considers reflexivity as "potentially more complex than being reflective, in that the potential for understanding the myriad ways in which one's own presence and perspective influence the knowledge and actions which are created is potentially more problematic than the simple searching for implicit theory."

Guba and Lincoln (1994) indicated that findings from qualitative research are not facts per se but are generated through the actions and interactions of research participants, the data, the researcher, and the evaluators of the research. The value systems of each member of the interactive group and their contexts thus also feed into research findings. As outlined by Fahey and Ippolito (2014) it is when doctoral participants surface, question, and challenge assumptions that are often taken for granted that their learning experience targets what is going on behind their practice—providing an opportunity for transformational learning. Mezirow (2000, p. 11) links transformational learning to reflective discourse and points to their connections with "collective experience." Through CFGs challenges to experimenting with new practices can be articulated and addressed collectively, maintaining focus on how difficult it is to make fundamental changes requiring old assumptions to be dropped and new ones to take their place.

Accessing Reliable First-Person Data

The extent to which the practitioner-researcher is transparent about the processes by which data on lived experience has been identified, collected, and analyzed and findings presented allows for readers of the research to consider the researcher's interpretations. Further, the plausibility of the research, the basis for confidence in the research, and the validity of findings can then be evaluated by the reader.

Piccinini (2009, p. 1) writes specifically on "the scientific use of first-person data," which he explains are usually (but not exclusively) generated from verbal reports relating to how issues of interest are perceived by an individual, or individuals, or what they mean. Both concurrent and retrospective accounts, or verbalizations, count as first-person data (Newell & Simon, 1972). Other types of first-person data are generated through selection of options such as subjects' levels of happiness and/or pain indicated by selection of various images or other indictors of perception. Piccinini (2009) explains why such data are scientifically legitimate by fulfilling the "epistemic role of (self-) measuring instruments" (p. 2) and that the degree of reliability of first-person data generated by perception can be established by public methods—for example, "correlating the reports of perceivers with the objects and events they perceive" (p. 7). He explains that, like all instruments, they are "limited in what they can measure. Like every measurement apparatus, the processes responsible for producing first-person behaviours can measure only some variables and not others. Of those they can measure, they may measure some better than others. And they measure what they measure only to some degree of approximation" (p. 12). Piccinini (2011) explains that making methods public requires searching for and minimizing risks of confounding factors, making assumptions explicit, and outlining procedures for encoding data. While this requires the "sharing" of information in terms of research methods, for example, the identification and sharing of assumptions is substantially dependent on relationships of trust between the cohort on the program and the program facilitators—and trust both in cohort members and the CFG process are requirements for successful CFGs.

First-Person Inquiry

Moustakas (1990, p. 9) outlines heuristic inquiry as one method appropriate to "exploration and interpretation of experience, which uses the self of the researcher," an approach similar to Heron's (1998) lived inquiry. Not only does it focus as a method on first-person data but it is the lived experience of the researcher that is at the heart of the research. It is a version of phenomenological inquiry and the essence of the approach entails the transformative impact of the inquiry on the researcher's experience.

Hiles (2001, p. 2) contends that heuristic inquiry is a demanding process requiring "self-commitment, rigorous self-searching and self-reflection" and should not be undertaken lightly. The core processes and phases of the method have been summarized by Hiles (2001), based on Moustakas (1990), as illustrated in Table 8.1. Arnsperger (2010, p. 8) identifies a "brand of economics which is inherently plural in its methodologies" summarizing his book *Full-Spectrum Economics* (2010a). He argues that in addition to the standard questions and methods used in economics, more focus should be placed on changing economists' assumptions about members of the economy as

> mostly unaware, unrealized humans who have no idea of how much of their internal capacities for knowledge they are leaving unutilized—it is an economy made up of . . . economists who believe their mission in life is to do narrow, positivistic . . . "science" and economic agents who function as unreflective, adaptive automata. (Arnsperger, 2010, p. 8)

Arnsperger (2010, p. 13) generates a matrix (2 × 2) of individual and collective perspectives against interior and exterior perspectives for which a range of research methods are appropriate—depending on the question or issue to be explored. By implication, where methods are not part of *economists'* toolbox, then some aspects of knowledge production are excluded from analysis. The result is a range of questions and issues requiring analysis of *economists' lived experience* and that of the economic agents they study. Such broadened consideration of questions based on a range of methods gives rise to "integral economists" engaging in "integral economics."

Integral economists may be directly engaged in two types of analysis—introspective where their subjective views are the focus of their research and extrospective when similar questions are posed to focus on economic agents' subjective views. First-person data is generated for both cases albeit from differing perspectives.

The novel, and challenging, context posed by the foregoing is in terms of bridging the subjectivism and practice of first-person themes more

Table 8.1 Core Processes and Phases in Heuristic Inquiry

CORE PROCESSES

Identify with the focus of the inquiry
Getting inside the research question, becoming one with it, living it.

Self-dialog
Self-dialog is the critical beginning, allowing the phenomenon to speak directly to one's own experience. Knowledge grows out of direct human experience and discovery involves self-inquiry, thus openness to one's own experience.

Tacit knowing
In addition, there is knowledge that is implicit to our actions and experiences. This tacit dimension is ineffable and unspecifiable, it underlies and precedes intuition, and can guide the researcher into untapped directions and sources of meaning.

Intuition
Intuition provides the bridge between explicit and tacit knowledge. Intuition makes possible the seeing of things as wholes. Every act of achieving integration, unity, or wholeness requires intuition.

Indwelling
Conscious and deliberate turning inward to seek a deeper, more extended comprehension of a quality or theme of human experience. It involves a willingness to gaze with unwavering attention and concentration into some aspect of human experience.

Internal frame of reference
Outcome must be placed in the context of the experiencer's own internal frame of reference.

PHASES

Initial engagement
Task—to discover an intense interest, a passionate concern that calls out to the researcher, one that holds important social meanings and personal, compelling implications. The research question emerges.

Immersion
The research question is lived in waking, sleeping, and even dream states. This requires alertness, concentration, and self-searching.

Incubation
Retreat from the intense, concentrated focus, allowing the expansion of knowledge to take place at a more subtle level, enabling the inner tacit dimension and intuition to clarify and extend understanding.

Illumination
This involves a breakthrough, a process of awakening that occurs naturally when the researcher is open and receptive to tacit knowledge and intuition. It involves opening a door to new awareness, a modification of an old understanding, a synthesis of fragmented knowledge, or new discovery.

(continued)

Table 8.1   (Continued)

Explication

Involves full examination of what has been awakened in consciousness, requiring organization and a comprehensive depiction of the core themes.

Creative synthesis

Thoroughly familiar with the data, the researcher puts the components and core themes in the form of creative synthesis—a narrative account, a report, a thesis, a poem, story, drawing, painting, etc.

Validation of the heuristic inquiry

The question of validity is one of meaning. Does the synthesis present comprehensively, vividly, and accurately the meanings and essences of the experience? Returning again and again to the data to check whether they embrace the necessary and sufficient meanings. Finally, feedback is obtained through participant validation, and receiving responses from others.

Source: Hiles (2001) based on Moustakas (1990).

explicitly. This is the requirement for a practitioner doctoral program aimed at supporting development of greater effectiveness of practitioners in delivering on their functions and their professional development over the course of a three-year program—while also in full-time employment. Working out the pathways through which effectiveness can be delivered and explored is the general orientation of the program that is mapped to meet the specific individual needs of each participant.

Conclusions

For the practitioner doctorate program (DBA Business Economics) the themes above point the way to a differentiated positioning where subjective lived experience in the professional and organizational contexts can be used to generate meaningful "data" for analysis. A genuine engagement is required to surface such experience and this represents a significant challenge for researchers, both student and supervisory, and demands appropriate support to guide the manner of accessing and reporting on such data.

It is possible to see how, for example, a subjectivist perspective on Penrose's theory of firm growth may be operationalized in the context of practitioners' experiences and their reflection on both their experience and the prompts generated by a Penrosean view of the firm. Since Penrose's "subjective productive opportunity" may be developed to the extent to which a firm sees opportunities for expansion, is willing to act upon them, and is able to respond to them, the translation of this process allows for consideration and analysis of the individual's role and potential role in qualitative growth of the firm. It also points to the role of team performance and its relation to team meaning-making capabilities and its consequence for the information processing capability of the firm—as a focal point for the growth process of organizations. Therefore, channels for accessing and working with the data are to be found also in the context of appropriate theory, which as in the case of Penrose may have been incompletely or partially used in terms of the implications of the concepts or for generating hypotheses of relevance in the context of lived practice and experience.

Paganelli (2010) pointed out, referring to the work of Adam Smith (1759), that commerce enlarges an individual's opportunities to interact with strangers and thereby introduces distance into interpersonal relationships. Greater interaction with strangers supports the development of self-command or autonomy, which balances self-interest (Smith, 1776). When reading Adam Smith's works the clear message is that far from eroding values and ethics, the processes required for commerce *demand* social cooperation and moral development can result in transformational development. Essentially, commerce emerges in an evolutionary process rather than through the design of any individual, group, or government. Similarly, personal and moral evolution is another unintentional outcome.

From consideration of the pedagogical positioning outlined here, an alternative perspective to Paganelli's (2010) also emerges. This view is that first-person perspectives focus not only on a process of distancing oneself from the commercial world, but in fact of *getting closer* to an understanding of one's personal and subjective experiences and how they govern and guide business practice. These experiences and their evolutions underlie "impartiality" as meant by Adam Smith (see Raphael, 2007), which involves examining oneself in relation to others to identify moral behavior and act on it. Within the safe environment of the CFG, engaging in such reflections is grounded in both subjectivity and, at the same time, a public or social behavior. When appreciating the reflexivity of individuals (Davis, 2003) this implies that subjectivity relates to an individual's self-appraisal of themselves as "I" as well as on an "object" within its social context. This would cover one's understandings of their own evolving identifications and relationships and how these adapt through time. Such understandings, as reflected in lived experience, are both relevant to and required for personal, professional, and organizational development. The unfolding and reorganization of meaning is at the heart of lived experience, as Perry explains it: "Organisms organize . . . and what human organisms organize is meaning" (cited in Kegan, 1994, p. 29).

Note

1. The author gratefully acknowledges financial support from the Research Fund of the College of Business and Law, University College Cork, to present an earlier version of this paper at the 4th International Conference on Professional Doctorates in Cardiff, April 2014. Thanks to attendees of that conference for comments on that version and to Connell Fanning, practitioners Paddy Crowe, Iaian Daly, and Keith Deats. Thanks to Stephen Brosnan for editorial assistance.

References

Arnsperger, C. (2010). Spelling out integral economic science. *Journal of Integral Theory and Practice, 5*(3), 174–192.

Arnsperger, C. (2010a). *Full spectrum economics: Toward an inclusive and emancipatory social science.* London: Routledge.

Boettke, P. J., Lavoie, D., & Storr, V. H. (2001). The subjectivist methodology of Austrian economics and Dewey's theory of inquiry. Paper prepared for the *First Annual Symposium on the Foundation of the Behavioral Sciences,* organized by the Behavioral Research Council (a division of American Institute for Economic Research) on "John Dewey, Modernism, Postmodernism and Beyond," at Simon Rock College of Bard, Great Barrington, MA, July 20–22.

Boulding, K. E. (1956). *The image.* Ann Arbor, MI: University of Michigan Press.

Breidenstein, A., Fahey, K., Glickman, C., & Hensley, F. (2012). *Leading for powerful learning: A guide for instructional leaders.* New York, NY: Teachers College Press.

Chen, Z., Doyle, E., & Fanning, C. (2012). Penrose's "unused services": A cross-cultural perspective on growth of firms. *Journal of Knowledge Generation in China, 44*(1), 66–79.

Davis, J. B. (2003). *The theory of the individual in economics.* London: Routledge.

Fahey, K., & Ippolito, J. (2014). *Towards a general theory of critical friends groups.* School Reform Initiative. Retrieved from http://www.schoolreforminitiative.org/research/general-theory-of-critical-friends-groups/

Fook, J. (2002). *Social work: Critical theory and practice.* London: Sage.

Foss, N. J., Klein, P. G., Kor, Y. Y., & Mahoney, J. T. (2008). Entrepreneurship, subjectivism, and the resource-based view: Toward a new synthesis. *Strategic Entrepreneurship Journal, 2*(1), 73–94.

Guba, E. G., & Lincoln, Y. S. (1994). Competing paradigms in qualitative research. In N. K. Denzin & Y. S. Lincoln (Eds.), *Handbook of qualitative research* (pp. 105–117). Thousand Oaks, CA: Sage.

Hayek, F. A. (1942). Scientism and the study of society. *Economica,* New Series, *9*(35), 267–291.

Hayek, F. A. (1945). The use of knowledge in society. *American Economic Review,* *35*(4), 519–530.

Heron, J. (1998). *Sacred science: Person-centred inquiry into the spiritual and the subtle.* Ross-on-Wye: PCCS Books.

Hiles, D. (2001). Heuristic inquiry and transpersonal research. Paper presented to CCPE, London, October.

Kegan, R. (1994). *In over our heads: The mental demands of modern life.* Cambridge, MA: Harvard Business Press.

Kegan, R., & Lahey, L. L. (2009). *Immunity to change.* Boston, MA: Harvard Business Press.

Kirzner, I. (1992). *The meaning of market process.* New York, NY: Routledge.

Kirzner, I. (2000). *The driving force of the market economy.* New York, NY: Routledge.

Knight, F. H. (1940). What is truth in economics? Reprinted in F. H. Knight, *On the history and method of economics* (pp. 151–178). Chicago: University of Chicago Press, 1956.

Lachmann, L. (1971). *The legacy of Max Weber.* Berkeley, CA: The Glendessary Press.

Lavoie, D. (1991). The discovery and interpretation of profit opportunities: Culture and the Kirznerian entrepreneur. In B. Berger (Ed.), *The culture of entrepreneurship* (pp. 13–33). San Francisco, CA: Institute for Contemporary Studies.

Lavoie, D. (1991a). The progress of subjectivism. In M. Blaug & N. de Marchi (Eds.), *Appraising modern economics: Studies in the methodology of scientific research programs* (pp. 470–486). Gloucestershire, UK: Edward Elgar.

Mezirow, J. (2000). *Learning as transformation: Critical perspectives on a theory in progress.* San Franciso, CA: The Jossey-Bass Higher and Adult Education Series.

Mindich, D., & Liebermann, A. (2012). *Building a learning community: A tale of two schools.* Stanford, CA: Stanford Center for Opportunity Policy in Education.

Mintzberg, H., & Waters, J. A. (1985). Of strategies, deliberate and emergent. *Strategic Management Journal, 69*(3), 257–272.

Mises, L. (2005). *An interpretation of social and economic evolution.* Ludwig von Mises Institute. Original publication 1957. Retrieved from https://www.mises.org/library/theory-and-history-interpretation-social-and-economic-evolution on February 3, 2015.

Moustakas, C. (1990). *Heuristic research: Design, methodology and applications.* London: Sage.

National School Reform Faculty. (2012). Self-guided tour to NSRF critical friends groups. Retrieved from http://www.nsrfharmony.org/ on January 22, 2015.

Newell, A., & Simon, H. A. (1972). *Human problem solving.* Englewood Cliffs, NJ: Prentice-Hall.

Paganelli, M. P. (2010). The moralizing role of distance in Adam Smith: The theory of moral sentiments as possible praise of commerce. *History of Political Economy, 42*(3), 425–441.

Penrose, E. (1995). *The theory of the growth of the firm* (3rd ed.). New York, NY: Oxford University Press. Original publication 1959.

Piccinini, G. (2009). First-person data, publicity and self-measurement. *Philosophers' Imprint, 9*(9), 1–16.

Piccinini, G. (2011). Scientific methods must be public, and descriptive experience sampling qualifies. *Journal of Consciousness Studies, 18*(1), 102–117.

Polanyi, M. (1966). *The tacit dimension.* Chicago, IL: University of Chicago Press.

Porter, M. E. (1985). *Competitive advantage.* New York, NY: Free Press.

Raphael, D. D. (2007). *The impartial spectator: Adam Smith's moral philosophy.* New York, NY: Oxford University Press.

Smith, A. (1759) [1982]. *The theory of moral sentiments* (Edited by D. D. Raphael & A. L. Macfie). Indianapolis, IN: Liberty Fund.

Smith, A. (1776) [1982]. *An inquiry into the nature and causes of the wealth of nations, Volumes I and II* (Edited by R. H. Campbell & A. S. Skinner). Indianapolis, IN: Liberty Fund.

Swaffield, S. (2003, October). *Critical friendship. [Inform No. 3.] Leadership for learning.* Cambridge: University of Cambridge Faculty of Education. Retrieved from http://www.educ.cam.ac.uk/centres/lfl/current/inform/InForm_3_Critical_Friendship.pdf on January 15, 2015.

Varela, F. J., & Shear, J. (1999). First-person methodologies: What, why, how? *Journal of Consciousness Studies, 6*(2), 1–14.

Weber, M. (1978) [1922]. *Economy and society: An outline of interpretive sociology* (Two volumes) (Edited by G. Roth & C. Wittich). Berkeley, CA: University of California Press.

9

Postgraduate Work-Based Learning for Nontraditional Learners: Focused across All Four UK Regions

Elda Nikolou-Walker

This chapter addresses the case of postgraduate university work-based learning (WBL) for nontraditional adult learners by considering the following: What does postgraduate university WBL mean? How has nontraditional WBL developed within the UK context? What does the term nontraditional adult learner mean? What conceptual or theoretical lenses should be adopted in order to make sense of the whole field?

Centuries of research regarding education have provided some experience on how to navigate through the field, according to the unique demands that each participant presents. WBL indicates that this uniqueness determines to a great extent the degree to which an individual will be inclined to engage with educational matters (or not), as an adult.

A productive approach in relation to postgraduate WBL has been the critical friends augmenting the positive aspects of the workplace as well as advocating critical reflective practice. Indeed, the methodology of the CFs can assist a usually established "top-down" approach within the business structure. Often, the latter does not help the creation of partnerships and the sharing of inevitably implicit and/or explicit knowledge that an adult individual would possess (without necessarily being in a leadership position), in order to transfer on a collegial level to others within the same workspace.

Research suggests that the critical friends model may be a very useful practice within postgraduate WBL. It also highlights the challenge that a lot of traditional leaders find themselves facing when examining their role in the workplace. It is not rare for leaders to realize that their knowledge stops within the absolute necessary in order to merely do the job. Hence, the delivery to others in a company is constrained by rather technical aspects without an emphasis on the human side of each distinctive individual and their capacity to engage in preferred learning style(s) at work.

In the current context, it is also important to highlight that the word "critical" is used not to replace but instead to complement a vital, reflective, and indispensable process regarding an individual's belonging in the workplace. A standard complaint among employees regarding the workplace, in general, has been the apparent resistance and unwillingness of the various bosses to tackle challenging issues within a business context. This might be due to lack of training that postgraduate WBL can possibly bridge.

What is University WBL: An Elastic Concept?

Nixon (2008) commented on the diversity of interpretations of the WBL concept and suggested that it was critically important to establish a shared understanding of it. The frequency with which the term is now being applied has tended to make WBL an elastic concept, and since it is being invoked as much in relation to further education as it is to higher education, its meaning within a university context needs to be clarified. Levy (1989, cited in Brennan & Little, 1996) defined three interrelated components. He reckoned that WBL was structuring learning in the workplace, providing appropriate *on-job* training and learning opportunities, and identifying and providing *relevant off-job* learning opportunities. More recently, Connor (2005) has defined WBL as the gaining of both knowledge and skills (in this case, competencies) sourced from the workplace.

Despite the fact that WBL has been defined in several different ways by numerous commentators and authors, generally speaking it is still viewed as a worthwhile attempt at combining the workplace's knowledge with the knowledge gained while in higher education. The objective of the exercise is consistent with the range in which students develop higher-level skills.

The old model of learning was one whereby the individual learnt all the theories in university and, hopefully, subsequently applied these to the workplace setting (*The Guardian*, April 8, 2014). On the other hand, WBL recognizes new forms of learning taking place outside of university disciplines and in new professions. The university then finds ways to recognize and to validate these forms of learning. An example of such a credential could be an individual piece of writing, or a dissertation in one's own preferred field that is driven by academic theory. This venue allowed WBL the flexibility to deal with a diverse group of people, including those who have not gone through the formal routes of education. Instead, university experts help individuals (or groups of individuals and companies) to convert work-based and experiential learning into academic credentials, such as an undergraduate and/or a postgraduate degree.

Some scholars have claimed that the problem with the WBL concept derives from the fact that people view it as a subject for study, although it is more appropriate to classify WBL as a mechanism for learning (see, e.g., Gray, 2001). Other scholars, though, view the combination of these two elements as a subject alone, as well as a means for studying *any* subject—as linking learning to the work role successfully.

Of the many definitions of WBL that have been developed, one which seems to be largely popular with universities is also the one shared by me (see Nikolou-Walker, 2009). This definition sees WBL not just as a mode of learning within a range of disciplines but also as an area of study in its own right. That is to say, WBL is centered on learning about learning; it is an educational program that equips students to develop a critical awareness of their own learning processes so that tacit knowledge gained in the workplace can be articulated in academic formats, and thus accredited within other programs.

The Development of UK WBL

The development of WBL in the United Kingdom can be traced back to two major educational innovations. The first, and most widespread, was the introduction of the Accreditation of Prior Experiential Learning (APEL or APL), a process by which experiential learning was given recognition and academic value. Experiential learning encompasses knowledge, skills, and behaviors acquired in a planned or unplanned way through life, especially work. In the 1980s, APEL in the United Kingdom was highlighted as an admission tool for higher education programs by demonstrating competency, against National Occupational Standards for the award of a National Vocational Qualification (NVQ).

In the higher education sector, the use of APEL developed from the pioneering work of the Learning from Experience Trust (e.g., Evans, 2004), and in 1986, earned the academic credit for mature entry provided by the

Council for National Academic Awards (CNNA, the academic awarding body for the polytechnics).

The CNNA stance was crucial as it legitimized APEL in higher education. The development drew heavily from the work of Council for Adult and Experiential Learning (CAEL) in the United States. APEL was driven by the perceived need to extend access to higher education to mature students at a time when it was feared that demographic trends would severely restrict the pool of 18-year-olds seeking entry to higher education. Thus, the initial primary purpose of APEL was to increase the supply of students to higher education.

The spread of APEL was facilitated in the early 1990s by the favorable policy and funding context needed to promote a dramatic expansion of higher education numbers. APEL was influential in highlighting the significance of flexible, credit-based program structures in order to meet the needs of an expansionist higher education agenda.

The second major educational innovation was the Education Development Projects funded by the UK Employment Department and focusing on higher education. Most of the first round of funded Projects, in the early 1990s, concentrated upon student placement. However, a distinctive approach was taken by the Middlesex University Project (London), which centered upon the identification and accreditation of the "curriculum in the workplace" (Naish, 1995).

Research since the early 1990s has indeed explored the option of WBL making a rich contribution to university education through meaningful development of employer and/or higher education partnerships. Garnett (2007) clearly discussed the plethora of benefits, which the intellectual capital of an organization might gain, if its employees engaged in experiences that explored both their professional and educational contribution in the workplace.

Who is the Nontraditional Adult Learner?

Considerable debate has taken place, both in academic and/or professional circles, in an attempt to define exactly "who" the nontraditional student is? For the purposes of this research (and in order to avoid possible confusion), a nontraditional student is here defined as a student who is 25 years of age and older and who returns to education primarily for work-based improvement of prospects through professional certification, in some cases returning for lifelong learning purposes that often include paid/unpaid and/or voluntary employment. Consequently, this chapter is very much concerned with adults' perceptions with respect to the experience of Higher Education for the first time, and certainly *after* the traditional age (e.g., 18 years old).

The National Centre for Education Statistics (NCES) officially reported that, though a precise definition was still to be derived, the following characteristics were common among nontraditional students:

- They do not enter higher education after leaving school, though attends higher education (and/or any form of education) on a part-time capacity.
- They continue working full-time, while studying.
- They are considered to be financially independent, but have dependents (other than a spouse), and frequently elderly and/or sick family members.
- They are often a single parent without a primary degree, and/or in some cases without having completed high-school study.

Frequently, the terms nontraditional and lifelong learners are intermingled, although it remains to be universally established exactly when the term nontraditional student entered the education vocabulary (Ross Gordon, 2011).

Table 9.1   Sample of Research Questions, or Foreshadowed Problems, Include the Following

---

1. Does becoming a member of a postgraduate WBL program influence personal and professional identities (identity issues)?
   - If so, how?
   - How do "nontraditional" learners make sense of university WBL?
   - Does it help them achieve a better understanding of the workplace?

2. Does postgraduate WBL engage nontraditional learners (participation issues)?
   - If so, how?
   - What are the unique features of university WBL as participants view it?
   - What relationships, if any, help or hinder engagement?
   - Does the work environment help or hinder?
   - Does university WBL participation differ from participation in other areas of university study?
   - Has a common language developed? (e.g., about postgraduate WBL)
   - Which access route do nontraditional learners prefer?

Literature on the Barriers When Participating in
Postgraduate WBL

The knowledge management and intellectual capital literature suggests that, despite the importance attached to knowledge and learning, and the rise of the corporate university, the university sector is not generally seen as having a significant role beyond the provision of general management courses, for example, the MBA. In contrast, the development of WBL in the UK university sector appears to offer a focus on facilitating Mode 2 knowledge production (see Table 9.2), and the opportunity to achieve a level of customization of provision, through partnership between the university and the organization.

Postgraduate WBL appears not only to be an imperative for individuals and their employers, but also for universities, as they seek continued relevance and funding in the twenty-first century and beyond.

Managing and delivering postgraduate WBL programs attracts a lot of positive attributes. These, however, should always be contrasted with the inevitable difficulties that postgraduate WBL encompasses. For example, a fuller picture of the process involved is included in a study conducted by the Scottish Executive Central Research Unit (2002). This involved a survey of over 500 employees that investigated the extent, nature, and perceived value of WBL. Employers in the study described "losing staff time when employees participated in training" and "the cost of course fees, and the need to pay for staff cover" as perhaps the most significant barriers when considering participation in WBL (pp. 68–76). However, though consideration of time and resources were always expected to be given priority by employers, the lack of information in relation to external funding opportunities and/or general information on "up skilling," training, and educational aspects were not mentioned by employers.

Regarding employer engagement, and the "hard to reach" people in this category, a study by Brennan and Little (2006) suggested that the various

Table 9.2   Modes of Knowledge (Brennan & Little, 1996)

Mode 1 knowledge	Mode 2 knowledge
Linear, causal, cumulative, a "closed system," rooted in disciplinary authority and therefore reductionist, publicly organized, and funded	Multivariate, unsystematic; an "open system" where the users are creative users, rather than passive beneficiaries, multidisciplinary, produced in the wider social context

policy bodies should put in place strategies for employer engagement and WBL in general that looked to more innovative forms of learning.

Workplaces and educational institutions merely represent different instances of social practices, in which learning occurs through participation. Therefore to distinguish between the two in terms of formalisms of social practice (i.e.: that one is formalized and the other informal) and propose some general consequences for learning, arising from these bases is not helpful. Describing workplaces, as "informal" learning environments is negative, inaccurate and ill focused. (Billett, 2002, p. 61)

Historically, the two learning arenas (academia and workplace) have been kept separate, each one fulfilling distinct functions regarding the theory and practice and/or the application of learning. However, there also seems to be a pattern emerging where the recognition that a combination of skills of learning that would simultaneously include theory and relevant practice would be more advantageous to the participant, rather than each component of learning being separately taught. The latter view was recognized by researchers as far back as Honey (1994) and Raelin (1997).

It is generally accepted that both academia and the workplace aspire to create both sustainability and continuity in the economy. However, an academic route, which includes a University qualification, still seems to be considered a more laudable direction for a candidate to take. (Raelin, p. 83)

An argument by Duckenfield and Stirner (1992) also surfaced in "Report of the Assessment and Accreditation of Work Based Learning Project within Academic Programs, in Higher Education Project." This report claimed that the obstacles to proper interaction between academia and the workplace were perhaps due to the learning gained in the workplace not being consistently defined nor gaining recognition and/or an award for a formal qualification.

Communities of Practice

The concept of postgraduate WBL has been enhanced by educational researchers, including Lave and Wenger, and linguists interested in, for example, theories of language in use, literacy practice, and discourse and power (see, in particular, Barton & Tusting, 2005). Barton and Tusting, for example, suggested that the Communities of Practice (CoP) concept could help to identify the differences between formal and informal education. Also, Gee (2005) illustrates in his paper "Semiotic Social Spaces and

Affinity Spaces" that an alternative usage to groups is needed to understand learning without the restrictions that belonging to a community would bring. Gee uses the original Wenger's learning pattern of CoP's as an inspiration when he argues that, due to the complicated nature of the membership concept, people might experience an inhibition regarding their learning if they do not identify with all the membership rules. According to Gee, a "semiotic social space" (SSS), which can be and very frequently is an affinity space, allows for participants to avail of the positive aspects of the related learning without the expectation of repeated, acknowledged, and/or revealed identity, which again can and should be verified against the true credentials of each individual. Gee also talks about the unhelpful notion of trying to label people in groups according to standard membership criteria, arguing that, as with WBL, different learners "can be good at a number of different things, or gain repute in a number of different ways" (p. 227). Results of empirical research on postgraduate work-based learners indicate that the participants have followed different routes to arrive where they are today. These individuals' form of participation to learning has been different and varied each time. It has been through not just subject-specific (intensive knowledge) routes, but also through knowledge, which is more general (extensive knowledge). All WBL learners, according to individual desire for its use and purpose, can uniquely share this type of knowledge.

Table 9.3 identifies some of the elements of the WBL field that should be taken into account when trying to understand its position within higher education and the broader communities of learners who might avail of a postgraduate qualification of the WBL area in the university sector.

Gee (2005) also argues that the actual notion of leadership is porous and it cannot be meaningfully achieved through traditional methods that follow a well-structured hierarchy. Today, work-based learners are frequently used as leaders themselves, depending on the actual situational context. The CoP argument indicates both the role and use of hierarchy, but as Gee argues there are commonalities in an affinity space that may be helpful in assisting disentangling the related concepts. For example, in an Affinity Space, as in postgraduate WBL, teachers can become resources themselves,

Table 9.3   Elements of the WBL Field

Work domain	University domain
Practical application	Verbal explanation
Output/Product-driven	Process-driven/Led
Practice defense	Theoretical input

therefore the relevance, as it is argued, of "many businesses which organize such spaces for their customers" (p. 228) can, indeed, be integral to WBL. Within the UK context, education recognized as useful by participants has always shown an emphasis toward vocationalism. The rise of polytechnics, with their clear and explicit vocational ethos, has assisted the move to WBL. Further, a number of related publications have emphasized the aforementioned development, such as the Dearing report (1997), the Green Paper "The Learning Age: A Renaissance for a New Britain" (1998), and the White Paper "Learning to Succeed: A New Framework for Past-16 Learning" (1999). These pieces of work were setting the government agenda for education, training, and work. But all of these reports have also provided a setting for the WBL concept.

It is, however, interesting to notice that the final Leitch Report in 2006 recommended that the United Kingdom should become a world leader in skills by 2020. Setting a similar benchmark by the government, with the aim of the United Kingdom being among the top eight countries worldwide for each skill level, means that the ultimate aim is to deliver qualifications to a much higher figure than the existing percentage of the workforce. For example, the actual target aims for 90% of adults to become qualified to above level 2, while also increasing the related number of adult apprenticeships.

By now, WBL has emerged on an international scale, both within Europe and beyond (Karamanos & Gibbs, 2012; Gibbs & Barnett, 2014). Similar projects (i.e., Lemanski's "Developing European Work-Based Learning Approaches and Methods," 2011, and Gibbs's work *Learning, Work and Practice: New Understandings*, 2013) are further attempts to relate WBL to the overall social good and wellbeing of people. For example, while Gibbs's contribution to the international dialog of WBL practice concentrates perhaps more on the philosophy of learning at work, it still teaches us a lot from an international perspective regarding the challenging meaning and value of ethics in the workplace. Apart from the specific effort to develop different models and approaches to WBL, within an international consortium of establishments the aim has always been to enable access to higher education qualifications for people who are currently in paid, unpaid, and/or voluntary employment.

Maclaren and Marshall also examined WBL in 1998. These authors highlighted the need for all academic institutions involved in WBL to adapt to the needs of what was starting to form, namely a new learning society required to satisfy the needs of industry as well as the needs of the learner. In other words, the encouragement to forge partnerships between universities and the world of commerce with the ultimate objective of creating and developing a learning workforce is certainly not new.

An additional aspiration was that the tripartite members (university, employer, and employee/learner) set up a type of "action plan" from the start of the partnership, so that the WBL experience would be able to take advantage of all existing and potential sources of knowledge (such as the university and the workplace). This almost invariably also includes prior learning activities that incorporate tacit (nonverbalized), but still very significant individual learning. The important aspect of the WBL success is the prior agreement in place regarding all parties. For example, it is usually expected that the employer will have consulted with the employee/learner.

WBL has not been sufficiently analyzed as a postgraduate qualification, which can become fully accredited and possibly standardized across the United Kingdom so that all interested participants, including employers, can make an informed choice, regarding educational and vocational funding, for their employees. Thus, the methods of self-completion of postal questionnaires, semi-structured interviews, and document evaluation were used for generating much-needed data.

Postgraduate WBL: Transformative Experiences-Sojourners!

Over 70 returned questionnaires referred to the WBL postgraduate qualification as a positive addition to the individuals' educational and vocational experience, some even going as far as calling it a life-changing experience. The data suggested that five out of the seven interviewees had engaged with WBL in such a way that it had implications for their own identities. Some people (around 50 questionnaires) expanded significantly on the specifics of the WBL's postgraduate qualification as "really useful," because of the importance of "vocational skills taught in a realistic manner." Fenton-O'Creevy has described the trajectory of these students through the academic-workplace boundary as sojourners (Fenton-O'Creevy, 2014).

Despite the fact that at times it remained quite difficult to cluster as one overall answer or even clearly decipher regarding the exact meaning of WBL, the overwhelming majority of those responding to this piece of research have described their postgraduate university WBL experience extremely positively, with only a small number of them offering an expression of confusion regarding the purpose of postgraduate WBL.

For example, consider what the following participants had to say:

> Work Based Learning did change my life. Honestly it did! Critical Friends supported me during my postgraduate University course. (Participant 7)
>   It was very good overall . . . but it would be easier to describe my own experience if I knew exactly what Postgraduate WBL was intending to do . . . I quickly understood though. (Participant 2)

It was a serious attempt to combine the workplace with academia, the best thing was to be able to talk about what I've learnt in the University, in a Postgraduate course, while at work. (Participant 3)

For me . . . WBL was the best thing ever completed as a Postgraduate University course, . . . and more relevant to work, compared to other stuff I've covered in the past. (Participant 1)

What is important here is that my experience in my Postgraduate WBL course was very positive, because of my new knowledge that links with work, not because of my first degree. (Participant 4)

My WBL Masters changed my attitude towards work . . . it was not always positive, some "challenges" I found irrelevant, but it worked because it was always useful. (Participant 5)

In other words, postgraduate WBL participants appeared to have actively engaged in integrating their understanding of academic and workplace practices, and ultimately reconciled various personal experiences in these different domains in ways that illustrate different trajectories in terms of the impact of postgraduate WBL regarding the participants' journey through the community of academic practice, as Fenton-O'Creevy would term it.

Prior Qualifications and "Common Language"

Despite the students' overall positive experience in the postgraduate WBL course, it remains a significant "stumbling block" that in order for WBL to gain an equal place next to the other academic disciplines a common language still needs to be constructed to describe postgraduate WBL. Some respondents felt that the roles of "employee and student" are regarded as quite distinct although that was not their experience.

One of the important elements of the Work Based Learning process was that it was changing according to the actual context. I've heard this word "context" used before, but I was never sure what it meant. (Participant 1)

What I did as an Undergraduate in the University, was no use to me at all . . . and as a WBL Master's student, I wouldn't have been successful in my efforts if I did not have somebody with vast vocational experience helping me along . . . and this colleague did not have a primary degree. (Participant 4)

It was clear to me that in the University, people were trying to emphasize—usually through the process of "Critical Friends" . . . more the higher level skills of thinking and reflecting. (Participant 6)

When, I was uttering the word "Work Based Learning," most of the people understood a lot more basic things than "University" Postgraduate provision. (Participant 2)

All of the research participants felt that being able to use university learning within the work environment was of utmost importance. They were all equally keen to refer to the need for further clarity of the WBL term. As explained earlier, the general term of WBL is part of a cluster of concepts including those of Lifelong Learning, employability, up-skilling, and flexibility. It is worth mentioning that the postgraduate participants were also using the term "workplace learning," when they simply meant WBL. The fact that the participants in this piece of research had successfully completed a master's course in WBL was not necessarily what the world understood, when they were starting to explain the qualifications acquired.

One participant commented:

> I would have liked people to understand easier that when we talk about a WBL Masters, we do not simply talk about an undergraduate Work Based Learning placement—something that the process of "Critical Friends" taught me . . . The system of "Critical Friends" in the university made me realize that my worth was more relevant at work than I thought. (Participant 3)

Therefore, a common language is required to understand overall WBL, and in this case it seems paramount to create one for postgraduate WBL.

Postgraduate WBL: Crossing Boundaries in "Work" and "Learning"

Most of the respondents experienced a degree of difficulty in defining consistently both the term "postgraduate WBL knowledge" and the concept of what constitutes a professional personality. The issue of language in postgraduate WBL was earlier referred to, but this section looks particularly at the capacity of the postgraduate WBL participants to successfully cross the boundaries of work, to those of learning and vice versa.

One would easily assume that the argument of identifying a common definition used by all in higher education for postgraduate WBL is as imperative as identifying something similar for the concepts of *postgraduate WBL knowledge* and *professionalism*. However, the capacity of the respondents to customize the terms, according to their individual experiences, might indicate that no matter how many definitions are available for each concept, individuals will tend to adopt the meaning closest to them and their vocational experience.

In this case, this was done for assistance in interpreting postgraduate WBL as a higher-level skill, dealing with postgraduate study, within a higher education setting.

Here are some of the participants' thoughts on that:

> In my Postgraduate WBL University course, work was combined with learning and new knowledge with work, it seemed so much easier to "play" between "work" and "learning." (Participant 1)
>
> Everything, my WBL knowledge was all used, and still is, on a daily basis at work. I could talk all day on how helpful it was for work but I better leave this now! (Participant 3)
>
> It is difficult to explain at work how useful my University learning was for work . . . My boss would like to think that it is all their doing at work that helps. (Participant 5)

While these points are very important in terms of indicating the value of combining work and learning, they also highlight that some participants could not, or did not want to, verbalize more specifically the particular aspects of the postgraduate WBL knowledge and its contribution to their overall professional identity. Some others, however, consistent with the theme of variation element in the participants' responses, said that their broad understanding of the meaning of work helped them to comprehend within their own context. Over half of the respondents felt that their professional personality was still "adjusting" according to the vocational area that they joined each time. These participants saw postgraduate WBL as a positive, inevitable growth experience, and expected it to inform forthcoming changes in the workplace.

Postgraduate WBL: New Directions in Learning and Assessment

To become able to negotiate both *assessment packages* and *content delivery* within the context of an agreed combination of university lecturers and workplace mentors also appears to be of paramount importance. In order to produce a worthwhile product, employers need to possess the knowledge of *what* exactly their employees will study and *how* relevant the latter will be to their understanding of their current working environment.

Some of the significant participants' comments were as follows:

> For me Work Based Learning was ideal! My Masters University assignment work was going "hand-in hand" with my working environment, you don't have the time to do things separately in life. I've experienced the meaning of "relevance." (Participant 4)
>
> I am married, I have kids and time is of essence. Postgraduate WBL was offering "blended" learning and I was able to use that directly at work, it was never the case of just one essay. My employer was telling me things that they

thought were important for "us" (work) and I was producing "combined" portfolios with the use of the internet. (Participant 2)

Work Based Learning was for me different, because it was useful. I had the opportunity to apply new learning at my work, not just learn irrelevant theory on a Masters level. (Participant 6)

You are "dead" if you stop learning, but the excitement of using my learning from Monday to Friday at work, was unique! We went "deeper" on the WBL Masters, and this helped me a lot with my career. (Participant 5)

If WBL is to become involved at the right level, it seems to be possible that a positive result appreciated both on an academic as well as vocational level will be produced. All of the questionnaires returned referred to the WBL postgraduate qualification as a positive addition to the individuals' educational and vocational portfolio, but the relevance that postgraduate WBL revealed during the participants' studies was associated with flexible and innovative assessment strategies. This is what appears to have made the difference between choosing *any* course to study and opting for WBL.

My experience at work was very useful but also quite inhibiting in a totally different environment. Postgraduate Work Based Learning was not at all like that: it was really inclusive and we've soon realized that all of us (the students), we were "on the same boat." That meant that even if somebody was an expert in a specific field at work, this "expertise" was not necessarily the same for another colleague. We were in a position to share our (I suppose I have to call them that), "working feelings" only to usually discover that even if the nature of work was different, the problems were uncannily similar! (Participant 7)

One participant commented in the questionnaire:

I liked the fact that I could use work as my main portfolio theme and that actually my knowledge of work could be supported so well by new academic theory. (Participant 3)

Another participant observed:

My professional experience was massive so I had to do the WBL Masters course. (Participant 1)

All postgraduate WBL research participants tend to positively point toward the argument that employer engagement has to constantly be on the higher education agenda, and that the cultural gulfs between university and workplace have to be bridged as much as possible.

Traditional Universities versus Newer Universities (Polytechnics)

A clearer distinction between research-intensive universities and those that are business-facing might also be worth exploring. As already clear from discussions, both on scholarly and nonacademic levels, postgraduate WBL is generally recognized as important, especially as it relates to the importance of combining work-based skills with academic knowledge.

However, no work has so far challenged the existing academic status quo by the standardized establishment of a master's program in WBL, especially within what is known as a traditional university setting.

Three of the participants' responses in relation to the assistance that the postgraduate WBL program has offered to its participants are worth quoting:

At the start I could not see if they were any (WBL aspects) at all . . . I am afraid it had to take a bit of time before "the penny dropped"! For me after this happened though, it was an absolute revelation. I've learnt not necessarily "how to say no" when I didn't like something . . . but how to understand why I could not say "no" . . . my understanding had already changed, instead of doing things "mechanically," I was now comprehending the rationale behind it all! I was pleased that all of this was happening in a University . . . even if mine used to be a Poly. (Participant 2)

I still think that some of the lecturers were "sticking to a more traditional" (safe??) form of delivery, as my University was a "Russell Group University" [elite, research-focused universities in the United Kingdom] and for a lot of teaching parts, I could not see the connection with my workplace at all, I still think that it was an experience though . . . (Participant 4)

I always considered myself an accomplished individual at work and I was sure that this would help my participation in the WBL Masters, but the acquisition of knowledge regarding research tools like "action-research" and the exploration of me being "central" to my research . . . also how to avoid conflict with my employers, all was phenomenally useful—my University, though I suppose is considered to be a "newer" University—specializes in the delivery of these concepts and despite the fact that these concepts would be considered more academic, I've used them, and keep using them at work all the time, the application was rather immediate and this "know-how" was necessary. (Participant 3)

Indeed, APEL seems to be working in different combinations of university and work-based environments (usually, resulting in an independent qualification at undergraduate level). Most of the time, the assumption is also made that since learning, especially for a nontraditional adult, is usually work based, it is acceptable to recognize the learning that takes place "outside" the university setting as part of a vocational and/or specialist qualification for each of the participating professionals.

It seems though to be the case that a full master's in WBL is rather rare to find within the traditional university provision and again in most cases, when found, additional actions need to be taken on the participant's part to ensure (i.e., through letters to employers where relevant claims are made) that the full academic and vocational recognition has been rightfully attributed. It appears that traditional universities, whose main emphasis in their work would be educational research, will not recognize postgraduate WBL in the same form as other universities (previously known as polytechnics) would, because of their immediate proximity to industry.

Three participants commented as follows on the existence of a primary degree:

> Some colleagues, even more senior to me, were approaching me for advice because they knew that I now have a WBL Masters into the bargain from a University! (Participant 5)
>
> Not having a primary degree usually creates havoc regarding consistency of the learner's understanding but my experience has shown that other APL means are better for Postgraduate WBL study. I want to see APL materializing fully, success is up to the lecturer(s), not up to a 1st degree. Others though might not think so . . . but what would really be their real workplace involvement is another matter. (Participant 7)
>
> To be able to join-in the University on the basis of evidential reports from work and APEL, boosted my confidence in relation to my capacity to study on a Postgraduate level in the University. (Participant 6)

Another quote regarding this theme comes from a WBL master's participant, who observed the importance of work-based choice within a profession, as well as the significance of underpinning theoretical knowledge to technical considerations:

> There are not a lot of jobs around and I had to think "long and hard" if this Postgraduate Work Based Learning University course would be relevant for me. This was a University close to industry anyway. But a University after all . . . but it was tremendous because it did really help me understand that there is always a "choice" when it comes down to what you do at work. A few things I've simply considered that I had to do even if I did not want! (Participant 5)

Therefore, it might be a safe assumption to make that higher education through postgraduate WBL now has, more than ever, a responsibility to closely identify the differing nature of these "new learners" and accommodate their needs in a diverse manner, which may not align with the way a "traditional" learner would be accommodated.

In addition a participant commented:

> Time is of essence as you might expect. Life at the moment is not very "smooth" at the home front either . . . to be able to study in the University, a Postgraduate course that helps my working life is nothing less than terrific. (Participant 1)

The following participants added:

> I don't think that there was even a "comma" that I did not use at work (I mean from the stuff that I've learnt in the University). A lot of University qualifications (even if the opposite is claimed), in essence they bear no relationship to the real world, particularly the ones that they are not directly related to the workplace. Ok you do "get an idea," but it is a "protected" idea, well "shielded" from all the mishaps that I am afraid, inevitably happen at work. (Participant 5)
>
> It is not the same to be young, "free" and in a placement, the challenge is to care for an entire family and study at the same time, my WBL Masters gave me that chance! I can understand that no quality can be compromised here . . . but why the heck would we ever think that a primary degree is a guarantee of quality. I'll never know . . . In my Postgraduate Work Based Learning class, the most timid students were the ones without University experience, not in a "traditional" form anyway and they were definitely the best students in the end. (Participant 1)

The above comments appear to speak positively to the benefits of a postgraduate WBL course in relation to students' professional development.

It seems to be the case that universities, which were previously polytechnics, always had a rather direct relationship with industry. On the other hand, more traditional universities always underscored an independent research role rather than a more direct relationship with business. Ideally, postgraduate WBL provision would hold that the involvement of a minimum of three stakeholders (the professional/learner, the workplace, and the university) increases the chances of counteracting positively any problems which might occur during the process of the postgraduate study in WBL. Proponents of postgraduate WBL would argue that the fact that three parties are involved (as opposed to two or even one exclusively at work) can help the "main professional player" to identify more creative solutions, when none appear to be presenting themselves as possibilities. Even if individual reluctance exists, on the part of the professional employee to continue in search of a productive solution, the fact that the work-based relationship involves by definition more "players" than the workplace, in terms of the adopted perspectives, can prove to be very useful.

Discussion

This research has tried to identify the ways in which postgraduate WBL has contributed to the participation and access to higher education for nontraditional adult learners. However, the boundaries between practices are never unproblematic in that they always involve the negotiation of how the existing business of a community of practice becomes relevant (or not) to that of another (Wenger, 1998, 2002). Therefore, if we accept that these boundaries can be potential places of confusion and misunderstanding, we will probably also accept that the existing different regimes of competence belonging to nonidentical cultures can be places with different values to the ones we immediately recognize and therefore different perspectives can ensue, leading to various practices which follow, often in an unexpected manner.

Though boundaries hold the potential for unexpected learning, the new insights that present themselves without warning by no means guarantee productive engagement by its members. Therefore, boundaries between practices are not necessarily peaceful, or collaborative! However, despite the fact that crossing a boundary always involves the question of how the perspective of one practice might be relevant or not in that of another, boundary crossing and boundary encounters are both aspects of living in a landscape of practice (Wenger, 1998, 2002).

Gee, however, also argues that the actual notion of leadership is porous and it cannot be meaningfully achieved through traditional methods that follow a well-structured hierarchy. Today, work-based learners are frequently used as leaders themselves, depending on the actual situational context. The CoP argument indicates both the role and use of hierarchy but, as Gee argues, there are commonalities in an Affinity Space with WBL, which might be ultimately helpful in assisting and disentangling the related concepts. For example, in an Affinity Space, teachers can become resources themselves, therefore the relevance, as it is argued, of "many businesses which organize such spaces for their customers" (p. 228) can be integral to WBL. I tend to conclude that postgraduate WBL identifies with a number of elements that the principle of Affinity Spaces offers, without (as Gee terms it) the related baggage. However, the CoP concept overall carries on an important originator of the general learning involved in this type of WBL research.

The data on work-based learners indicate that the participants have followed *different* routes to "arrive" where they are today. These individuals' form of participation to learning has been different and varied each time. It has been through not just subject-specific (intensive knowledge) routes, but also through knowledge, which is more general (extensive knowledge). This type of knowledge can be *uniquely* shared by all WBL learners according to individual desire regarding its use and purpose.

Results also reveal the successful transition that facilitated participants through this study in order to affect a new work and/or educational identity and role. In other words, the critical expectation integral to deep learning suits the postgraduate work-based learner who already can use the existing working experience in order to produce a blended amalgamation of knowledge, as opposed to simply surface learning (The Higher Education Academy, 2010). Most of the work completed to date in WBL refers to the benefits of employer-led careers, with formal qualifications waiting at the end of it (Blundell, Dearden, Goodman, & Reed, 1997). The Higher Education Academy has also argued that we will understand the WBL's pedagogy better if we all start using similar or even identical terms to describe WBL. Until that happens, it appears to be quite difficult to use students' positive experiences on a postgraduate WBL course in a productive way since it is dangerous to conclude that *all* stakeholders assume the same understanding regarding the term "work-based learning."

"An Introduction to Work-Based Learning," a report commissioned by the Higher Education Academy in February 2011, acknowledges that the multiplicity of definitions and therefore functions of WBL can be varied and confusing for the user, unless the context of WBL is specifically defined. The Leitch review of skills has set a rather challenging target: the prediction of the review is that by 2020 the United Kingdom will be within the top eight regions worldwide for each skill level, with a strong emphasis placed in delivering work-based qualifications to a far bigger section of its workforce than what is currently occurring. It appears that it would be worthwhile for academics to take heed of the issue of students returning to the workplace and adopting a kind of superior attitude to colleagues or, to put it less pejoratively, the phenomenon of the person feeling a sense of fulfillment through WBL that could, on return to the workplace, crumble into frustration if it was felt that this achievement was not appreciated or properly recognized, and especially if the person's role in the workplace has not changed and become more responsible, or challenging, on account of it. This would seem to be a relatively underresearched part of the postgraduate WBL experience.

The literature still does not seem to have a standard definition for a nontraditional student and this category (the same as the concept of WBL) needs to be defined according to context. Almost invariably though, definitions tend to incorporate the fact that a nontraditional student is usually at work and over, on average, 18–21 years of age. There are, of course, additional traits, for example, family commitments. The latter usually includes elderly parents, underage children, and educational background (this is frequently also described as nontraditional)—it often means poor or even nonexistent background in education, and/or experiential professional evidence available, as well as a lack of a primary degree in a recognized university discipline.

Boud (1985) has argued that after full-time education, most learning occurs in the context of work. *All* respondents to this piece of research felt that it is a better idea for WBL postgraduate study to be based on an examination of APEL, rather than a "traditional way of assessment." It will be extremely significant to observe this development, particularly when considering the multidefinitional aspect of WBL. It might have been several decades since work and learning have started being theorized in a combined form; but until recently there has been little scholarly evidence to allow for an analysis of fully accredited postgraduate programs in WBL, and their benefits for the participating professional.

Currently, there are different types of models for postgraduate WBL, and the concept assumes various definitions according to the context that surrounds the term. Unwin and Fuller in 2003 (cited in Evans & Kersh, 2006), argue that WBL needs to be distinguished from Workplace Learning. They suggest that Workplace Learning is a "form of learning that occurs on a day-to-day basis at work, as employees acquire new skills to develop new approaches to solving problems. No formal education recognition normally accrues to such learning, whether or not it is organized systematically" (Evans & Kersh, 2006).

It is the case that a few scholars believe that perhaps one of the challenging issues with postgraduate WBL is that all stakeholders involved still try to distinguish if WBL is a field of study in itself or a direct learning experience. For example, the benefits of WBL were admired for being able to distinguish among different professional issues and deal with each one of them *directly*. Duckenfield and Stirner (1992) have claimed that adults who engage in further study with institutes of higher education bring the benefits of much experience and prior learning. In the past, while this has been widely recognized, it has rarely been assessed or accredited. It also seems to be the case that as far as the graduates of this WBL master, it counted for a lot in terms of time, money, and useful skills to be able to engage in a program, which was leading to a postgraduate qualification in its entirety (master's in WBL).

Conclusion

This chapter has outlined the development and context of postgraduate WBL and its context mainly within the British, but also the international post compulsory, education system. There is an examination of the status and distinctive characteristics of knowledge underpinning postgraduate WBL. There is also an evaluation of the potential contribution of the postgraduate WBL to the specific task of widening participation in postgraduate higher education and the extent to which postgraduate WBL contributes to the policy debate on both national competitiveness and globalization. The potential impact of postgraduate WBL on the tripartite relationship of the professional, nontraditional, adult learner, the employer, and the university is very significant.

The postgraduate WBL's contribution to participation and access to higher education for the nontraditional student is potentially enormous. The data suggest that if postgraduate WBL were not available, there would be an unbridgeable gap and a vocational and educational lost opportunity for all of its participants.

> Humans thrive when we feel valued as partners in meaningful relationships, doing relevant work towards a common goal. Partnership fosters ownership; ownership sparks motivation; motivation drives learning. (Beattie, 1995)

References

Barton, D. & Tusting, K. (Eds.). (2005). *Beyond communities of practice: language, power and social context.* Cambridge, UK: Cambridge University Press.

Beattie, M. (1995). New prospects for teacher education: Narrative ways of knowing teaching and teacher learning. *Educational Research, 37*(1), 53–70.

Billett, S. (2002). Workplace pedagogic practices: Co-participation and learning. *British Journal of Educational Studies, 50*(4), 457–481.

Blundell, R., Dearden, L., Goodman, A., & Reed, H. (1997). *Higher education, employment and earnings in Britain.* London, UK: London Institute for Fiscal Studies.

Brennan, J., & Little, B. (1996). *A review of work-based learning in higher education.* London: Quality Support Centre & OU Press.

Brennan, J., & Little, B. (2006). *Towards a strategy for workplace learning: Report of a study to assist HEFCE in the development of a strategy for workplace learning.* London: Centre for Higher Education Research and Information.

Connor, H. (2005). *Workforce development and higher education: Summary document.* London: The Council for Industry and Higher Education.

Dearing, R. (1997). *National committee of enquiry into higher education.* London: HMSO.

Duckenfield, P. & Stirner, M. (1992). *Learning through work*. Sheffield, UK: Employment Department.

Evans, K. (2004). The challenges of making learning visible: Problems and issues in recognizing tacit skills and key competences. In K. Evans, P. Hodgkinson, & L. Unwin (Eds.), *Working to learn: Transforming learning in the workplace*. London, UK: Kogan Page.

Evans, K., & Kersh, N. (2006). *Competence development and workplace learning: An overview for the UK and Ireland*. Project Report. London, UK: Institute of Education, University of London.

Fenton-O'Creevy, M. (2014). Students at the academic workplace boundary: Tourists and sojourners in practice-based education. In E. Wenger-Trayner, M. Fenton-O'Creevy, S. Hutchinson, C. Kubiak, & B. Wenger-Trainer (Eds.), *Learning in landscapes of practice: Boundaries, identity and knowledgeability in practice-based learning*. Abingdon: Routledge.

Garnett, J. (2007). Challenging the structural capital of the university to support work based learning. In D. Young & J. Garnett (Eds.), *Work based learning futures*. Bolton: UVAC.

Gee, J. P. (2005). Semiotic social spaces and affinity spaces: From the age of mythology to today's schools. In D. Barton & K. Tusting (Eds.), *Language, power and social context: Beyond communities of practices* (pp. 214–242). Cambridge, UK: Cambridge University Press.

Gibbs, P. (2013). *Learning, work and practice: New understandings*. London, UK: Springer.

Gibbs, P. & Barnett, R. (Eds.). (2014). *Thinking about higher education*. London, UK: Springer.

Gray, D. (2001). *A briefing on work based learning: LTSN Generic Centre Assessment Series*, No. 11. New York, NY: Learning and Teaching Support Network.

Higher Education Academy (2010). From small acorns, to big trees grow – common interests, shared goals and collaboration, languages, linguistic and area studies, by Brathwick, K. and Dickens, A. (Presentation). UK: Higher Education Academy.

Honey, P. (1994). Establishing and learning regime. *Organisations and People*, 1(1), 1–11.

Karamanos, N., & Gibbs, P. (2012). A model for student adoption of online interactivity. *Research in Post-Compulsory Education*, 17(3), 321–334.

Leitch, L. (2006). *Leitch review of skills: Prosperity for all in the global economy – World class skills*. Norwich: Her Majesty's Stationery Office.

Lemanski, T., Mewis, R., & Overtone, T. (2011). An introduction to work-based learning. *New Directions in the Teaching of Physical Sciences*, Issue 6 (September), 3–10.

Maclaren, P., & Marshall, S. (1998). Who is the learner? An examination of the learner perspectives in work-based learning. *Journal of Vocational Education and Training*, 50(3), 327–337.

Naish, J. (1995). *Auditing, accrediting and assessing employees' work based learning*. Report of Middlesex University Employment Department Development Project Middlesex University: National Centre for Work Based Learning Partnerships.

Nikolou-Walker, E. (2009). *The expanded university: Work based learning and the economy*. Harlow, Essex: Pearson.

Nixon, I. (2008). *Work-based learning: Impact study*. York: The Higher Education Academy.

Raelin, J. A. (1997). Work-based learning in practice. *Journal of Workplace Learning*, *10*(6/7), 28.

Ross-Gordon, J. M. (2011) Research on adult learners: Supporting the needs of a student population that are no longer nontraditional. *Association of American College and Universities*, *13*(1) (Winter), 26–29.

Scottish Executive Central Research Unit. (2002). Edinburgh, Scotland: Scottish Executive.

Wenger, E. (1998). *Communities of practice: Learning, meaning, and identity*. Cambridge: Cambridge University Press.

Wenger, E. (2002). *Cultivating communities of practice*. Cambridge, MA: Harvard Business School Press.

10

Transforming Doctoral Leadership Program Design through Cross-National Dialog

Carol Kochhar-Bryant

Introduction

Educational leadership preparation programs in the United States are generally noted for preparing leaders to appreciate and influence the larger national political, social, economic, and cultural contexts. However, few give systematic pedagogical attention to underlying values and personal motivation in the development of leadership behavior. This chapter explores "educational identity" as a core construct in the development of educational leaders and the instrumental value of a broader cross-national understanding in developing its potential. It describes a process of reinvention of the doctor of education (EdD) leadership program, shaped partly by a multiyear continuing conversation between US and Israeli educators. Visits by the author, along with faculty colleagues, to several academic institutions in Israel has ignited a transformation of perspectives of educators in both countries in addressing challenges and issues currently being encountered. Conversations are rooted in acknowledged commonalities between the nations about educational problems, issues of equity and access, and the challenges of preparing and retaining scholar-leaders for meaningful change. These interchanges are forming a critical friendship group (Storey & Richard, 2013) and colleagueship that is propelling the academic and clinical redesign of our EdD.

Theoretical foundations that are connected include (1) Nisan and Pekarsky's "educational identity," (2) the "civic courage" of Freire (the educational process is never neutral), (3) Lee Shulman's "pedagogies of engagement," (4) Schon's reflective practice, and (5) Bandura's "cognitive apprenticeship." The chapter describes the transformative impact of integrating these constructs into the design and development of a new EdD vision.

The Broadening International Context for Institutions of Higher Education

The terms "international dialog," "intercultural dialog," and "cross-cultural communication" refer to communication that creates the conditions for dialog among civilizations, cultures, and peoples based upon respect for commonly shared values (UNESCO, 2014). Educational leadership development programs are greatly enriched by educational and policy dialog between countries and can help emerging leaders gain perspective on internationally shared educational concerns. For example, the "Education for All" movement led by UNESCO is a global commitment to provide quality basic education for all children, youth, and adults. At the World Education Forum in Dakar in 2000, 164 governments pledged to achieve education for all and identified six common goals to be met by 2015. As the leading agency, UNESCO (2014) focuses its activities on six key areas: policy dialog, monitoring, advocacy, mobilization of funding, national education systems, and capacity development. These key areas align with educational capacity building in the United States and can lend a broader perspective to US education policy making and implementation strategies.

The strategic dialog that many institutions of higher education (IHE) are embarking on, including ours, is also shaped by increased public interest in the engagement of IHEs at the local and regional levels. Education is a powerful driver of development and one of the strongest instruments for reducing poverty and improving health, gender equality, peace, and stability (World Bank, 2014). This realization demands more extensive involvement of academic institutions in scaling up investment in effective educational practices, improving access and equity, ensuring the provision of quality higher education, and increasing contextually relevant research in the region.

Why a Collaboration with Israel?

The United States and Israel share many common cultural and economic features. Like the United States, Israel has developed a strong economy with an entrepreneurial and technology-propelled drive, but the socioeconomic divide between subpopulation groups continues to grow. In some regions such as northern Galilee, about half of the population is Arab. A central challenge for these regions is the disparity between Arab and Jewish populations' employment and education outcomes (OECD, 2011b). Israeli society has also absorbed and integrated immigrants from 79 different countries, who speak 39 languages.

Similarly, according to the 2010 US Census, in the United States approximately 36.3% of the population belongs to a racial or ethnic minority group: American Indian or Alaska Native, Asian American, Black or African American, Hispanic or Latino, and Native Hawaiian or Other Pacific Islander (Humes, Jones, & Ramirez, 2011; US Census Bureau, 2010). Based on the 2011 Census Bureau American Community Survey, of 291.5 million people aged five and over, 60.6 million people (21% of the population) spoke a language other than English at home and over 300 different languages are spoken (US Census Bureau, 2013).

In Israel, there is a growing social and economic divide between the center and periphery—the Galilee in the north and the Negev region in the south—and between population groups. The socioeconomic gap is evidenced in the rate of unemployment, the disparities in salaries, the lack of absorptive capacity in traditional industries, negative migration, poverty, which is highest among youth, and the fundamental disparity between the Arab and Jewish populations (OECD, 2011b). This uneven development poses a threat to the long-term sustainable development of Israel.

Similarly, in the United States the economic gap among races and other barriers to social mobility are the most compelling indicators that geography is all too often destiny. The United States faces several economic threats: stagnant growth in standard of living for some, a growing gap between the rich and the rest of the population, and low rates of upward mobility (Reeves, 2014). Real incomes for the top 1% of households have tripled since 1979, compared to a rise of 50% for the bottom fifth and just 36% for those in the middle (Mishel, 2011; Mishel, Schmitt, & Shierholz, 2014). The OECD found that the gap between the rich and poor in 30 OECD countries has widened over the past three decades, and in 2008 it reached an all-time high, with the United States having the highest levels (OECD, 2011a). Furthermore, the poorest children (black and white alike) receive the worst public education and during the K-12 years the achievement gaps between poor and affluent children tend to widen, rather than narrow (Reardon, 2011; Reeves, 2014).

Important questions that both countries are seeking to answer are: How can governments ensure equitable investment in education for different population groups? How can universities and colleges fuel local growth by developing relevant skills and improving educational attainment levels across the multiethnic, multireligious population? For example, the University of Haifa in northern Israel provides an example of success in broadening access to multiethnic populations. It is among the most pluralistic IHEs in Israel, bringing together students from older cities as well as newer development towns, kibbutzim and moshavim, new immigrants, Jews, Arabs, and Druzes.

The public's faith in knowledge production, research and development, and innovation has heightened expectations that IHEs engage with the social and economic challenges facing the communities of which they are a part (Pasque, 2010; Pasque, Hendricks, & Bowman, 2006). As higher education has become central to the development of nations, it is increasingly viewed by the public as key to achieving educational equity, access, and social mobility. In short, IHEs are being challenged to reexamine their public purposes and commitments (Chambers, 2005; Pasque et al., 2006; Pasque & Rex, 2010).

These expectations have great implications for educational leadership development, begging questions such as: How can we do more with our research, teaching, and service in order to strengthen the relationship between higher education and society? How can we establish pedagogy that can engender the motivation for sustained civic participation in complex and pluralistic societies? Higher education is uniquely positioned in both Israel and America to help future leaders understand the histories and contours of their respective challenges as diverse democracies. Both countries recognize that pluralism is a source of strength and vitality that will enrich their leadership education and help students work for the common social good (Presidents' Declaration on the Civic Responsibility of Higher Education, 2012). Furthermore, engagement of the IHE with the wider society will influence its pedagogical frameworks for leadership development (Avila, 2010; Bloom, Hartley, & Rosovsky, 2007; National Strategy for Higher Education to 2030, 2011).

During our trips to Israel, and their visits to the United States, our dialog with Israeli educational leaders allowed us to get to know each other on a much deeper level and to realize the value of mutual understanding about respective people and society. In Israel we were directly exposed to the many complex and nuanced issues of distinct regions, including the status of Israeli minorities, the plight of migrant workers and refugees, the tensions surrounding settlements in the West Bank, and Israeli government structures. The US-Israel collaborative began in 2010 with a series of informal faculty exchanges and seminars, followed by visits to Israel by US educators and visits to the United States by Israeli educators. The initial goal was to establish professional and personal exchanges, and to identify educational issues of common interest and importance. These exchanges have also provided opportunities to form a critical friendship group (Storey & Richard, 2013) to enrich the leadership training of doctoral students in the United States and in Israel.

Lessons from the Mandel School for Educational Leadership, Jerusalem

A key aspect of our dialog with Israel is with leaders of the Mandel School for Educational Leadership, founded in 1991 in collaboration with the Ministry of Education. The institute places the educator's vision at the center of professional development and nurtures motivated professionals who bring vision to the Israeli education system. Graduates serve in key positions in educational and communal organizations, filling senior positions in government ministries, local authorities, and educational and social organizations. Some graduates lead schools while others have spearheaded a variety of educational initiatives.

The program is a two-year course that is personalized and takes place in individual and group settings and combines theoretical and practical studies. The program has four objectives:

1. To facilitate clearer understanding of one's personal and professional identity;
2. To provide a thought-out, multifaceted formulation of one's vision;
3. To acquire skills for operating in complex situations, in an effort to translate ideas into reality;
4. To deepen the knowledge and expertise in one's professional areas of competence.

The courses rest on three main pillars: humanities and Jewish studies (the world of ideas and knowledge), studies in education, and policy studies (the world of action and policy). Fellows are exposed to various content and worldviews, and receive personal mentoring based on their individual development needs. The goal is to enhance the fellows' ability to navigate between the theoretical and practical worlds, to step outside the world of action they came from, and to develop a new and complex perspective on their personal and professional identity.

Mandel Program for Leadership Development in the Haredi (Ultra-Orthodox) Community

An additional component is the Mandel Programs for Leadership Development that prepares senior educators, entrepreneurs, and social leaders in the Haredi (Ultra-Orthodox) Community. The program, launched in 2011, prepares leaders who serve as go-betweens, bridging the Haredi community and the Israeli society at large (Mandel Leadership Institute, 2014). The program is grounded in several assumptions: (1) in aiming to influence Israeli society as a whole, it could not ignore the growing role of the Haredi community; (2) the problems within the Haredi community must be taken on by the community itself; and (3) public leadership must grow from within, informed by its values and experience. Thus, the programs aim to develop civic leadership in the Haredi community using those who are visionaries and practitioners, who possess a rich and thorough knowledge of Jewish law and tradition, who have strong intellectual capacity, and who are an integral part of the Haredi community (Mandel Leadership Institute, 2014).

The program brings together the new languages and terminology of the secular world with the richness of the Torah and Jewish tradition to develop vision and action, which draw upon both worlds. The program was uniquely developed to serve the ends of developing leadership capacity, articulating a personal and communal vision on education, translating that vision it into action, and developing a personal project intended to improve and advance the Haredi community and its connection with the larger Israeli society (Mandel Leadership Institute, 2014). The nature of the pedagogy that leads to effective translation of vision into action is of core interest to our faculty.

Critique of Traditional Leadership Programs in the United States: Toward a New Set of Assumptions

Leadership is a complex process that is still not well understood as a construct or as a set of behaviors (Bennis, 2009; Derue, Nahrgang, Wellman, & Humphrey, 2011). Most of what is labeled "leadership" has been considered "good management" (Heifetz, 1994). Leadership as a field of study began with a trait–behavior model that emphasized production and efficiency, and evolved to emphasize the power of the single leader (Stand and Deliver), in which power derived from the authority of the individual in the position of leadership (Avolio, 2007; DeRue, Ashford, & Cotton, 2009; Sithole & Mbele, 2008).

The postindustrial paradigm reflects globalization and an interconnected world (Bekker, 2010; Rost, 2007). It required new ways of leading that are principle-centered, express collaboration, moral purposes, and that can *transform followers into leaders* (transformational leadership). Leadership was redefined as a relational process of people accomplishing change together to benefit the common good (Komives, Lucas, & McMahon,

1998; Morgeson, DeRue, & Karam, 2010). Leadership now includes concepts of inclusiveness, empowerment, ethics, and purposefulness—ideas that are reflected in initiatives such as turn-around schools and community engagement.

According to Nisan and Pekarsky (2009) and Freire (1998), most educational leadership programs express the "training view" which emphasizes technical preparation and the provision of instruments and tools needed for practice. Critics agree that the training that school principals typically receive in university programs and in their districts does not adequately prepare them for their roles as leaders of learning (Darling-Hammond, Meyerson, La Pointe, & Orr, 2009; Morgeson et al., 2010; Rost, 2007). More than 80% of superintendents and 69% of principals think that leadership training in schools of education is out of touch with the realities of today's districts, fragmented, incoherent, and absent requirements of building communities across diverse school stakeholders (AACTE, 2001; Darling-Hammond, LaPointe, Meyerson, Orr, & Cohen, 2007; Peterson, 2002).

Initial leadership preparation programs are collections of courses that typically include management principles, school law, administrative requirements, and procedures, with little emphasis on student learning, effective teaching, professional development, curriculum, and organizational change (AACTE, 2001; Morgeson et al., 2010; Usdan, McCloud, & Podmostko, 2000). Few have strong clinical training components linked to academic course work and that pair prospective leaders with skilled veteran leaders, providing them experiences that enable them to learn the full complexity of their jobs.

Emergent Theories that can Enhance Program Design

The work of several educational philosophers are highlighted here as their ideas interconnect around the construct of identity and commitment in leadership development—Nisan and Pekarsky, Freire, Shulman, Schon, and Bandura.

Educational Identity

Mordecai Nisan and Daniel Pekarsky (2009) articulated the core philosophy of the Mandel School for Educational Leadership in Jerusalem, which develops influential leaders with vision to advance education in Israel. Nisan and Pekarsky contend that "educational identity" is an essential characteristic of an educational leader. The unique "identity view" of educational leadership emphasizes the development of a considered system of goals, values, and self-definition to which a person commits (p. 6). This view is not given adequate expression in the field of leadership training, but rather is eclipsed by an opposite view, the *training view* that focuses on the instruments and tools of management.

The *identity view*, which places goals and values at the focus of the development of educational leadership, along with opportunity to actualize them through self-realization, is the basis for developing personal commitment and educational leadership.

> Such leaders' commitment to their profession is built upon their self-definition as people involved in education, their view of education's goals and values, their vision of the good person and the good society, their perception of the area in which they are meant to act in this regard, and their self-perception—the beliefs, feelings, plans and abilities connected with their work that they have developed over the course of their lives. I will call this sort of commitment "educational identity." (Nisan & Pekarsky, 2009, p. 32)

Nisan and Pekarsky contend that leaders are expected to make and carry out decisions on the basis of their value-based educational identity rather than outside pressures or personal interests.

Civic Courage

Paulo Freire, a Brazilian educator, philosopher, and leading advocate of critical pedagogy, argued that education cannot be neutral, but rather demands that the educator address issues of values, beliefs, and commitments (1985, 1998). The teacher or educational leader is by his or her presence an *intervener* in the world and is destined to choose among alternative courses of action. Freire's term "intervention" refers to the aspiration for radical changes in society in areas such as health, education, economics, employment, and others. Freire speaks to the political nature of that intervention, proposing that "education cannot be neutral or indifferent in regard to the reproduction of the dominant ideology or the interrogation of it" (1998, p. 91). He also refers to modern business leadership development as including technical and scientific preparation but failing to address their "human and ethical presence in the world" (p. 92). The leader, therefore, needs to engage in the process of becoming a citizen, which does not happen as a consequence of "technical efficiency," but is a result of a political struggle to create a society that is humane and just. Freire's (1998) construct of *civic courage* connects learning and activism, which he views as the essence of human life. The educational leader takes a public stance, with integrity and at some personal risk, to challenge prevailing conditions and conventional ideas in pursuit of the common good.

Pedagogies of Engagement

Lee Shulman's (2004) construct of the "pedagogies of engagement" intersects with the construct of identity. A family of problem-based pedagogies, first defined by Edgerton (1997) was expanded by Shulman to include six features or claims. These include pedagogies of engagement, understanding, performance, reflection, generativity, and commitment. These pedagogies begin with real problems that *engage* students and deepen *understanding* of research-based and practical knowledge. They lead to *performance*—knowledge of how to act—that requires decision, judgment, and action. Performance must also be interrupted or disrupted to allow for *reflection* upon performance (e.g., How did I reach this decision? What did I do that makes this performance effective?) Active performance then must be balanced with strategic and intentional reflection (meaning-making) on one's performance.

The pedagogies create a *generativity*, or powerful desire to know more and to value engagement in order to learn. Finally *commitment* encompasses the affective and moral component of learning and development, a commitment not just to cognitive growth but also to *new dispositions*, habits, and values (Shulman, 2005, pp. 55–56). These pedagogies assist the emerging leader to continuously forge new connections between ideas and effective practice, and to perform with a sense of personal and social responsibility. The performances of practice must not only be skilled and theoretically grounded, they must be characterized by integrity and by a commitment to responsible, ethical service (Shulman, 2005, p. 2).

Cognitive Apprenticeship and Social Learning Theory

Constructivism or experiential learning is a theory of knowledge based on the proposition that knowledge and meaning are generated from an interaction between one's experiences and their ideas. Based on Jean Piaget's research on early childhood development, constructivist pedagogical approaches to learning have led to the development of a theory of cognitive apprenticeship (Ginsburg & Opper, 1969). The theory posits that when one has mastered a skill he or she often fails to take into account the implicit processes involved in carrying out complex skills when they are teaching novices (Brown, Collins, & Duguid, 1989). Cognitive apprenticeships, therefore, are designed to make the tacit explicit by enabling learners to observe, enact, and practice them with help from the coach or teacher. The cognitive apprenticeship model is supported by Albert Bandura's theory of modeling (Bandura, 1963, 1989), or *social learning theory*, which posits that people learn by observing others. Successful modeling requires the learner to be attentive, to retain the information presented, be motivated to learn, and able to accurately reproduce the target skill. People learn through observing others and develop self-efficacy, or the belief in oneself to take action. Bandura (1993) and other researchers have found an individual's self-efficacy plays a major role in how goals, tasks, and challenges are approached. Individuals with high self-efficacy are more likely to believe they can master challenging problems and they can recover quickly from setbacks and disappointments, whereas those with low self-efficacy are less confident and often avoid challenging tasks. Models are an important source for learning new behaviors and for achieving behavioral change in institutionalized settings (Miller, 2005). People learn by observing others, and each behavior witnessed can change a person's way of thinking (cognition).

Knowing in Action and Reflective Practice

Schön (1983, 1987) articulated the constructs of "knowing in action" and "reflective practice," suggesting that reflective practice is the capacity to reflect on action so as to engage in a process of continuous learning (Bolton, 2010; Schön, 1983). It requires attention to the practical values and theories, which inform everyday actions, by examining practice reflectively and reflexively. This leads to developmental insight, which is the centerpiece of experiential education (Itin, 1999). Experiential education is a philosophy of education that describes the process that occurs between a teacher/mentor and student that interconnects content with direct experience with the learning environment.

These theories and philosophies, along with the cross-national dialog with Israeli educators, have provided intellectual grounding for reevaluating the assumptions upon which our leadership EdD programs are predicated.

What it All Means for the Redesign of the Education Doctorate

While our leadership EdD program has undergone considerable change over the past two decades, we find ourselves in a crucible of sorts. Over the past two years, our dialog with Israeli educators provided an impetus for an analysis of our EdD program—the intellectual content, relevance to our consumers, and most of all, relevance for preparing our consumers to face the dominant challenges in education today in the United States and internationally. Our mutual exchanges are forming a critical friendship group (Storey & Richard, 2013) and colleagueship to shape our exploration of the academic and clinical elements of our EdD redesign.

Other concerns and aims also contributed to the redesign effort. These included (1) practical issues such as the desire to reduce students' time to completion, introduce preparation for the dissertation early in the program, and the provision of mentorship and support to guide students through and (2) issues of quality and rigor such as deepening students' readiness for leadership in their field, promoting dissertations that move beyond study of a problem to impacting a problem in context.

In 2012 a faculty critical friends learning community was formed to examine literature on leadership training programs and identify core features of effective programs. Since then, faculty has worked toward purposeful transformation as we rethink the foundations of our program. Such transformation has not meant reinvention for the sake of change, but faculty recognized the need to nurture a new generation of courageous educational scholar-practitioners or *scholar-pioneers* who can harness their creativity to solve crucial social problems. *Scholar-pioneers* are leaders who redraw or expand the boundaries of practice and policy because they are guided by a powerful vision of the future and can translate that vision into reality regardless of the environment.

As we evaluated our leadership EdD we paid particular attention to the strength of our curriculum and our field experiences to prepare leaders for a new paradigm of leadership—making a difference in contributing to the "common good" (Komives et al., 1998; Morgeson et al., 2010). We asked: Are we incorporating the pedagogies of *engagement, understanding, performance, reflection, generativity,* and *commitment* (Shulman, 2004)? Are we expecting students to move beyond the "armchair" study of a problem at a distance to actually enter into the often-messy context of the problem and work to affect a change? We asked: What strategies are we using to help students crystallize an "educational identity" (Nisan & Pekarsky, 2009), a "civic courage" (Freire, 1998), and to engender an aspiration for radical change in society and an ability to challenge prevailing conditions and conventional ideas in pursuit of the common good (Freire, 1998)? This self-interrogation led to another set of questions related to the assumptions, content, and processes of our curriculum and pedagogy:

1. How can a scholar-practitioner oriented EdD program cultivate a sense of "identity" for social commitment to the community and help students clarify values associated with their identity?

2. What is the developmental and transformative process for crystalliz-
ing a leadership identity and how does it deepen over time?

3. What are the pedagogical strategies and instructional environments
for creating committed leaders?

We will continue to work over the coming two years to work as a faculty
community, in dialog with our Israeli partners, and to integrate the concepts and processes related to educational identity and civic courage as
central to the development of the effective educational leader.

Framework for an Emerging Doctorate of Practice

Several teams of faculty are participating in EdD redesign projects, and
sharing their experiences along the journey. The framework for our EdD—
which is partly drawn from Carnegie Project on the Doctorate (CPED)
principles and partly from lessons learned from our Israeli friend—
emphasizes individual development of the leader, crystallization of an
"educational identity" and commitment to change leadership, inquiry as
practice in authentic settings, and attention to significant issues in education policy and practice. The individual development of the leader centers on leader as innovator, principled decision maker, policy developer,
and implementer. Candidates are challenged to (1) define an educational
"identity," (2) reflect on their capacity to attack complex education policies,
(3) explore their commitment to policy leadership and the improvement
of education at various levels, and (4) examine their commitment to seek
imaginative solutions to today's challenges.

The doctoral program will prepare both an emerging and ascend-
ing generation of top leaders who can challenge conventional policies
and practices and seek imaginative solutions, marshal research evidence
in decision-making, create pioneering and enterprising opportunities,
and manage resources strategically within the context of complex
organizations.

Identity View of Leadership

This rigorous program of study employs innovative instructional strategies
for leadership development as well as focusing on the individual development of the leader, specifically on the process of how leadership capacity
or *leadership identity* is created and changes over time. This program is
anchored by several philosophical principles:

1. Educational identity is a central factor in the development of educational leadership (Nisan & Pekarsky, 2009).

2. Exceptional leaders must be guided by a powerful vision of the future, inspired by profound ideas, and energized by imaginative resolutions to today's challenges.
3. Leadership identity can be cultivated and therefore, a leadership program must create the conditions and processes through which those characteristics are developed.

Design features include the following:

1. Design the curriculum to build fluency in research-based and experiential knowledge.
2. Combine experiential and critical analytic learning to address actions and choices in educational leadership. Since the leader's value-commitments deeply affect and guide his or her actions and choices in the education policy arena, the program challenges leaders to reflect on the use of power and position to influence the quality of education in their domain of authority (Komives, Owen, Longerbeam, Mainella, & Osteen, 2006).
3. Prepare leaders to identify and explore ethical complexities in policy formation and important values that underlie policy choices and the manner of their implementation.
4. Create "laboratories of practice" as authentic field-based settings in which theory and practice inform and enrich each other and allow students to address complex problems of policy and practice (Shulman, 2005; Copland, 1999).
5. Ensure that students exit the program with greatly enhanced capacity and interest in the design of innovative solutions to address the problems of policy and practice.
6. Recognize the potential power and assets of the cross-national experience; provide opportunities for students to engage with the social and economic challenges of the global community.
7. Deepen students' skills in using data to understand the effects of innovation, and prepare them to gather, organize, judge, and analyze situations, literature, and data through a critical lens (Shulman, 2005).
8. Prepare students to target social change through their professional and applied research activities to improve social conditions within the community, particularly for vulnerable populations (Yates & Youniss, 1999).

This doctoral model is designed to:

- Provide scholar-leaders with an advanced curriculum that focuses on relevant and current topics and issues in executive leadership and human capital development.

- Focus on the core leadership competencies, dispositions, and applied research that leaders need to be effective in various organization settings.
- Provide opportunities for candidates to focus their dissertations on actual problems within their organizations, making the dissertation relevant and practical and thereby encouraging support from host organizations.
- Provide candidates with access to a network of successful practicing scholars and organizations to support their intellectual, professional, and career development.
- Challenge students, from the moment of entry into the program, to (1) explore their identity for leadership and their social commitment to community, (2) examine their commitment to seek imaginative solutions to today's challenges, and (3) develop a world view and internalized set of values.
- Prepare socially conscious, morally grounded leaders who respect and embrace diversity.
- Provide sustained opportunities to struggle with difficult questions of goals and values.

The Capstone Project

Practitioner-scholars draw on the knowledge, skills, and understanding that they have acquired in the course of their doctoral studies to examine and address a *significant problem of practice*. A capstone project is intended to be of direct benefit to practitioners and, ultimately, the public. It is also a demonstration of a student's ability to carry out disciplined investigation and argumentation in accordance with the highest standards of academic inquiry, key ingredients in preparing students for leadership. The capstone project is designed as "embedded" or "in-vivo" research.

The Challenge to Create Scholar-Leaders Who can Respond to the Needs of Society

Several recommendations have been offered to IHEs as they prepare scholar-leaders for a greater responsiveness to the needs of society: (1) encourage involvement of the wider community in IHE activities, (2) respond to professional development needs of the wider community, (3) focus on consequences of the work of higher education and relevance for society, (4) emphasize civic skills and leadership in the curriculum and foster a deep commitment to the public good within the professorate,

(5) encourage students and faculty to target social change through their professional and applied research activities to improve particular social conditions within the community (Rex, 2006), (6) provide opportunities for international education experiences, and (7) ensure that accreditation processes include civic engagement and social responsibility criteria (Hollister et al., 2012).

References

American Association of Colleges for Teacher Education (AACTE). (2001, March). *PK-12 educational leadership and administration* (white paper). Washington, DC.

Avila, M. (2010). Community organizing practices in academia: A model, and stories of partnerships. *Journal of Higher Education Outreach and Engagement, 14*(2), 37–64.

Avolio, B. J. (2007). Promoting more integrative strategies for leadership theory-building. *American Psychologist, 62*, 25–33.

Bandura, A. (1963). *Social learning and personality development.* New York, NY: Holt, Rinehart, and Winston.

Bandura, A. (1989). Human agency in social cognitive theory. *American Psychologist, 44*, 1175–1184.

Bandura, A. (1993). Perceived self efficacy in cognitive development and functioning. *Educational Psychologist, 28*(2), 117–148.

Bekker, C. J. (2010). Prophet and servant: Locating Robert K. Greenleaf's counter-spirituality of servant leadership. *The Journal of Virtues & Leadership, 1*(1), 3–14. School of Global Leadership & Entrepreneurship, Regent University.

Bennis, W. (2009). *On becoming a leader* (3rd ed.). Jackson, TN: Perseus Books.

Bloom, D. E., Hartley, M., & Rosovsky, H. (2007). Beyond private gain: The public benefits of Higher Education. In J. J. Forest & P. G. Altbach (Eds.), *International handbook of higher education* (pp. 293–308). Dordrecht: Springer.

Bolton, G. (2010). *Reflective practice, writing and professional development* (3rd ed.). California, CA: SAGE Publications.

Brown, J. S., Collins, A., & Duguid, P. (1989). Situated cognition and the culture of learning. *Educational Researcher, 18*, 32–42.

Chambers, T. (2005). The special role of higher education in society: As a public good for the public good. In A. J. Kezar, T. C. Chambers, & J. Burkhardt (Eds.), *Higher education for the public good: Emerging voices from a national movement* (pp. 3–22). San Francisco, CA: Jossey-Bass.

Copland, M. A. (1999). Problem-based learning, problem-framing ability and the principal selves of prospective school principals (Doctoral dissertation, Stanford University). *Dissertation Abstracts International, 60*(8), 2750.

Darling-Hammond, L., LaPointe, M., Meyerson, D., Orr, M. T., & Cohen, C. (2007). *Preparing school leaders for a changing world: Lessons from exemplary leadership development programs.* Stanford, CA: Stanford Educational Leadership Institute.

Darling-Hammond, L., Meyerson, D., La Pointe, M. M., & Orr, M. T. (2009). *Preparing principals for a changing world.* San Francisco, CA: Jossey-Bass.

Derue, D., Nahrgang, J., Wellman, N., & Humphrey, S. (2011). Trait and behavioral theories of leadership: An integration and meta-analytic test of their relative validity. *Personnel Psychology, 64*(1), Spring, 7–52.

DeRue, D. S., Ashford, S. J., & Cotton, N. (2009). Assuming the mantle: Unpacking the process by which individuals internalize a leader identity. In L. M. Roberts & J. E. Dutton (Eds.), *Exploring positive identities and organizations: Building a theoretical and research foundation* (pp. 213–232). New York, NY: Taylor & Francis.

Edgerton, R. (1997). *Higher Education* (unpublished white paper). Philadelphia, PA: The Pew Charitable Trusts Education Program.

Freire, P. (1985). *The politics of education.* Westport, CT: Bergin & Garvey.

Freire, P. (1998). *Pedagogy of freedom: Ethics, democracy and civic courage.* Lanham, MD: Rowman & Littlefield Publishers.

Ginsburg, H. P., & Opper, S. (1969). *Piaget's theory of intellectual development.* New York: Prentice Hall.

Heifetz, R. A. (1994). *Leadership without easy answers.* Cambridge, MA: Belknap Press.

Hollister, R. H., Pollock, J. P., Gearan, M., Reid, J., Stroud, S., & Babcock, E. (2012). The Talloires network: Building a global coalition of engaged universities. Global University Network for Innovation, 21. *Journal of Higher Education Outreach and Engagement, 16*(4), 81–101.

Humes, K. R., Jones, N. A., & Ramirez, R. R. (2011). *Overview of Race and Hispanic Origin: 2010.* 2010 Census Briefs. US Census Bureau. Accessed 8/30/15 from: http://www.census.gov/prod/cen2010/briefs/c2010br-02.pdf

Itin, C. M. (1999). Reasserting the philosophy of experiential education as a vehicle for change in the 21st century. *The Journal of Experiential Education, 22*(2), 91–98.

Komives, S., Lucas, N., & McMahon, T. (1998). *Exploring leadership for college students who want to make a difference.* San Francisco, CA: Jossey-Bass.

Komives, S. R., Owen, J. E., Longerbeam, S., Mainella, F. C., & Osteen, L. (2006). A leadership identity development modal: Applications from a grounded theory. *Journal of College Student Development, 47*(4), 401–418.

Mandel Leadership Institute. (2014). *Jerusalem.* Accessed 12/15/14 from: http://www.mli.org.il/english/MhlLeadership/Pages/HarediLeadershipPrograms.aspx

Miller, K. (2005). *Communication theories: Perspectives, processes, and contexts* (2nd ed.). New York, NY: McGraw-Hill.

Mishel, L. (2011). *We're not broke nor will we be: Policy choices will determine whether rising national income leads to a prosperous middle class.* Washington, DC: Economic Policy Institute Briefing Paper #310. Accessed 8/2/14 from: http://www.epi.org/publication/were_not_broke_nor_will_we_be/

Mishel, L., Schmitt, J., & Shierholz, H. (2014). Wage inequality: A story of policy choices. *New Labor Forum, 1*(6), 1–6. New York, NY: The Murphy Institute, City University of New York. Accessed 7/23/14 from: http://nlf.sagepub.com/content/early/2014/08/04/1095796014544325

Morgeson, F. P., DeRue, D. S., & Karam, E. P. (2010). Leadership in teams: A functional approach to understanding leadership structures and processes. *Journal of Management, 36,* 5–39.

National Strategy for Higher Education to 2030. (2011). Department of Education and Skills, Dublin.

Nisan, M., & Pekarsky, D. (2009). *Educational identity as a major factor in the development of educational leadership.* Jerusalem, Israel: Mandel Institute, Hebrew University.

OECD. (2011a). *Divided we stand: Why inequality keeps rising.* Paris.

OECD. (2011b). *Higher education in regional and city development: The Galilee, Israel.* Paris.

Pasque, P. A. (2010). *American higher education, leadership, and policy: Critical issues and the public good.* New York, NY: Palgrave Macmillan.

Pasque, P. A., Hendricks, L. A., & Bowman, N. A. (Eds.). (2006). *Taking responsibility: A call for Higher Education's engagement in a society of complex global challenges.* Ann Arbor, MI: National Forum on Higher Education for the Public Good, University of Michigan.

Pasque, P. A., & Rex, L. A. (2010). Complicating "just do it": Leader's frameworks for analyzing higher education for the public good. *Higher Education in Review, 7,* 47–79.

Peterson, K. D. (2002). The professional development of principals: Innovations and opportunities. *Educational Administration Quarterly, 38*(2), 213–232.

Presidents' Declaration on the Civic Responsibility of Higher Education. (2012). *Campus compact.* Boston, MA. Accessed 1/15/15 from: http://www.compact.org/wp-content/uploads/2009/02/Presidents-Declaration.pdf

Reardon, S. F. (2011). The widening socioeconomic status achievement gap: New evidence and possible explanations. In R. J. Murnane & G. J. Duncan (Eds.), *Whither opportunity? Rising inequality, schools, and children's life chances* (pp. 91–116). New York, NY: Russell Sage Foundation.

Reeves, R. V. (2014). *Saving Horatio Alger: Equality, opportunity and the American dream.* Washington, DC: Brookings Institution.

Rex, L. A. (2006). Higher Education has done well, we can do more: A report from the Wingspread Access, Equity and Social Justice Committee. In P. A. Pasque, L. A. Hendricks, & N. A. Bowman (Eds.), *Taking responsibility: A call for Higher Education's engagement in a society of complex global challenges* (pp. 30–36). Ann Arbor, MI: National Forum on Higher Education for the Public Good, University of Michigan.

Rost, J. (2007). Moving from individual to relationship: A postindustrial paradigm of leadership. *Journal of Leadership & Organizational Studies, 4*(4), 3–16.

Schön, D. (1983). *The reflective practitioner, how professionals think in action.* New York: Basic Books.

Schön, D. (1987). *Educating the reflective practitioner.* San Francisco, CA: Jossey-Bass.

Shulman, L. (2004). *Teaching as community property: Essays on higher education.* San Francisco, CA: Jossey-Bass.

Shulman, L. (2005). Pedagogies of uncertainty. *Liberal education, 91*(2) Spring. Washington, DC: Association of American Colleges and Universities. Accessed 8/15/15 from: https://www.aacu.org/publications-research/periodicals/pedagogies-uncertainty

Sithole, P., & Mbele, T. (2008). *Fifteen year review on traditional leadership: A research paper*. South Africa: Human Sciences Research Council, Democracy and Governance.

Storey, V. A., & Richard, B. M. (2013). Critical friends groups: Moving beyond mentoring. In V. A. Storey (Ed.), *Redesigning professional education doctorates: Applications of critical friendship theory to the EdD* (pp. 9–24). Hampshire: Palgrave Macmillan.

UNESCO. (2014). *Introducing UNESCO: What we are*. Paris. Accessed 8/14/14 from: http://www.unesco.org/new/en/unesco/about-us/who-we-are/introducing-unesco/

US Census Bureau. (2010). *American community survey*. Washington, DC: US Department of Commerce, Economics and Statistics Administration. http://www.census.gov/2010census/data/

US Census Bureau. (2013). *American community survey*. Washington, DC: US Department of Commerce, Economics and Statistics Administration.

Usdan, M., McCloud, B., & Podmostko, M. (2000). *Leadership for student learning: Reinventing the principalship*. A Report of the Task Force on the Principalship School Leadership for the 21st Century Initiative Institute for Educational Leadership. Washington, DC: Institute for Educational Leadership.

World Bank. (2014). *Education overview*. Washington, DC. Accessed 8/15/14 from: http://web.worldbank.org/WBSITE/EXTERNAL/TOPICS/EXTEDUCATION/0,,contentMDK:20575742~menuPK:282393~pagePK:210058~piPK:210062~theSitePK:282386,00.html

Yates, M. B., & Youniss, J. (1998). Community service and political identity development in adolescence. *The Journal of Social issues, 54*(3): 495–512.

11

The Transition from Discipline-Based Scholarship to Interdisciplinarity: Implications for Faculty

Siomonn Pulla and Bernard Schissel

Introduction

The Doctor of Social Sciences (DSocSci) program at Royal Roads University, Victoria, British Columbia (BC), Canada, is now in its fifth year of operation. In the spring and fall of 2014 we graduated our first six doctoral students. The program is based on a scholar-practitioner model with an interdisciplinary academic framework. Most of our students are highly placed, full-time working professionals who are also pursuing full-time doctoral work and find it necessary to blend their professional activities with their doctoral research. The students bring an amazing variety of experiences and research foci to the program as, in many ways, their professional careers demand interdisciplinary epistemologies.

The interdisciplinary framework of the DSocSci program presents an exciting context for students and for faculty. It also, however, presents challenges for faculty who participate in the delivery of the program, given that all of our faculty members come from rather strict disciplinary backgrounds. This chapter, and the experiences upon which it is built, focuses on the complexity of faculty transition from discipline-based scholarship to interdisciplinarity, a transition that has implications for their own research, their colleagues' evaluations of them, and their professional development. The transition exceeds professional implications and has profound implications for pedagogical approaches that normally shift through the development of online pedagogy and in response to interdisciplinary teaching and learning.

This chapter is based on our own reflections and some informal interviews with faculty who have made the transition to our program and to the interdisciplinary mandate of the applied scholar model. We focus on career implications, which include the following: (1) research funding, (2) research development, (3) the role of critical friends in program dissemination, (4) colleague approval, (5) colleague collaboration, and (6) internal university acknowledgement. In addition, we explore pedagogical implications for faculty including teacher satisfaction, skill development, student-professor challenges, and transformative approaches to doctoral supervision.

The Doctor of Social Sciences Program: An Overview

DSocSci is a four-year structured program designed on a cohort model—with an average of 15 students per cohort. Each cohort of students journeys together through six core courses. Four of these courses are delivered thorough a blended learning model: the students start with a three-week initial online component, followed by three weeks of intense face-to-face learning through two residencies in the first year of study, and then six weeks of online learning post-residency. In between the two residencies, the students take a full online course to explore epistemological and methodological issues in applied interdisciplinary social sciences research. Subsequently, they develop directed studies with their chosen supervisors. Once all the course work is completed in the beginning of their second year, the students are required to pass their candidacy exam. After successful completion of the exam, they work with their committees to develop their research proposals, and seek approval for their doctoral research projects through the department that evaluates research ethics. By the beginning of their third year, students are engaged in the data collection phase of their research (see Figure 11.1).

As you can see from our program data in Table 11.1, more females than males are enrolled in the program but overall most students are in their mid-forties. As a result of this demographic, the students bring a variety of experiences and research projects to the program.

And interestingly, our data also show that the majority of our students are coming from education organizations: this typically includes teachers, instructors, and professors from secondary and postsecondary institutions who are seeking to upgrade their credentials from a master's to a doctoral level (Table 11.2). We also see a high concentration of students from the

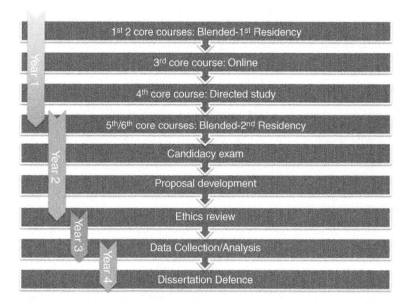

Figure 11.1 DSocSci Program Timeline

Table 11.1 DSocSci Gender and Age Statistics

	2010	2011	2012	2013	2014	2015a	2015b	Total
Male	2	1	5	7	6	5	4	30
Female	6	5	6	6	8	9	7	40
Age	35–63	38–54	44–60	31–63	28–58	26–70	28–60	

environmental sector, as well as from backgrounds such as government, consulting (unknown in Table 11.2), and social science research. What you can ultimately derive from the data is that we continue to attract well-placed professionals from a variety of sectors and backgrounds making the program truly applied and interdisciplinary.

The scholar-practitioner model we embody is based on an applied interdisciplinary academic framework that helps integrate the diverse backgrounds and experiences of our students. Typically, our students enter the program with a strong practitioner focus; one of our major challenges as faculty is to help our students engage in the rigors of scholarship and ultimately to draw links between their practitioner selves and the demands of rigorous scholarship. We do this by supporting the students in

Table 11.2 Represented Organizations

	2010	2011	2012	2013	2014	2015a	2015b	Total
Education industry	1	1	3	3	3	4	2	17
Environment	1	3	1	1	1	1		8
Government	2		2	1	1			6
Social sciences				2	2	1	1	6
Health/Social services	1	1		1			2	4
Human resources			1			2		3
Justice/Public safety			1		1		1	3
Arts and culture			1		1			2
Energy				1		1		2
Finance/Insurance	1						1	2
Manufacturing/Production						1	1	2
Business/Administration				1				1
Communication	1							1
Legal	1							1
Marketing					1			1
Services						1		1
Technology						1		1
Trades/Transportation				1				1
Unknown			2	1	2		1	6

the design of research helping them to focus on translating abstract scholarly theories and concepts into applied and action-oriented projects that focus on tangible deliverables, usually associated with their professional positions. This action-oriented, iterative process ensures that students not only consult with their committees as part of their research design, but that they involve their practitioner communities in the design, collection, and dissemination of their research. Their active research colleagues come from within academia and from outside.

Shifting to an Interdisciplinary Pedagogy: A Critical Friends Approach

The interdisciplinary framework of our doctorate program presents an exciting context for students and for faculty. As already noted, it also, however, presents challenges for faculty who participate in the delivery of the program, especially given that all our faculty members come from rather strict disciplinary backgrounds. Our traditional training, especially the idea of a discipline-based pedagogy, in many ways can seriously constrain our ability to address adequately the diversity of needs within an applied interdisciplinary program. And the development and delivery of online interdisciplinary pedagogy introduces additional issues. While the form of asynchronous learning we employ in DSocSci addresses the fact that almost all of our students are full-time professionals, the online delivery format destabilizes traditional student-professor relationships, roles, and responsibilities, as well as require new virtual space roles and responsibilities of faculty to facilitate learning.

The epistemology or the pedagogical philosophy of the conventional educational world assumes that students know very little, and that we, as teachers know much more. Furthermore, the conventional assumption is that knowledge can ultimately be put into subject matter silos or disciplines—such as anthropology and sociology—with complete academic integrity and investigative credibility. Indeed, for centuries the whole educational universe has been organized around predetermined subject areas.

A truly effective interdisciplinary pedagogy, however, requires that we embrace the destabilizing spaces required to break free from disciplinarity, especially when these new interdisciplinary-based approaches are more policy and action based than isolated disciplinary endeavors. Manathunga, Lant, and Mellick (2006, p. 371) argue that interdisciplinary pedagogy is threatening emotionally, socially, and cognitively for both teachers and students because it deliberately seeks to engage students in controversy and asks them to develop an appreciation for ambiguity. Manathunga et al. (2006) suggest that there are four key dimensions that support interdisciplinary doctoral pedagogy. These are (1) providing relational, mediated, transformative, and situated learning experiences; (2) focusing on development of the critical skills in students to help them move beyond disciplinary cultural relativism to interdisciplinary synthesis; (3) strengthening higher order thinking and metacognitive skills in students to help them critically unpack multiple disciplinary perspectives; and (4) enhancing students' epistemological understandings of their original discipline (p. 368).

Instead of the subject matter being the structure for learning, the interdisciplinary pedagogy underlying the DSocSci focuses on connecting the learning outcomes we are trying to achieve for our students with the social challenges they want to be working on, whether those challenges are related to indigenous community work, leadership, or environment and sustainability. Interestingly, most of the research endeavors of our students have a social and/or environmental justice focus. This means that our applied interdisciplinary pedagogy becomes highly practice-centered: our teaching is based on both practice and scholarship and we focus on learning as an interactive process. The general framework for our courses and the discussions that ensue revolve around the professional and research needs of our students. The quality of our curriculum therefore is not based on what is de rigueur in a discipline but on emerging knowledge, and knowledge that is relevant to the unique professional challenges of each of our students.

Unfortunately, students may initially perceive gaps in our subject matter expertise as a limiting factor in their learning experiences that in turn may negatively influence teaching evaluations and their application to our professional development and promotion requirements. Furthermore, gaps in our subject matter expertise challenge our ability to evaluate the diversity of learning styles and backgrounds of our students. As professors in an applied interdisciplinary program we therefore need to be profoundly aware of the literature that is required to support the learning outcomes of our students. We need to be able to articulate and connect often disparate and sometimes contradictory ontologies, epistemologies, and methodologies, and we need to understand how other people are articulating these same ideas. We also need to be able to choreograph learning experiences for our students to bring the learning alive and add that extra layer of insight and understanding that comes from diversity in knowledge claims.

Employing a critical friends approach to interdisciplinary learning provides an opportunity to tap into the power of both our cohort and blended learning models. The critical friends model has more than 30 years of use in education (Costa & Kallick, 1993; Gibbs & Angelides, 2008; Kember et al., 1997; Storey & Richard, 2013; Swaffield, 2007; Wachob, 2011). Costa and Kallick's (1993) classic definition suggests that a critical friend is "a trusted person who asks provocative questions, provides data to be examined through another lens, and offers critiques of a person's work as a friend" (p. 50). After over two decades, this definition of the critical friend still resonates deeply. Researchers, too, have been building constructively upon Costa and Kallick's critical friend concept. Swaffield (2007), for example, suggests that the critical friend role is not just a supportive role, but also one that encourages and cultivates constructive critique. Such relationships rely heavily on trust, commitment, and knowledge of the professional context of the "friends." Storey and Richard (2013) in fact highlight how trust is really the key element in the critical friends approach; trust provides the framework to provide and receive constructive criticism more effectively than a top-down pedagogical style might.

In one of the core classes on applied qualitative research methodologies being taught during the second residency, students spend much of their three weeks together providing critical feedback to each other. Feedback is accomplished through a series of assignments designed on a snowball technique in which the students work together through tangible issues related to their research; that research cumulates in a polished 20-minute presentation outlining their doctoral research project. Throughout these assignments, the students provide deeper and deeper critical feedback to each other. The power of this interdisciplinary critical friends approach is that each student receives a host of different critical perspectives on the gaps and successes of their project designs; the deep trust built between the students through the intense residency format of our program facilitates a much greater reception to the criticism than if we—their professors— provided it to them. Therefore, in the space of three weeks, the students are able to transform this critical feedback into tangible insights into their research projects—a process that would take months to achieve through a typical student–professor dialog. In short, our program fosters collegiality among all of us at a very profound level that fosters learning equity in opposition to authoritative teaching.

Embracing Interdisciplinary Research Methodologies

Being an applied interdisciplinary researcher necessitates a true willingness to engage in reading outside rigid disciplinary backgrounds. Such readings mean ongoing searches for, and sometimes frustrating confrontation with, bodies of literature that change regularly and rapidly. In many instances, as interdisciplinary novices, we often focus our research on substantive issues in lieu of larger interdisciplinary theoretical frameworks, and in some ways, this is a comforting approach for us. Many disciplinary-based scholars question the legitimacy of this research and characterize it as a-theoretical. Unfortunately, it is these same scholars who frequently make up the adjudication boards of granting bodies. As a result, much applied interdisciplinary scholarship is left underfunded, underrepresented at conferences, and underpublished by top peer reviewed journals. To address these challenges it would certainly help to have a new category of scholarly funding that recognizes the importance of practical research complemented by a new approach to adjudication that can address the incredibly complex, and often policy-driven nature of applied interdisciplinary research design.

We strongly feel the need to continue to push the envelope in terms of how we do research without relying on traditional scholarly grants to legitimize our knowledge production. We need to be proactive in how we disseminate our research to ensure that any knowledge created is accessible to multiple sectors and communities of practice. As applied interdisciplinary scholars we typically have a very strong practice-based research program. This means that much of our research is driven by policy needs, practical issues, and even activism, instead of merely an intellectual curiosity. It is this applied nature of our research, combined with the integration of multiple scholarly epistemological and methodological approaches to scholarship that drives our applied interdisciplinary scholar-practitioner model. And where there is a willingness to work together in teams with colleagues who are very much not alike with respect to disciplinary thinking and modernist-postmodernist orientations, the possibility for innovation and systemic local and national change is incredible. And as we continue to build our international networks of applied interdisciplinary scholar-practitioners, the possibilities to tackle and even solve the increasingly complex and global social issues of the twenty-first century become not only doable but also necessary. We also have to acknowledge that building a truly engaged, applied interdisciplinary research community may take a generation or two and that the work we do today will benefit our students and their students in the years to come.

Interdisciplinary Doctoral Supervision

As doctoral supervisors in an applied interdisciplinary program, one of our biggest challenges is maintaining openness to our students' needs to incorporate complex ways of conceptualizing their research that involves both the social and natural sciences and in some cases the humanities, and often includes indigenous epistemologies. There is no denying that power relations play a significant role in many aspects of the student–supervisor relationship (Deuchar, 2008, p. 491), including being supportive (or not) of our student's unique perspectives on and approaches to their research projects. In many instances, as much as students look up to us as the subject matter experts who are supposed to be guiding them through their learning journey, we need to be able to admit to our students that they are in fact teaching us something new. Our teaching and/or learning and research development are certainly more reciprocal than anything we have experienced to date.

We also need to be transparent, making it clear that as much as we are engaged in supporting our student's learning journeys, we are also there to ensure that they are meeting the program requirements in terms of timing as well as rigor. Based on extensive research into supervisory styles (Delamont et al., 2000; Gurr, 2001; Kam, 1997; Pearson & Brew, 2002; Taylor & Beasley, 2005), Deuchar (2008) points out that two key variables of supervision are foundational: structure and support (p. 490). Based on these two variables, Deuchar suggests that within this foundation four key styles of doctoral supervision occur: (1) the "laisser-faire" style makes the assumption that students "are capable of managing both the research project and themselves"; (2) the "pastoral style," as distinct from the former, assumes that the student is able to manage the academic aspect of the doctorate, but requires personal support; (3) the "directorial" style, is the opposite of the pastoral and assumes that the supervisor needs to support only the management of the project; finally, (4) the "contractual" style assumes that supervisors and students need to negotiate the extent of the support in both project and personal terms (p. 490). The alignment of supervision styles and student needs are further illustrated by Gurr (2001) in a two-dimensional graph (see Figure 11.2) outlining the importance of ensuring that students' needs match the abilities and styles of supervisors. The importance of student and/or supervisor alignment highlights the reality that as much as we may feel we *should* be able, or need to be able to work with a potential student—or that a potential student *should* work with us—we need to be brutally honest with students about our availability, our interests, and our abilities.

The complexity of providing adequate structure and support through doctoral supervision also needs to be contextualized within the debates circulating about the veracity of the role of student autonomy and independence in doctoral studies. An increasing neoliberal "consumerist service ethic" within education is shifting the discourse on supervision toward a model of efficiency, adding pressure to provide students with "quick fix" solutions to their academic difficulties (Deuchar, 2008, p. 490; Holligan, 2005, p. 268; Lucas, 2006). As a result of this focus on efficiency, supervisors may now be compelled to overdirect their students' research in

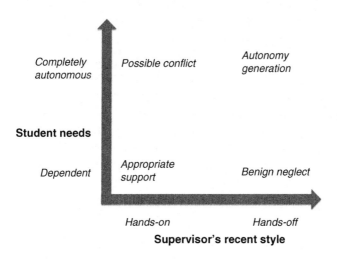

Figure 11.2   Alignment of Supervision Styles with Student Needs
Source: Adapted from Gurr (2001, p. 87)

order to meet program deadlines (Deuchar, 2008, p. 490). We have found that supervisory guidance on applied interdisciplinary doctoral research projects largely depend on the students being able to bring their theoretical and applied work together. It is the students who ultimately drive the research—and this kind of student entrepreneurship demands supervisors to be much less directive than in the past. We are somewhat like consultants, helping to guide the research and writing processes while allowing the students to be highly independent researchers. We do, however, need to continue to manage the expectations of our students in terms of program outcomes and processes. This does not mean overdirecting their research, but rather ensuring that their research projects are not overly ambitious and that we are able to help them to get back on track if it becomes too divergent from their original plans.

We have found that applying a critical friends approach to supervision allows us to build trust with our students, trust that helps to break down the often opaque power relations associated with supervisor-student relationships and helps open the student up to receiving critical feedback without taking it personally.

Conclusion

While the literature of our students' research projects typically lies outside of our expertise, as supervisors we need to cultivate a willingness to build teams of expertise. This means working together and helping to manage a diverse range of modernist and postmodernist orientations as well as disciplinary thinking processes, which will ultimately help our students connect the dots between perspectives to strengthen their research design and data analysis. In the end, the type of collegiality and cooperation that interdisciplinary work demands—as indeed does our program—is based on an academic humility that is framed around our rather new approach to teaching and research; we have become conscious lifetime learners as professors and supervisors and, in fact, we learn as much from our students as they learn from us. The foundational demand of interdisciplinarity is that we are committed to lifetime learning and, over the course of four years and beyond, we pass that commitment on to our students.

References

Costa, A. L., & Kallick, B. (1993). Through the lens of a critical friend. *Educational Leadership, 51*(2), 49–51.

Delamont, S., Atkinson, P., & Parry, O. (2000). *The doctoral experience success and failure in graduate school.* New York: Falmer Press.

Deuchar, R. (2008). Facilitator, director or critical friend?: Contradiction and congruence in doctoral supervision styles. *Teaching in Higher Education, 13*(4): 489–500.

Gibbs, P., & Angelides, P. (2008). Understanding friendship between critical friends. *Improving Schools, 11*(3), 213–225.

Gurr, G. M. (2001). Negotiating the 'rackety bridge': A dynamic model for aligning supervisory style with research student development. *Higher Education Research and Development, 20*(1), 81–92.

Holligan, C. (2005). Fact and fiction: A case history of doctoral supervision. *Educational Research, 47*(3), 267–278.

Kam, B. H. (1997). Style and quality in research supervision. *Higher Education, 34*(1), 81–103.

Kember, D., Ha, T., Lam, B., Lee, A., Ng, S., Yan, L., & Yum, J. (1997). The diverse role of the critical friend in supporting educational action research projects. *Educational Action Research, 5*(3), 463–481.

Lucas, L. (2006). *The research game in academic life.* Berkshire, UK: Open University Press.

Manathunga, C., Lant, P., & Mellick, G. (2006). Imagining an interdisciplinary doctoral pedagogy. *Teaching in Higher Education, 11*(3), 365–379.

Pearson, M., & Brew, A. (2002). Research training and supervision development. *Studies in Higher Education, 27*(2), 135–150.

Storey, V. A., & Richard, B. (2013). Carnegie Project for the Educational Doctorate: The role of critical friends in diffusing doctoral program innovation. In C. A. Mullen & K. E. Lane (Eds.), *Becoming a global voice—The 2013 yearbook of the National Council of Professors of Educational Administration* (pp. 52–65). Ypsilanti, MI: NCPEA Publications.

Swaffield, S. (2007). Light touch critical friendship. *Improving Schools, 10*(3), 205–219.

Taylor, T., & Beasley, N. (2005). *A handbook for doctoral supervisors.* London: Routledge.

Wachob, P. (2011). Critical friendship circles, the cultural challenge of cool feedback. *Professional Development in Education, 37*(3), 353–372.

12

Dissertation in Practice: Reconceptualizing the Nature and Role of the Practitioner-Scholar

Valerie A. Storey and Bryan D. Maughan

Introduction

The richness of dialog about the differing approaches to doctoral educational research from the viewpoint of a scholar and from the viewpoint of the professional has been inspiring and continues to shed new light on the role of the practitioner who performs research under the aegis of the academe (Butlerman-Bos, 2008; Drake & Heath, 2011; Hochbein & Perry, 2013; Jarvis, 1999b; Shulman, Golde, Bueschel, & Garabedian, 2006). However, there continues to be a curious lack of understanding about the signature product of a practitioner performing scholarly research who must satisfy the demands of both viewpoints (Dawson & Kumar, 2014; Willis, Inman, & Valenti, 2010). Accountability to traditionally disparate institutions—the academe and professional practice stakeholders (decision-makers)—decries innovative approaches to the capstone product—the dissertation. We will continue this discussion by outlining the unique characteristics of the dissertation produced by a practitioner who performed educational research. We refer to a dissertation produced by a practitioner while in practice as the Dissertation in Practice (DiP) (ProDEL, 2012; Storey & Maughan, 2014). We continue the discussion about how methodologies of applied or practice-oriented research assists the researcher in professional preparation, public service, outreach, and organizational change (Shulman, 2010). We will also briefly discuss the place of collaborative research among professionals in different disciplines and its purposeful contribution to the DiP.

The Dissertation

It has been argued that the traditional doctorate is more symbolic than pragmatic and that the need to do research is not driven by a shared research problem or set of problems but instead by the need to maintain the status of the degree (Margolin, 2010). In a similar vein, Shulman (2010) described the dissertation process as a marathon designed to measure whether a candidate has the stamina to stay the course, but not particularly useful for the real work that individuals with doctorates are called upon to do. Because the majority of practitioners pursuing doctoral education are middle-aged, mid-career, and full-time professionals, they have different motivations for returning to school (Costley & Lester, 2012). Motivation is the catalyst for innovation and a "doctoral marathon" as an eight-year independent research project resulting in a "classic monologue-as-dissertation" is not often motivating to the practitioner (Shulman, 2010). Professional practitioners are intrinsically motivated toward action, a desire to improve practice (i.e., policies, procedures, and productivity), and are guided by authentic problems, or noted opportunities for improvements. They thrive when organizational vision and mission is aligned to the research project.

Shulman (2010) encourages colleges to develop professional doctoral degree programs in a more purposeful and efficient way that recognizes the collaborative nature of practice in the field, and meets the needs of practitioners who seek to improve their trade. While Shulman's challenge was addressed to educational leadership professors it has not gone unnoticed by faculty from other domains. This shift in educational research has emboldened universities across the world. Though a gradual shift, through the development of a consensual vision and entrepreneurial leadership, we have witnessed transformations within colleges in miraculously short periods.

There is now evidence that a variety of alternative dissertation models and formats are desirable (Holmes, Seay, & Wilson, 2009), and are being designed and applied that reflect a deep understanding and critical perspective on complex problems from professional fields (Storey & Maughan, 2015). Within alternative formats may be found action research, clinical portfolios of assessments, electronic portfolios, e-books, film and video production, position papers, problem-based investigations, practitioner handbooks, program evaluations, projects designed to address specific client needs, research manuscripts submitted for publication, various types of social media, and white papers (Storey & Maughan, 2015). These alternative formats and the elements that may be found within them will be further discussed below.

Professional Doctorate

"Professional doctorate" is a generic term that covers a wide range and type of doctorates (Willis et al., 2010). The first professional doctorate program is said to have begun in the United Kingdom in 1980. This suggests the doctorate is yet in an embryonic stage in its development (Drake & Heath, 2011). Costley and Lester (2012) differentiate between the occupation-specific professional doctorate and the practice-led professional doctorate. Practice-led professional doctorates are focused on the development of work-based practice. On the other hand, professional doctorates are better described as those with "specific professional boundaries, which may be strongly discipline-based (such as engineering, medicine, psychiatry, and psychology)" (p. 257) and we would argue, education. There are also many similarities between professional doctorates and the practice-led PhD, as found in the arts (QAA, 2011).

Professional practice doctorates, sometimes called clinical doctorates, generally are completed in a shorter period of time than PhDs and do not require original research, but they typically include a clinical component; beyond this, there is little agreement on what they are or should be (Council of Graduate Schools, 2007). In the United States, many of the new professional practice doctoral programs are being offered at institutions that a decade ago had no doctoral studies (Zusman, 2013). As a result, these institutions are necessarily facing significant challenges as they transition into doctoral education. Two key challenges confront the program design model for the final capstone or dissertation.

The first is that doctoral programs must be perceived as both rigorous and relevant, without which they are perceived as weak and less credible. The second is to ensure faculty has the capacity to model scholarly research and practice while at the same time instructing their students in research methods fit for the students' field of practice. This second challenge becomes a key deterrent when the focus of faculty on scholarly pursuits does not coincide with the problem of practice that becomes the focus for the professional practitioner. This dual focus suggests a need for innovation on the image of the doctorate.

The research community defines the epistemologies of research and also controls its image. Image has been traditionally controlled by the methodologies through which it is generated (Choo, 2006). In other words, academe guides the underpinning *nature* of the knowledge that is generated. The way knowledge is generated with professional practitioners is a natural social process, but it takes time for traditional images to change and new conceptions to come to the fore. The traditional view is that theory emerges as a result of scientific research and should define practice. The theoretician, looking through the lens of a particular methodology informed by ideology, was the legitimator of the authentic knowledge (Bauman, 1987) and had a higher status than the practitioner who merely applied it.

With the drive for more practitioner research today, traditional and newer conceptions of research are developing a symbiotic relationship resulting in varied dissertation/capstone models in doctoral programs. Following the tradition of academe, there is a developing realization that a practitioner must have researched and discovered the most recent knowledge about their practice in order to be authentically perceived as an expert practitioner. Researching practice, and problems in practice, is a necessity to which every organization that wishes to have a place in our competitive world must respond. While knowledge generated by a practitioner may not necessarily fulfill the criteria of empirical science, new approaches to research suggest that the field benefits from immediate communication of research outcomes and the opportunity to speedily apply new knowledge, gathering data to measure impact. Such a process not only bridges a research practice divide but provides a signposted path from practice to research to practice. It characterizes a learning society and enables research to become a community activity rather than a discrete activity between a doctoral candidate and a university advisor.

But as doctoral programs begin to design their final capstone what does this mean for their doctoral candidates—the practitioner-scholar?

The Practitioner as a Scholar

During doctoral coursework and research, professional practitioners are not far removed from the methods of career-bound PhD researchers. Practitioners received the scholarly tools necessary to guide deep inquiry into relevant situations where change or improvement is needed. They are trained in the use of theory, various approaches to data gathering methods, and analysis techniques. The difference is that the practitioner, although mentored by a professor from the academe, is uniquely positioned to address problems of practice. The research becomes highly contextualized. With the combination of the academy and situational research, the practitioner is poised to become what may be referred to as a practitioner-scholar. In this case, one primary role of the practitioner is to address problems of practice that are deeply relevant to their background, role, and responsibilities within their settings and where the analysis of data reflects both the conceptual frameworks of the researcher and the related transdiscipline academic literature.

In practice the typical practitioner-scholar working on a doctorate is encouraged to publish in a professional journal. They will have developed the tools for research that produce useful knowledge. This sustainable model of research allows them to continue to inquire about problems of practice long after graduation (Archbald, 2010; Fulton, Kuit, Sanders, & Smith, 2012; Jarvis, 1999a). Because of the pragmatic nature of this kind of research, active practitioners pursuing a graduate degree on a part-time basis are expanding in numbers. They are seeking out practice-based programs that enable them to craft a dissertation that addresses significant and immediate issues found within their field (Finch, 1998).

The design of such a doctoral program is no longer solely the domain of the university professor focusing on theory with the understanding that practice will follow. Instead it is designed in partnership with the profession and because the practitioner-scholar is committed to the well-being of their clients and colleagues as well as academe they learn to balance (1) understandings from within professional practice, (2) higher education practices, and (3) the researcher's individual understanding of themselves in context of their day-to-day activities (Drake & Heath, 2011). Balancing the roles of professional practitioner, practitioner-scholar, and reflective-practitioner calls for innovative approaches to knowledge generation within, not separate from, the professional workforce. It also calls for a way to approach inquiry and a way to represent knowledge generated and actualized (Guthrie, 2009). A practitioner-scholar has the role of mediator and change-agent. They must mediate the demands of both academe and stakeholders in professional practice. At the same time they must present their knowledge in a signature capstone product—the dissertation—in a manner acceptable to both.

However, the student who performs research on-site (in context of their profession) discovers *how* things happen and *what* changes are necessary when things do not go as planned. Both paths to knowledge discovery are critical, so why pursue one path at the expense of the other? We believe that carefully pursuing knowledge within the context of the profession is complementary and critical for the survival of education. For the sake of this chapter, we will discuss the role of the practitioner who seeks to use the tools of the academe to produce generative and actionable knowledge and seeks to understand *what* is happening, *why* it is happening, and *how* it happens and how it can change (i.e., improve) if necessary.

Competing Demands

There is a tension, however, in performing two roles simultaneously, especially when the roles are not recognized. Some practitioners have difficulty gaining a sense of their new identity as a practitioner-scholar and are unable to transfer their newly learned skills to their practice, viewing the scholarly portal they are entering as different from, and separate to, their practice. The identity of a practitioner-scholar is bound up in a complex web that constitutes who they consider themselves to be as a professional. They are connected to social groups (gender, race, generation, ethnicity) and work roles (leader, manager, colleague, client) and each group has a set of goals, values, language, and priorities (Kram, Wasserman, & Yip, 2012). Once they see themselves as researchers in conjunction with being a professional, their own role identity may change and that in turn affects their performance as a practitioner due to their changing lens of perception as a result of the application of a research theory, and increasing self-reflection. As the dual roles begin to merge, conflict may occur, affecting relationships with coworkers, colleagues, and even family (Bouck, 2011). A feeling of isolation characterized by confusion surrounding professional roles and perceptions of coworkers may impact self-esteem and impede the research process if not carefully managed. They begin their process under scrutiny as colleagues and members of the academe question whether practitioner-scholars can realistically distance themselves enough from the problem to provide unbiased, meaningful alternatives to practice.

Traditional standards of research rigor demand that they put aside the attachments to their organizations, the allegiance that years of employment have engendered, and their socialized way of viewing the world through the lens of the organization and adopt a stance of neutrality. Alternatively, it can be argued that one key method for performing academic research in practice, and ensuring honest inquiry, is the need to disclose all biases. Expounding on limitations informs the reader about the perceptions that may bias data gathering and analysis. Thus, the practitioner-researcher's intimate knowledge of their craft including their technical, tacit, and tribal knowledge is identified as a virtue.

Performing dual roles also raises ethical issues in that the practitioners are dealing with colleagues and clients as practitioners. Should they also be using this role to act as researchers (Jarvis, 1999a)? There are times when asking the research questions have been subsumed with issues of practice resulting in the researcher's problem of practice being modified or no longer occurring. While this is obviously a benefit for professional practice it can cause frustration to the scholarly researcher.

Despite intrinsic difficulties the role of the practitioner-scholar benefits the profession.

The Nature of Practice

The theory of practice as practice insists, contrary to positive materialism, that the objects of knowledge are constructed, not passively recorded and, contrary to intellectual idealism, that the principle of this construction is the system of structured, structuring dispositions, the *habitus* which is constituted in practice and is always orientated to practical functions. . . . To do this, one has to situate oneself *within* real activity as such that is in practical relation to the world.

(Bourdieu, 1990, p. 52)

A field of practice is an area of operation or activity, a site at which the occupation is performed (Jarvis, 1999a, p. 28). In the twenty-first century the field of practice is transitory rather than empirical and static. It is possible to see fields of professional practice in terms of both internal structures and external boundaries, and the changes are having their effects on both by blurring boundaries and demanding greater interdisciplinary communication and transdisciplinary knowledge and skills (Davis, 1995; Klein, 2005). Shifts in healthcare, education, and social welfare have meant an adjustment in practice to incorporate new technology, new specialisms, standardization, data-driven decision-making, and public accountability. The fact that practice is a locus of change means that learning and researching practice are essential for practitioners.

Though every practice situation is unique there are reoccurring patterns. Bourdieu (1990) pointed out the importance of being involved with the practice, having an agreed understanding of common vocabulary and a consistent lens for viewing a situation, that it is possible to understand the complexities of every unique situation. It is in this context that the role of the practitioner-scholar is a necessary if practice is to evolve to meet the changing environments.

Dissertation Formats for the Education Doctorate

DiP is the showcase for the impact of the practitioner-scholar's work through dissemination-ready components. Dissertations build from a number of theoretical sources and draw them together in a configuration unique to the particular study since context (macro and micro), role, positionality, and methodology come together in unique ways that form the broader conceptual ecosystem. Insofar as practitioners in any field have traditionally been assumed primarily receivers of knowledge from the university, the movement toward generating knowledge by practitioners represents a constructive disruption of some understandings of the relationships of knowledge and practice, in and out of the university (Cochran-Smith & Lytle, 1999).

To borrow a phrase from Clayton Christensen, leading Harvard scholar on disruption, we might identify the DiP as the disruptive dissertation. Christensen (2008) believes that disruptions in education, and the dissertation is included in education, will "change the way the world learns." He teaches, "Disruption is a positive force. It is the process by which an innovation transforms a market whose services and products are complicated . . . into one where simplicity, convenience, [and] accessibility" (p. 11). Scholars have criticized the dissertation for being too complicated, which makes it problematic for the practitioner (Duke & Beck, 1999; Gross, Alhusen, & Jennings, 2012).

Originally, the purpose of the dissertation was to train young scholars for the professoriate—full-time professor mentoring the next generation of researchers (Willis et al., 2010). While the professor-bound scholar grapples with philosophical dilemmas, the practitioner-scholar addresses complex problems of practice from a field-based perspective. Dissertation formats may change to meet the needs of industry stakeholder, but the practitioner-scholar must continue to exhibit scholarly competence through a variety of available approaches. Inquiry, no matter the selected methodology—action or applied research, translational, program evaluation—may use either qualitative, quantitative, or mixed-method approaches. These scholarly tools do not need to be sacrificed in the name of innovation.

These innovations do not suggest the standard of the dissertation be compromised. Practitioner-scholars must remember doctoral research contributes to the improvement of science and society. A practitioner-scholar contributes by addressing authentic and researchable problems of practice, asking relevant research questions, gathering meaningful data, and proposing timely solutions—the sine qua non of the practitioner-scholar. Practitioner-scholars demonstrate that they have developed habits of mind that help them conceptualize the system within which their research problem is situated in their organization and organize a compelling argument.

Meeting the demands of academe and the preferred format of information sharing from leaders from the workplace invites a disruption in the dissertation formats. For example, computer technologists, engineers, and scientists often receive new information through white papers, trade magazines, or professional journals. Business executives and government leaders value executive summaries or portfolios. Communication or marketing professionals prefer a digital format such as a website. Historians and those in the humanities field might value a documentary or video presentation.

Dissemination

The scholarly role of the practitioner-turned-scholar is to disseminate their information in a way that is respected by both academia and industry. Scholars have long criticized the dissemination strategy of the dissertation (De Jong, Moser, & Hall, 2005; Gross et al., 2012; Robinson & Dracup, 2008). Although it is a public document, it has a very low readership. It is traditionally more accessed by early graduate students learning to format their own dissertations (Duke & Beck, 1999; Reid, 1978). Traditionally, the conclusion of a dissertation offers implications for future research, and, occasionally, implications for practice, but theoretical language, epistemological underpinnings, methods and methodology, and analysis techniques are often complex and uninteresting to the practitioner. It often lacks a clear path to operationalize the new knowledge. A dissertation should not only provide implications for future inquiry, but a strategy to implement new knowledge.

Another criticism of disseminating knowledge from a dissertation is the traditional five-chapter format. Because the original format does not conform to journal publication guidelines, students are required to rewrite (Thomas, 2015). From a survey of 12 institutions in the United States, Thomas, West, and Rich (2015) conclude that most doctoral graduates do not publish in an academic journal. They claim many graduates see little authenticity in their dissertation because of the writing style and academic process.

Many criticisms may be alleviated by the choice of the dissertation format. As part of the process of a working professional to become a practitioner-scholar, she or he must be aware of what is acceptable by their workplace leaders, major professor, and doctoral committee members. This awareness will help them discern the most valuable ways to disseminate the results of their research for the benefit of the industry. Because of the unique blend of theory in context of practice, the practitioner-scholar might publish in academic journals, as well as trade magazines, professional journals, targeted websites, technical papers, or other industry-recognized publications. Other outlets may be considered due to the preferred formats for disseminating new information from each discipline.

Alternative Dissertation Formats

Three-Article Dissertation

The three-article dissertation (TAD) is gaining in popularity among doctoral programs. The TAD has been used in the life sciences since 1968 (Reid, 1978) and is commonly used among engineers, scientists, and many other disciplines. Although the TAD is a relatively new convention for the doctor of education (EdD), it is well established within the science, engineering, and nursing communities. The TAD resolves the concern of meeting the demands and competing interests of decision-making stakeholders and academe. Articles can be independent and may be presented for publication either before or after the dissertation defense. Each article is usually related with regard to topic or theme, but may be the result of inquiry into differing aspects of a single situation. Depending on the needs of the clientele and professors, the articles in the TAD may also be separated into different aspects of a similar issue. They might probe different topics surrounding the issue in question. They might perform different analyses on similar topics.

An example of the TAD addressing separate topics but on a similar issue was in a three-year EdD program at the University of Idaho. Between 2011 and 2014 a doctoral cohort of 23 students were encouraged to complete a TAD. They were invited to work collaboratively during data gathering and analysis stages following the methods of Action Research (Stringer, 2014) and Rapid Assessment Processes (Beebe, 2001). Research teams found that although they came from different disciplines within the educational industry, they shared similar problems within their relative practices. The outcome of their TAD consisted of (1) Chapter 1, introduction, conceptual framework, (2) Chapter 2, independent inquiry into a specific and contextualized problem of practice, (3) Chapter 3, cross-disciplinary article—qualitative meta synthesis, or secondary analysis (Erwin, Brotherson, & Summers, 2011; Zimmer, 2006), of all team members' independent inquiries, (4) Chapter 4, white paper directed toward selected industry stakeholders, and (5) Chapter 5, conclusion, applications for practice, and invitation for continuous inquiry.

Although there are clear benefits, the TAD has also been criticized by scholars. Academia generally requires that scholarly research be embedded within extant literature. Because in a TAD each article generally has its own literature review, methods section, analysis, and conclusion it is assumed that each of these sections will be less rigorous than the traditional five-chapter format. The assumptions are that TADs have shorter literature reviews and lack depth in methods theory. This can be alleviated with the addition of an appendix that offers in-depth information where it is deemed necessary by the major professor and committee (Thomas et al., 2015).

Academe is typically pleased with the likelihood of publication soon after, or before, graduation, which is significantly increased with a TAD format (Thomas et al., 2015). In this case the practitioner-scholar and professor stand to benefit academically and professionally from a published article. The nature of the practitioner-scholar is to continue iterative cycles of research during practice. This provides a structure for continued publication possibilities.

Though the TAD was introduced in 1968 it continues to struggle to gain traction in some research disciplines, particularly in the social sciences. It is clear, however, that the demand for alternative formats is growing (Smith, Sanders, Fulton, & Kuit, 2014). A study by Thomas et al. (2015) found that of the select group of alumni from doctoral programs across the United States, 19% would recommend the traditional five-chapter monograph-as-dissertation to upcoming doctoral students; 81% recommended alternative dissertation formats. While alternative formats are gaining traction, information about each of them is scarce.

Digital Formats

Increasing numbers of universities require students to download dissertations in digital formats. Digitizing allows students to include videos, pictures, three-dimensional maps, flash animation, interactive web links, and recordings. Some digital options used in dissertations at Emory University and Stanford include "infrared scans and geolocation mapping to build interactive maps that tell the history of cities and important events in visually creative ways" (Patton, 2013, n.p.). Consequently, digital formats have the potential to reach a broader population and shape cultural narratives, and have a powerful effect on how the knowledge will be received for the current and future generations. Professional-practitioners using digital formats may enter the metanarrative and discover deeper meanings within a larger social network. Gregory Donovan (2013) of the City University of New York provides an excellent example of a digital dissertation (see: http://mydigitalfootprint.org/dissertation/). Some universities now hire faculty with electronic expertise to hold digital boot camps to train their graduate students (Patton, 2013).

Graphic Arts

Nick Sousanis's (2015) disruptive dissertation defies conventional formats by using graphic art. His manuscript is entirely built of drawings that depict ways humans construct knowledge. This format was accepted by Teacher's College at Columbia University and published by the Harvard University Press (2015).

Executive Summary or Management Consultant Report

The capstone project for the EdD program at the Peabody College of Education at Vanderbilt University is another disruptive dissertation format. This is an independent research project that is performed as a group project (Stevens, 2010). Vanderbilt's Peabody College (2015) "believes the capstone, rather than the traditional dissertation, brings to bear the analytic abilities, professional understanding, contextual knowledge and teamwork skills that are accrued throughout the Ed.D. program, and more closely mirror the challenges of contemporary education practice" (n.p.). A team of doctoral students creates a client-centered capstone project that culminates in a written report for a particular stakeholder (Stevens, 2010). One of the contentions of Vanderbilt's model is that rather than students being embedded in practice, they are invited as external clients to bring problems within which the students have limited familiarity, if any. The final capstone product is "written as a management-consultant format that is consistent with the actual reports that leaders will use in the field of education" (Stevens, 2010). Although there is controversy, it has proven to be a powerful tool to inform practice and affect positive change.

Practitioner-Scholar's Methodology and the Role of Critical Friendship

With appropriate tools of research, the goal of a practitioner-scholar should be to continue to address real-time problems and generate innovations long after the formal process of graduate school ends. Doctoral programs are too often framed in a way that discourages research after graduation unless the graduate continues a career in academia. Original research should impact practice initially, but as time moves forward and new problems arise, the practitioner-scholar will have the tools to address challenging situations with the confidence gained from the graduate research process. Therefore, by the time of graduation, the practitioner-scholar should be fluent with the iterative learning and development cycle. The practitioner should know how to introduce change, test it, learn its weaknesses and strengths, enhance or correct the situation, and with each iteration generate new professional knowledge. This process is a learned skill and, like any skill, requires practice. In a graduate program, it should be developed simultaneously with coursework. In this way graduates foster and hone habits of hearts and hands that continue to lead positive change long after completing their formal doctoral training.

A methodology for a practitioner-scholar should help them develop as skilled artisans of their craft. Practitioners typically enter doctoral programs with skills and habits that are honed because of their work-a-day tasks. As Knowles, Holton, and Swanson (2012) suggest, these adult learners are self-directed and often problem-centric. Naturally, they are self-determined, can readily engage with complexity, and are accustomed to responding to random and unpredictable circumstances (Bhoyrub, Hurley, Neilson, Ramsay, & Smith, 2010). As artisans of their craft, they possess intellectual prowess, cultural competence, and professional know-how and wisdom. The tacit realm of knowledge is a space of mastery where "we can know more than we can tell" (Polanyi, 1966, p. 4). Therefore, the background, knowledge, and skills of a practitioner-scholar must be considered when selecting a research methodology.

Because practitioner-scholars are client-centric and perform research in situ, they are positioned to use a methodology that allows iterative experimentation. A systematic but less restrictive design is recommended for a researcher who is expected to perform specific job functions while conducting research, a design that allows the researcher to collect and analyze data simultaneously. The research process should help the practitioner-scholars combine research techniques with experiential knowledge and deepen their ability to think about problems and search for practical solutions simultaneously. Like an athlete, they adjust to the ball wherever it is kicked, tossed, or thrown. They also adjust to other players on the field or court. A research methodology for the fast-paced executive or the school change-agent must guide them toward timely solutions so they need a methodology that will help them. Methodologies we recommend include action research, rapid assessment processes, and translational research.

In addition, the practitioner-scholar needs to be able to explain current dilemmas, but they also should to do so with complete transparency about their biases. This is done well through the help of critical friends—fellow researchers who bring an "enlightened eye of accumulated wisdom" (Reardon & Shakeshaft, 2013; Storey & Hartwick, 2010) to the "befriended" (Swaffield, 2004, p. 44). A critical friend as defined by Costa and Kallick (1993, p. 50) is a trusted person who asks provocative questions, provides data to be examined through another lens, and offers critique of a person's work as a friend. Consequently, the critical friend can be vital in developing the practitioner-scholar's reflective skills, and in the promotion of generative learning, planning, acting, and sharing.

In a critical friend protocol developed by Storey and Richard (2013), for graduate students a willingness to ask hard questions, learn from differences, and change one's mind is highlighted. It can lead to new learning, and the questioning of established assumptions. Each practitioner-scholar can be encouraged to identify a critical friend during the first semester of a doctoral program. Throughout the process, the applied critical friend protocol (Storey & Richard, 2013) and the critical friend dialog can provide strategies that allow the practitioner-scholar to implement incremental changes as part of day-to-day operations, evaluate those changes, reflect on relationships and systems, and submitted improvements all as a result of supportive dialog and penetrating questions emanating from a trusted critical friend. Such support by the critical friend encourages incremental risks, which inevitably means the practitioner-scholar experiences some failures. But it also means that the critical friend is able to offer support to overcome setbacks, which might be overwhelming when faced alone. After a few iterations of change, the practitioner-scholar is ready to approach stakeholders to implement the larger change with the knowledge that the rate of failure would be significantly lower (Langley, Moen, Nolan, Nolan, Norman, & Provost, 2009).

As we have seen, supported by a critical friend, practitioner-scholars must combine their self-determined and self-directed nature with a mindset that requires the absorption of theoretical and philosophical constructs. Naturalistic inquirers offer methods that may be helpful for the practitioner-scholar in their role as a real-time researcher. Lincoln and Guba (1985) boldly claim that naturalistic inquirers

- perform research in their natural settings—wholes cannot be understood in isolation from their context;
- gather data themselves, because they are capable of grasping and evaluating meaning during data gathering;
- utilize tacit knowledge, because there are tacit interactions between investigators and respondents, and because tacit knowledge mirrors that value patterns of the investigator;
- prefer qualitative methods because these are more adaptable to multiple realities pertaining to circumstances;
- sample purposively in order to gather as much data as is possible;
- analyze data through induction, because this makes interactions explicit, describes settings fully, makes transferability to other settings easier, identifies mutually shaping influences. Values can be an explicit part of the analytic process;
- ground theory in data because no a priori theory could encompass multiple generalizations, and because shaping in a context may be completely explicable in terms of the context;
- allow emergent themes to become known through the research process rather than predicting in advance (learning in the workplace is situation-specific and new forms of knowledge cannot be predicted in advance);

- negotiate meaning through the process, "because it is their constructions of reality that the inquirer seeks to reconstruct";
- report case studies;
- allow concepts to arise from contexts rather than underlying laws or
  rules. Tentatively applies the research from within the context rather
  than overly generalized;
- ensure trustworthiness of the work, which is that it is credible, transferable, dependable, and can be confirmed. (Adapted from Lincoln &
  Guba, 1985, pp. 39–43)

Given the constructs of the naturalistic inquirer we submit that it provides
a helpful framework for the practitioner-scholar to conduct actionable,
transformational, and timely inquiry. Applied research in the form of action
research tends to provide the practitioner-scholar valuable tools that combine their experiential know-how with scholarly research methodologies
(Gutierrez & Vossoughi, 2010). It may assist with the problem-based learning
(PBL) approach, program evaluation, policy analysis, or product development. Applied research may incorporate research traditions such as phenomenology, case study, grounded theory, or ethnography methodologies.

Critical friendships developed in the first semester of the program
highlight the collaborative nature of practice as opposed to the traditional
individualist nature of scholarship. Completing the dissertation monograph is likely to leave students unprepared for the increasingly collaborative scholarly world of the future and for new ventures in collaborative
public scholarship (Smith et al., 2014). Professional activities are developed
based on collaborative exchanges in working and learning communities.
Practitioner-scholars are at the point of immediate contact with authentic
problems. In most work environments, team members will pull together
to create, innovate, design, develop, share, support, and comfort. Given
the speed of change and the need for solutions, it is not a good use of time
to languish in isolation over methods, methodologies, and data analysis.
According to Prewitt (2006), "Building doctoral training around practices
that are interdisciplinary and collaborative is our future" (p. 33). The recent
trend toward collaborative research is redefining and democratizing the
concept of research (Jarvis, 1999b). Educators who teach in varied disciplines such as mathematics, history, English, computer sciences, and more
can perform research in situ. They can bring together fresh perspectives
about both the common and idiosyncratic nature of educational practices
among and within their disciplines. Collaboration in this way may be the
ingredient for practitioner-scholars to sustain their networks and continue
the iterative cycles of research and learning together with their colleagues
long after the formal doctoral research program ends. Such a process provides a signposted path from practice to research to practice.

Become a Practitioner-Scholar

If not careful, we contend that a tight focus on epistemology—what a student knows—and the utility of that knowledge—what is done with what is known—might miss the ontological considerations for what a practitioner-scholar becomes. It may also miss the deep transformations that occur within the student during the research journey. When reviewing the outcomes of six major US universities with students in professional practice doctoral programs we noticed a consistency in expectations for what a practitioner-scholar should become (Storey & Maughan, 2014). When a program is completed a practitioner will prove their scholarship and professional capabilities by

- leading change and affecting positive change;
- innovating new strategies for improved teaching and learning;
- generating independent original professional knowledge that confirms a theory;
- producing generative knowledge;
- proposing further inquiry that builds upon their findings;
- publishing in refereed journals, trade publications, and professional outlets;
- impacting policy;
- improving vision and performance;
- collaborating effectively with other professionals;
- mentoring colleagues and decision-makers while actualizing results;
- analyzing and disseminating reflections on practice;
- framing an educational dilemma;
- demonstrating knowledge with extant theory and literature;
- understanding action plans, logic models, and evidence-based practices;
- articulating complex realities;
- building professional connections and sustaining and nurturing educators' well-being.

The purpose of professional practice doctoral programs as a source of both professional development and knowledge generation should be to help practitioners to reconceptualize their identity as contributing members of society rather than simply a resource of knowledge (Dall'Alba, 2009). The dual nature of the demands from stakeholders from practice and academe clearly symbolizes the research's ability to make strong contributions in both directions.

We propose applied methodologies such as action research, translational research, and rapid assessment processes for the practitioner-scholar because they are useful for both small and large projects. They lend themselves to individual or collaborative research projects. Qualitative, quantitative, or mixed-method research approaches may be used with these methodologies. With the combination of these inquiry approaches and applied research methodologies the practitioner-scholar will break the mold and become a leader of change.

References

Archbald, D. (2010). "Breaking the mold" in the dissertation: Implementing a problem based, decision-oriented thesis project. *Journal of Continuing Higher Education, 58*(2), 99–107.

Bauman, Z. (1987). *Legislators and interpreters*. Cambridge: Polity Press.

Beebe, J. (2001). *Rapid assessment process: An introduction*. Walnut Creek, CA: Rowman & Littlefield.

Bhoyrub, J., Hurley, J., Neilson, G. R., Ramsay, M., & Smith, M. (2010). Heutagogy: An alternative practice based learning approach. *Nurse Education in Practice, 10*, 322–326.

Bouck, B. M. (2011). Scholar-practitioner identity: A liminal perspective. *Scholar Practitioner Quarterly, 5*(2), 201–210.

Bourdieu, P. (1990). *The logic of practice*. Cambridge, UK: Polity Press.

Butlerman-Bos, J. A. (2008). Will a clinical approach make education research more relevant for practice? *Educational Researcher, 37*(7), 412–420.

Cochran-Smith, M., & Lytle, S. L. (1999). The teacher research movement: A decade later. *Educational Researcher, 28*(7), 15–25.

Choo, C. W. (2006). *The knowing organization: How organizations use information to construct meaning, create knowledge, and make decisions* (2nd ed.). New York: Oxford University Press.

Christensen, C., Horn, M. B., & Johnson, C. W. (2008). *Disrupting class: How disruptive innovation will change the way the world learns*. New York: McGraw-Hill.

Costa, A., & Kallick, B. (1993). Through the lens of a critical friend. *Educational Leadership, 51*(2), 49–51.

Costley, C., & Lester, S. (2012). Work-based doctorates: Professional extension at the highest levels. *Studies in Higher Education, 37*(3), 257–269. doi: 10.1080/03075079.2010.503344

Council of Graduate Schools. (2007). *CGS task force report on the professional doctorate*. Washington, DC: Council of Graduate Schools.

Dall'Alba, G. (2009). Learning professional ways of being: Ambiguities of becoming. *Educational Philosophy & Theory, 41*(1), 34–45.

Davis, J. R. (1995). *Interdisciplinary courses and team teaching: New arrangements for learning*. Phoenix, AZ: American Council on Education, Oryx.

Dawson, K., & Kumar, S. (2014). An analysis of professional practice Ed.D. dissertations in educational technology. *TechTrends, 58*(4), 62–72.

De Jong, M. J., Moser, D. K., & Hall, L. A. (2005). The manuscript option dissertation: Multiple perspectives. *Nurse Author & Editor, 15*(3), 7–9.

Donovan, G. T. (2013). *MyDigitalFootprint.ORG: Young people and proprietary ecology of everyday data.* Retrieved from: http://mydigitalfootprint.org/dissertation/.

Drake, P., & Heath, L. (2011). *Practitioner research at doctoral level: Developing coherent research methodologies.* New York: Routledge.

Duke, N. K., & Beck, S. W. (1999). Education should consider alternative formats for the dissertation. *Educational Research, 28*(3), 31–36.

Erwin, E. J., Brotherson, M., & Summers, J. (2011). Understanding qualitative metasynthesis: Issues and opportunities in early childhood intervention research. *Journal of Early Intervention, 33*(3), 186–200.

Finch, B. (1998). Developing the skills for evidence-based practice. *Nurse Education Today, 18*(1), 46–51.

Fulton, J., Kuit, J., Sanders, G., & Smith, P. (2012). The role of the Professional Doctorate in developing professional practice. *Journal of Nursing Management, 20*(1), 130–139.

Gross, D., Alhusen, J., & Jennings, B. M. (2012). Authorship ethics with the dissertation manuscript option. *Research in Nursing & Health, 35*(5), 431–434.

Guthrie, J. W. (2009). The case for a modern doctor of education degree (EdD): Multipurpose education doctorates no longer appropriate. *Peabody Journal of Education, 84*(1), 3–8.

Gutierrez, K. D., & Vossoughi, S. (2010). Lifting off the ground to return anew: Mediated praxis, transformative learning, and social design experiments. *Journal of Teacher Education, 61*(1/2), 100–117.

Hochbein, C., & Perry, J. A. (2013). The role of research in the professional doctorate. *Planning & Changing, 44*(3/4), 181–195.

Holmes, B. D., Seay, A. D., & Wilson, K. N. (2009). Re-envisioning the dissertation stage of doctoral study: Traditional mistakes with non-traditional learners. *Journal of College Teaching and Learning, 6*(8), 9–13.

Jarvis, P. (1999a). *The practitioner-researcher: Developing theory from practice.* San Francisco, CA: Jossey-Bass.

Jarvis, P. (1999b). Global trends in lifelong learning and the response of the universities. *Comparative Education, 35*(2), 249–257. Retrieved from http://search. proquest.com/docview/195149382?accountid=98

Klein, J. T. (2005). Interdisciplinary teamwork: The dynamics of collaboration and integration. In S. J. Derry, C. D. Shunn, & M. A. Gernsbacher (Eds.), *Interdisciplinary collaboration: An emerging cognitive science* (pp. 23–50). Mahwah, NJ: Lawrence Erlbaum Associates.

Knowles, M. S., Holton, E. F., & Swanson, R. A. (2012). *The adult learner: The definitive classic in adult education and human resource development.* Burlington, MA: Elsevier.

Kram, K. E., Wasserman, I. C., & Yip, J. (2012). Metaphors of identity and professional practice: Learning from the scholar–practitioner. *Journal of Applied Behavioral Science, 48*(3), 304–341.

Langley, G. J., Moen, R. D., Nolan, K. M., Nolan, T. W., Norman, C. L., & Provost, L. P. (2009). *The improvement guide: A practical approach to enhancing organizational performance.* San Francisco: Jossey-Bass.

Lincoln, Y. S., & Guba, E. G. (1985). *Naturalistic inquiry.* Newbury Park, CA: Sage.

Margolin, V. (2010). Doctoral education in design: Problems and prospects. *Design Issues, 26*(3), 70–78.

Murphy, J., & Vriesenga, M. (2005). Developing professionally anchored dissertations: Lessons from innovative programs. *School Leadership Review, 1*(1), 33–57. Retrieved from http://www.tcpea.org/slr/2005/murphy.pdf

Patton, S. (2013). The dissertation can no longer be defended. *Chronicles of Higher Education.* Retrieved from: http://ida.lib.uidaho.edu:2282/article/The-Dissertation-Can-No-Longer/137215/

Polanyi, M. (1966). *The tacit dimension.* Chicago, IL: Random House.

Prewitt, K. (2006). Who should do what? Implications for institutional and national leaders. In C. Golde & G. Walker (Eds.), *Envisioning the future of doctoral education* (pp. 23–33). San Francisco: Jossey Bass.

Professional Doctorate in Educational Leadership [ProDEL]. (2012). *Dissertation in practice guidelines* (DP-2.2-Fa12). Duquesne University, Pittsburgh, PA: Author.

QAA. (2011). *Doctoral degree qualifications.* London, UK: QAA.

Reid, W. M. (1978). Will the future generations of biologists write a dissertation? *Bioscience, 28,* 651-654.

Reardon, R. M., & Shakeshaft, C. (2013). Criterion-inspired, emergent design in doctoral education: A critical friend perspective. In V. A. Storey (Ed.), *Redesigning professional education doctorates: Application of critical friendship theory to the EdD* (pp. 177–194). New York, NY: Palgrave Macmillan.

Robinson, S., & Dracup, K. (2008). Innovative options for the doctoral dissertation in nursing. *Nursing Outlook, 56*(4), 174–178.

Shulman, L. S. (2010, April 4). Doctoral education shouldn't be a marathon. *The Chronicle of Higher Education, 56*(30), B9–B12.

Shulman, L. S., Golde, C. M., Bueschel, A. C., & Garabedian, K. J. (2006). Reclaiming education's doctorates: A critique and a proposal. *Educational Researcher, 35*(3), 25–32.

Smith, S. (2014). Beyond the dissertation monograph. Reprinted from the Spring 2010 *MLA Newsletter.* Retrieved from http://www.mla.org/blog&topic=133

Smith, S., Sanders, G., Fulton, J., & Kuit, J. (2014). An alternative approach to the final assessment of professional doctorate candidates. Paper presented at *4th International Conference on Professional Doctorates,* April 10–11, 2014, Cardiff, Wales: United Kingdom Council on Graduate Education.

Sousanis, N. (2015). *Unflattening: A visual-verbal inquiry into learning in many dimensions.* Harvard, MA: Harvard University Press. Retrieved from http://www.hup.harvard.edu/catalog.php?isbn=9780674744431.

Stevens, D. A. (2010). *A comparison of non-traditional capstone experiences in Ed.D. programs at three highly selective private research universities* (Order No. 3418175). Available from ProQuest Dissertations & Theses Full Text: Social Sciences; ProQuest Dissertations & Theses Global: Social Sciences (750445117). Retrieved from http://search.proquest.com/docview/750445117?accountid=9817

Storey, V. A., & Hartwick, P. (2010). Critical friends: Supporting a small, private university face the challenges of crafting an innovative scholar-practitioner doctorate. In G. Jean-Marie & A. H. Normore (Eds.), *Educational leadership preparation: Innovative and interdisciplinary approaches to the EdD and graduate education* (pp. 111–133). New York, NY: Palgrave MacMillan Publishers.

Storey, V. A., & Maughan, B. D. (2014). *Beyond a definition: Designing and specifying Dissertation in Practice (DiP) models.* Pittsburgh, PA: The Carnegie Project on the Education Doctorate. Retrieved from: http://cpedinitiative.org/findings

Storey, V. A., & Richard, B. (2013). Critical friend groups: Moving beyond mentoring. In V. A. Storey (Ed.), *Redesigning professional education doctorates: Application of critical friendship theory to the EdD* (pp. 9–25). New York, NY: Palgrave Macmillan.

Stringer, E. T. (2014). *Action research.* Thousand Oaks, CA: Sage Publications.

Swaffield, S. (2004). Critical friends: Supporting leadership, improving learning. *Improving Schools, 7*(3), 267–278.

Thomas, R. (2015). *The effectiveness of alternative dissertation models in graduate education.* Unpublished master's thesis. Brigham Young University, Provo, UT.

Thomas, R., West, R., & Rich, P. (2015). *The effectiveness of alternative dissertation models in graduate education.* Under Review. Brigham Young University, Provo, UT.

Vanderbilt University Peabody College (2015). Ed.D. Capstone Experience. Retrieved from http://peabody.vanderbilt.edu/departments/lpo/graduate_and_professional_programs/edd/capstone_experience/index.php

Willis, J., Inman, D., & Valenti, R. (2010). *Completing a professional practice dissertation: A guide for doctoral students and faculty.* Charlotte, NC: Information Age Publishing.

Zimmer, L. (2006). Qualitative meta synthesis: A question of dialoguing with texts. *Journal of Advanced Nursing, 53*(3), 311–318.

Zusman, A. (2013). *How new kinds of professional doctorates are changing higher education institutions.* Research & Occasional Paper Series: 8.13. Center for Studies in Higher Education, University of California, Berkeley.

13

Critical Friendship as a Pedagogical Strategy[1]

Joan Smith, Philip Wood, Gareth Lewis, and Hilary Burgess

Critical Friendship and Academic Writing

Academic writing is challenging for many students and academics working in higher education (HE), yet it tends to be something of a "secret activity" (Murray, 2015, p. 2). The processes and practices of writing are not normally discussed or shared, while wanting to talk about writing can even be seen as a weakness (Murray, 2015, p. 2). This chapter provides an overview of a project in which we devised pedagogies to facilitate doctor of education (EdD) students' engagement in peer assessment, and discussions about writing, in order to develop their critical writing and reviewing skills.

As Storey (2013) illustrates, critical friendship theory has usefully informed the development of innovative pedagogies in EdD programs, and has included students acting as critical friends to EdD directors in the development of programs. We sought to engage students in critical friendships with each other, enabling them to develop their critical writing and peer reviewing skills within their own supportive but intellectually rigorous community of postgraduate researchers.

Context for the Study

The University of Leicester's EdD program is a part-time course designed for full-time teachers, school leaders, and other educational professionals. Our students include professional educators mainly from the United

Kingdom, but also from Europe, Canada, Africa, Asia, and the Caribbean. It includes teachers from all phases of education and a variety of educational support and advisory services. The age range of the students is broad, from mid-twenties to mid-fifties, although the majority of our students are mid-career professionals in middle or senior leadership positions.

The EdD program offers students a structured induction into academic research and writing. During the first two years, students complete five formally assessed written assignments, before embarking upon their thesis. Most EdD students undertake practice-based research in the classroom or institution in which they work, resonating with Jones' (2013, p. 155) notion of the students' workplaces as *laboratories of practice*.

The university offers sessions during an initial induction weekend and an annual summer school, which includes the annual Postgraduate Research Conference. The taught sessions and the conference afford students enjoyable opportunities to get to know each other and to discuss their work together. In autumn 2014, a group of year one EdD students set up their own support group. They meet monthly, and their aim is to support each other with assignments. Six of the students who attend the support group participated in this project along with four other students who joined at later stages of the program.

The Issues

A combination of issues led us to identify the focus for the project. First, many doctoral students find it difficult to write critically, and many supervisors find it hard to help students to develop critical writing skills. Criticality is clearly identified in the EdD assessment criteria, yet it is rarely explicitly addressed in our teaching and supervisory pedagogies. While we frequently advise students to be more "critical" in their writing, we do not explicitly define what we mean by "criticality," nor do we clearly identify the steps our students might take to become critical writers. Therefore, we saw a need to be more explicit in addressing criticality, and to develop pedagogical strategies to support and empower students to develop their ability to write critically.

A second challenge for our EdD students can be that of accepting critical feedback on their developing work. Two supervisors, who provide detailed written feedback, assess their five written assignments. In some cases, formative feedback from supervisors had been interpreted as negative and hurtful, resulting in defensiveness, demoralization, and alienation of some students. This led us to a realization that there is a need to be proactive in addressing potential affective barriers to accepting supervisory advice and feedback delivered in a professional manner. Given the importance and centrality of peer review in academic life, we wondered how we might support students to develop both their emotional resilience as researchers, and their capacity to heed and act upon constructive criticism. We realized that the skills and dispositions that positive engagement with critical review requires tend to be assumed, but not explicitly addressed or articulated. We wanted to be proactive in developing researcher resilience, so that engagement with critical review might come to be viewed as an integral and valuable part of the critical writing process. We appreciated that establishing an atmosphere of trust and mutual support would be crucial if we were to engage students in peer assessment as an induction into peer review.

Third is the issue of isolation. While EdD students appreciate being able to attend the schools and the conference, the long gaps in between events can leave them feeling cut off from the doctoral research community. As Jones (2013, p. 147) notes, the experience of writing a thesis "can be isolating when there is no longer the camaraderie felt from being in classes with other students." Once the students return to the workplace, in many cases, their only university contact is through email or Skype tutorials with their lead supervisor. We wanted to find ways to engage students more meaningfully in the academic community and to "cultivate a culture of collaboration among scholars and practitioners" (Hamann & Wunder, 2013, p. 163).

Drawing on Kamler and Thomson's (2006, p. 5) notion of "writing as social practice" and Murray's (2015, p. 1) work on "making writing relational," we devised pedagogical strategies to engage students in peer assessment designed to develop their critical writing skills. In so doing, we sought to foster a sense of belonging and to facilitate students' engagement in critical friendships that would afford them opportunities for mutual support and development in sustainable ways.

Aims and Purposes of the Project

The aims of the project were:

- to develop students' understanding of criticality and their critical writing skills;
- to foster students' engagement in a research community founded on critical friendship;
- to develop students' ability to give, receive, and act upon constructive critical feedback;
- to develop researcher resilience and overcome affective barriers to giving and receiving critical feedback;

- to equip students with the necessary skills to become effective peer reviewers and become inducted into the culture of academic writing.

The Project

The project was launched with an intensive, residential critical writing weekend. All EdD students were emailed and invited to take part, and ten volunteered. The ten included students at all stages of the research journey, although six of the ten were year one students. There were eight women and two men.

Prior to attending the "weekend writing seminar," participants were asked to email us a writing draft that they would like to develop. Each draft was then sent out to two other participants, who were asked to read the working draft and provide constructive feedback to its author. Thus, each participant reviewed the work of two other students and received feedback on their own draft from two other peer reviewers. Reviewers were asked to use the following criteria as a basis for structuring their feedback to the authors:

- clarity of language and expression
- critical engagement with and evaluation of literature, theory, and/ or concepts
- development of argument
- two or three strengths
- two or three points for improvement.

On the first day of the critical writing weekend, all ten students engaged in a formal roundtable discussion, during which they were required to communicate their observations publicly and provide feedback on their colleagues' written draft. While the atmosphere at this stage was a little tense, the mutual feedback was delivered with the utmost professionalism and sensitivity. After the session, students were encouraged to take opportunities during the weekend to redraft their work and engage in further exchanges of mutual review.

On the second day, three workshops were scheduled: "Positive criticality," "Writing clearly and critically," and "Preparing for the editorial board meeting."

In the first workshop, we explored notions of criticality. Aiming to move students away from the idea of criticism as negative and attacking, we suggested that criticality involves not just deconstruction, but communication and synthesis. It involves evaluating and combining ideas in novel ways to offer new insights.

Drawing on the work of Dweck (2006), we discussed the implications of "fixed" and "growth" mindsets, opening up discussion about why students might have a negative and emotional response to feedback, and how they might shift mindset from fear of failure toward a readiness to learn. The capacity to make this shift depends in part on students' ability to distance themselves emotionally from criticism: instead of viewing feedback as a personal attack, adopting a rational perspective on constructive criticism enables them to see it as an evaluation of their work that invokes improvement.

We suggested that thinking develops through writing, and the need to spend time developing ideas, reading, and redrafting was strongly emphasized. One of the researchers shared with students two drafts of a paper he had recently published—the first draft and the final version—and asked them to estimate how many drafts there had been in between. A few ventured suggestions. None came near the actual number: 27. This seemed to be a light-bulb moment for many students as they realized that "even academics" had to work on draft after draft in order to tease out clear narratives and improve the standard of their writing.

The second workshop, "Writing clearly and critically," focused mainly on the use of language, the development of argument, and clarity of communication. In preparation for the workshop we sent students a link to a journal article (Page, 2013) and asked them to read and make notes on the article, identifying as specifically as possible what makes this an effective piece of writing. Students were asked to comment in response to a number of prompts, relating to structure, use of language, use of literature, clarity, use of data and quotes, and ways in which the paper might be improved.

The ensuing group discussion afforded students an opportunity to communicate explicitly their implicit understanding of criticality and effective writing: they were able to articulate and give examples of how Page's work was critical and clearly written. To recap, following on from the discussion of the article, students were asked to "quick-list" the characteristics of effective, critical, academic writing. In so doing, they became conscious of their own knowledge, which they would need to apply to their own developing work.

In a simulated peer feedback exercise, we then shared with students short extracts from two doctoral researchers' developing theses (borrowed from Kamler & Thomson, 2006). We asked workshop participants to work in pairs to read, annotate, and discuss the two extracts to decide what feedback they could provide to each student in order to help improve their work. By engaging in the "safe" discussion of the unknown students' work, participants were able to express freely their evaluation of the drafts, which tended to be phrased in a negative manner in the initial stages. However, the insistence from the tutors moved them toward phrasing feedback in ways that were constructive. This simulation prepared them for the next stage of the workshop, which involved working within the group to engage in mutual feedback, building on the roundtable session on the first day.

The session ended with a plenary in which students were invited to reflect on what they had become aware of in their own writing during the workshop discussions. At this point, students were able to identify concrete and positive ways in which they could seek to improve their own writing, and several reported feeling more confident about how to go about redrafting and improving work. Interestingly, throughout the discussions, no student or researcher referenced a "need" to "plan" writing. It seemed to be taken as a given that the process of writing was complex and organic rather than linear.

In the third session we explained that the challenge for the rest of the weekend was for the ten students to work together in order to establish an editorial board and to devise an online journal, for and by EdD students. While tutors provided some guidance, however, it was made clear that the journal was to be student-led, with tutors acting only in a supportive manner. This approach echoes to an extent that of Hamann and Wunder (2013, p. 165), who used a "complex, critical collegiality building assignment" to enable EdD students to develop critical friendships as a group.

Students were expected to present us their plan for action by lunchtime on the third day. Tutors suggested points to consider, and we then withdrew, and were only available to conduct consultations for the rest of the weekend. The research assistant stayed with the editorial board to observe and note developments.

The board worked late into Saturday evening and all morning on Sunday. There were tense moments. However, roles were allocated, jobs identified, editorial policy agreed upon, and a coherent plan established. By Sunday noon, the students presented us with an impressive plan to develop the journal, entitled *The Bridge*, as it serves to link research and practice. As promised, issue one came out in June 2014 and issue two in January 2015 (please see https://journaleducationalresearchinformed-practice.wordpress.com).

Interviews

Prior to taking part in the weekend writing sessions, students were interviewed about what they understood by "criticality" and what they hoped to gain from their participation in the project. After the weekend the students were reinterviewed to establish what they felt they had learned or gained from their participation.

We draw here on the pre- and post-critical writing weekend interview data to ascertain how participation in the critical writing weekend impacted on students' understanding of criticality and on their dispositions to giving and receiving critical feedback. As a part of this, we consider their perspectives on their experiences of critical friendship.

Initial Findings and Discussion

A comparison of post- with pre-weekend interview data indicates certain shifts in students' thinking. First, participants reported that they had moved from seeing critical feedback as negative, hurtful, and destructive to appreciating that it can be supportive, evaluative, and developmental.

Second, they perceived that their understanding of the notion of criticality and critical writing was considerably enhanced through their engagement with the peer assessment and critical friendship process. For many students, the shift in understanding moved in tandem with a shift in identity, progressing from initial alienation and feelings of inadequacy before the weekend to a growing sense of positive researcher identity afterward. The key difference and the keyword marking the before and after was "confidence."

Third, it was apparent that this dual shift was much more bound up with affect, anxiety, and belonging than we had anticipated. There was strong evidence that learning was enhanced via social aspects of the peer assessment and review experience, and engagement in a community. Critical friendships were established through the peer assessment and review process, and the student journal provided a meaningful basis for sustained engagement in the peer review community.

These three factors in combination allowed sustainable critical friendships to emerge. Changes occurred at the individual level but also at the level of the group, with particular benefits for the EdD support group. The students had established the support group with the desire to form critical friendships. However, in not fully understanding criticality before the project, they had not been able to make the group function quite as intended. As students reflected back on this they were able to understand why it was not as effective as it might be, and how this could now change.

In order to illustrate some of these initial findings, we have included, below, extracts from the interviews of two participants, Ellie and Peter (both pseudonyms). In order to protect their anonymity, minimal biographical details of the two are provided, but both are very experienced educational professionals who hold positions of significant responsibility in their institutions. Both are year one students, and both have been involved in the students' support group since the start of the year.

Shift in Understanding of Critical Feedback

Typically students' pre-weekend interviews reflected a view of critical feedback as damaging and hurtful. They were reluctant therefore to provide critical feedback to others in the group, seeing this as a negative and destructive process. Yet, they were aware that this meant that the students' support group was not as constructive as it might be. Peter, for example, commented,

> I've read some of the other students' stuff . . . but the problem is . . . you don't want to upset anyone. You look at their work . . . but you just say, "Oh, it's good," and . . . we're not really doing anyone any favours there. (Peter, interview one)

The post-weekend interviews reflected a shift in thinking, as participants now framed critical feedback as evaluative and developmental. For example,

> I thought that [the roundtable feedback session] was illuminating . . . I think we were all scared to begin with, but the context in which it was carried out allowed us, I think, to be receptive to listening to constructive . . . critical feedback, and . . . to give it in a constructively critical way . . . [It was] very calm, professional, sitting around a table, "This is what we're going to do," you know? It's just how you have to do it properly and . . . not getting upset because someone said your writing was rubbish, it's about listening to . . . how it could be better. (Ellie, interview two)

Ellie had also felt unsure initially about how she would find the experience of peer reviewing articles for the student journal. However, by drawing parallels with her professional work as a teacher, she was able to construct peer feedback as caring and nurturing, rather than as hurtful and destructive.

> I didn't find [giving critical feedback] as difficult as I thought I was going to find it . . . by the end I thought, "I've got clear things and I know what I've got to say" . . . I used the same principles as I would use marking children's work, you know, "you said this, so for example, where you said such and such a thing, you could add this or that, or you might have referenced such and such a thing, which is really—it struck me actually that it's not a whole lot different from giving [pupils] feedback on you know, cohesion between

paragraphs. The same principle, if you're going to comment on something then you've got to back up your comments and suggestions." (Ellie, interview two)

Students perceived that they had shifted from a pre-weekend unwillingness to hurt others, even though they knew their polite positivity was not helpful to peers' development, to a realization that well-thought out feedback pointed others to recognize the worth of their work and improve it in constructive ways. Their induction into peer review had helped them to understand that "the point is not to tear down, but rather to show how critique can be an iterative vehicle of advance and improvement" (Hamann & Wunder, 2013, p. 169).

Confidence, Criticality, and Developing Researcher Identity

Students perceived that, through their involvement in the critical writing weekend, their understanding of criticality and critical writing had been greatly enhanced. Ellie commented,

> I think beforehand, we'd had a couple of meetings at the library, my little . . . support group, and I'd not really felt able to give anybody any meaningful feedback about their writing, and we didn't know where to start. And it's just having that structure, in a pro-forma that was provided to . . . give the feedback in the beginning, and emailed out before the course started, that just helped to . . . I understood what I was being asked to comment on and how. (Ellie, interview two)

Like Ellie, Peter reported feeling that he had gained a better understanding of criticality through his experiences at the critical writing weekend, and moreover that this would improve the quality of mutual feedback at the students' support group meetings:

> We're all going to be meeting up again in about a week or so—we tend to, as a group, before the assignment, and that's one of the first times we've met up having done [the critical writing weekend] . . . we always read through each other's work, so that is going to be really interesting. But yeah, I think what we're able to do . . . what I'm able to do now is be, you know, really critical. I can be critical with people. (Peter, interview two)

Shifts in understanding of criticality, critical writing, and critical feedback seemed to be accompanied by important shifts in identity. Students typically moved from feelings of inadequacy, lack of confidence, and, in some cases, alienation before the weekend to a more confident, positive researcher identity thereafter. Ellie's lack of self-belief as an academic was evident in her first interview:

> I've found [critical reading and writing] very, very difficult, particularly, for both assignments, the literature review, because I find it very difficult to be critical about something I am reading. To disagree with something I am reading, in that critical sense: "That sounds so incredibly academic and difficult to read and therefore it must be right!" So that, I have found that hard . . . this incredibly clever person has done this research into this particular topic and has found this and has drawn these conclusions. Who am I to disagree with that? Because I don't have any experience . . . [and I] haven't done my own research in order to be able to do it. And you can't really formulate an opinion about something you didn't have an opinion about in the first place until you've read enough. You have to build up, I feel, a breadth of reading to then start thinking, "Ah, now I know what I think about that because I have read him, him and him." (Ellie, interview one)

Ellie had experienced a sense of alienation as a result of the frustration of tackling academic reading:

> One of the first books I read for my second assignment was a book that was just completed last year about complexity theory. Oh my word! I spent about three hours reading five pages, because I had to keep stopping and looking up every other word in the dictionary. Eventually I started to feel quite cross. To start off with, I was quite intimidated by that—"Oh I'm just not clever enough for this" . . . Part of me feels exasperated with academic writing. (Ellie, interview one)

Peter's first interview was also characterized by his self-doubt and lack of confidence:

> When I sit down at the table with our peers, really, I'm probably the least confident of anyone there, you know, because I'm not always that confident in my ability . . . In the past I've worked on group stuff before and I haven't really contributed that well, because I haven't felt . . . everyone's seemed to understand what's going on except me . . . it's always in the . . . back of my head really . . . when I read my work and read . . . others' in the group . . . peers', sometimes I feel mine is just too simplistic . . . I tend to use straightforward words, let's say non-academic words . . . that's something that I know I need to get away from. (Peter, interview one)

However, by the second interview, both Peter and Ellie, like most other students, talked about their increased confidence as well as their improved understanding.

I felt much more confident by the end of the weekend. I understood what critical writing looked and felt like. (Ellie, interview two)

You know, when I look back on [the critical writing weekend] now, I thoroughly enjoyed it and I got a lot of things out of it, and the thing is, like I mentioned ... before, ... to me it's a confidence thing, and towards the end of it I certainly felt a bit more confident in me, about my own ability. (Peter, interview two)

Data from the second interviews seemed to indicate that students were moving from initial feelings of inadequacy and alienation to a more positive identity as capable, confident researchers, and academic writers. Students' self-perceptions had altered since the start of the project: they considered that their understanding of criticality had been enhanced and thus their confidence in their ability to read, write, and think were critically improved.

Learning Enhanced by Social Aspects of Engagement

Students perceived that their understanding of criticality and critical writing had improved through their involvement in the weekend and subsequent peer review activities. However, it was also clear that students already had some understanding of the notion of criticality, and were already challenging themselves to ensure criticality in their writing prior to the preweekend interviews, for example:

I do a lot of writing in the context of my work. But [critical writing is] ... a different discipline altogether ... because you can't be too descriptive. You can't be passionately committed to something ... So you have to suggest that things *might* be the case, based on evidence and research ... You just can't express an opinion, really, without backing it up ... It's a bit like critical appreciation of poetry. You're not criticizing the poetry. You're analysing it and thinking about its meaning and what relevance the words have on the point you decided to choose. So, it's not about being negative ... it's analytical. OK, it's a bit like playing devil's advocate isn't it? ... thinking about a particular point of view from different perspectives. (Ellie, interview one)

This suggests that the more significant shift was not in the students' understanding of criticality per se, but in their confidence and perceptions of being capable of criticality. This change appeared to result from their engagement in peer assessment and review. This suggests that students' learning was enhanced through the social aspects of critical friendship, and belonging to a research community in which they were able to play a meaningful role. Feeling a sense of belonging was an important factor in students' positive perceptions of the weekend:

> I think it was really great. Really enjoyed that, really enjoyed meeting [all the other participants] . . . they're all just such lovely people and . . . I think it helps that we're all distance learners, even people like me who live nearby. Everyone's all scattered to the four winds that it, it just gives you a feeling of belonging to somebody, that you don't get as the kind of student we are. (Ellie, interview two)

Importantly, this sense of belonging entailed sustainable relationships based on trust, which were prerequisites for critical friendship and peer review. Peter perceived that the quality of mutual review in the students' support group would be much improved as a result of the activities undertaken and the relationships established during the writing weekend:

> Most of the people [from the support group] were [at the critical writing weekend] . . . and we do meet up, we talk about the assignment normally, we normally make comments about what the supervisor has said to try, and give guidance to other people and then we always try and read each other's. But before it was a case of reading it and you might say, "Oh yeah that's good . . . maybe a couple of grammatical mistakes"—you wouldn't go too deep. Whereas I think now we don't mind stepping that little bit further, you know what I mean? And I think . . . two or three meetings' time, I think we'll be quite OK with it. It is just being prepared to . . . let's say there's something bad in what you've done, and they're really going to point these things out then, you know, you want to have that little bit of a bond . . . you want a reasonably good bond with them. (Peter, interview two)

It is evident from Peter's comments that he sees a qualitative difference between how the students' own support group had been operating up until the critical writing weekend, and how it would function thereafter. Before the weekend, the group had been providing what Murray (2015, p. 3) describes as relief or camaraderie, as in "It's good to know we are all in the same boat." However, participation in the critical writing weekend enabled the group to move from camaraderie to critical friendship. There is a fundamental difference between the two in terms of the nature of the mutual support. A critical friend offers "both intellectual and moral support" (Miller, 2013, p. xv), providing "constructive critique through a mix of both support and challenge" (Storey, 2013, p. 1). It was interesting to observe that the student group had been offering moral support but not challenge, and the students perceived that this had meant it had been relatively ineffective in offering the intellectual support necessary for students to develop their writing. An important shift occurred after the weekend. The foundations for critical friendships had been laid, enabling the group to be more strategic and rigorous, with each member assuming the role of critical friend in ways that resonate with Miller's (2013, p. xv) definition, as

a trusted colleague who provides objective feedback, identifies challenges and opportunities, and raises more questions—questions that should strengthen what one proposes to do or sharpen one's thinking.

Through their experiences of peer assessment during the critical writing weekend, the students had become aware of the need to move beyond providing emotional support for each other, and to use their conversations as an academic community to develop members' writing skills. The relationships established at the critical writing weekend provided ongoing formal and informal reasons for the community of students to come together, including the following: (1) editorial board meetings, (2) support group meetings, and (3) informal contacts among the group. While the establishment of the journal provided a basis for students' ongoing meaningful engagement in peer review, the added benefit for the year one students was that the practices and relationships in the group they had already set up, themselves were enhanced and given direction as a result of the participation of several members in the critical writing weekend. This would shift the group toward a more rigorous focus on writing, to the long-term benefit of its members. This was in a sense an unexpected outcome of the project. Encouragingly, it was consistent with the principles of self-sustaining, autonomous critical friendships, and resonant with the experiences of students in Hamann and Wunder's (2013, p. 170) study, who found that "the collegiality and related accountability to peers had helped them persevere and persist."

Summary, Conclusions, and Recommendations for Program Design: EdD and Beyond

We embarked upon this project with a will to engage students meaningfully in a community of scholars that would afford them opportunities to engage in mutual support and review, in order to develop their critical writing skills. From the interview data collected before and after the critical writing weekend, it is apparent that there have been clear benefits for students. Affective barriers to giving and receiving critical feedback have been significantly reduced by engaging students in peer assessment processes founded on the principles of critical friendship. Students' learning and their confidence in themselves as researchers, reviewers, and critical writers appear to have been enhanced through the social aspects of the peer assessment and review process. Importantly, formal and informal opportunities for the students to come together in the spirit of critical friendship seem likely to endure beyond the life of the project, with the journal *The Bridge* providing a useful basis for their sustained, meaningful engagement in the postgraduate research community. This is in addition to the now more strategic and critical student support group. This leads us to conclude that the empowerment of EdD students through self-sustaining, critical friendships is too important to leave to chance, and should form an integral part of our programs and pedagogy.

Based on this research, we would like to make two key recommendations for the design of professional practice doctorates. The first is that it is imperative that programs are consistent in explicitly addressing notions of criticality and critical friendship. The second is that programs should schedule formal and informal opportunities for students to engage in peer assessment and review, and to discuss the practices and processes of academic writing.

Notions of criticality and critical friendship need to be explored and discussed with students from an early stage. Program designers need to be strategic in building into their courses points at which these ideas can be revisited, on a spiral curriculum basis, throughout the program. This will support students in developing a deeper understanding over time and enable them to apply their developing understanding to their own and others' work.

The difference between camaraderie and critical friendship needs to be clearly articulated and exemplified, as a shared understanding of this cannot be assumed. This research has indicated that criticality can be re-conceptualized as caring work and as a part of the collective responsibility of a community of researchers. Useful parallels can be drawn between students' responsibilities as teachers who provide helpful feedback to pupils, and their responsibility to each other as postgraduate students and critical friends.

Students need to be enabled to experience critical friendship in order to appreciate how this works and to manage their own working relationships as researchers. Program leaders should therefore plan formal and informal opportunities, face-to-face and online, for students to engage in dialog. It may be helpful to adopt a blended learning approach, which might include pre- and post-workshop readings and tasks, online activities, taught sessions, and peer-assessed work as part of the formal program. For example, a date might be calendared by which paired students are to exchange draft assignments and provide mutual feedback, to inform a redraft ahead of formal submission. In this way, peer feedback provides students with a stepping-stone toward the formal assignment, while drafting and redrafting become a part of the normal process of writing.

Program leaders might consider scheduling a succession of events (e.g., student conferences, residential courses, writing retreats, and so on) at which students can come together. These might usefully be supplemented by online fora. In order to secure students' engagement and a sense of meaningful involvement, a concrete purpose is required. For example, the students might be engaged in a collaborative writing project leading to a joint publication (see Hamann & Wunder, 2013), or the setting up of an editorial board of a student journal, as in this project. The aim is to set challenges and to provide a basis for engagement in a postgraduate community that is supported by academics, but led by students. Practical considerations include the need to provide readily available physical and online spaces in which students can meet and organize autonomously. For example, in an earlier project on peer assessment (see Burgess, Smith, Wood, & Scalise, 2014), we engaged students in constructing research posters, which they displayed in an online gallery, serving as a virtual conference venue. Each student gave and received critical feedback on the posters, and then further developed their own poster, presenting it face-to-face at the postgraduate conference in the summer term.

Finally, we would recommend that the process of inducting students into critical writing, critical friendship, and peer review should start at the master's level. We are currently engaged in another pedagogical project focusing on innovative approaches to teaching research methodology to a group of international students following the MA in international education (MAIE) program at the University of Leicester. We have moved away from a model in which students attended research methods classes for two hours per week, to a series of blocks of time of between one and three days, during which students were engaged intensively in considering philosophical underpinnings of research, as well as the practicalities of undertaking field work as a lone researcher. A key part of the experience for students is their engagement in mutual critique of research design. At the time of writing, the students are not quite half way through the year and have just taken part in a mini-conference in which they presented orally or in poster format a research design for a proposed project. Questioning by and conversation with peers was rigorous and challenging and, interestingly, seemingly unhindered by the traditions of polite understatement we encountered with those (mainly UK nationals) involved in the EdD project described in this chapter. As the MAIE program includes Chinese, Vietnamese, American, Nigerian, Kazakhstani, Saudi Arabian, and Kurdish students, this raises some interesting questions about possible cultural influences on students' dispositions to criticality, and would provide a useful focus for further research.

Engagement in critical friendship can significantly enhance students' learning and experience of postgraduate study, building researcher expertise and resilience. As we have shown in this chapter, this has been an important development in the EdD program. We are now moving beyond the EdD, shifting our focus to master's level (arguably a somewhat neglected area in pedagogical research), in order to deepen students' understanding and provide them with a strong basis for doctoral research.

Note

1. Project funded by the UK Higher Education Academy Social Sciences strategic priorities teaching research methods in the social sciences.
   We are grateful to University of Leicester (UK) for permitting study leave time to enable this work to be completed.

References

Burgess, H., Smith, J., Wood, P., & Scalise, M. (2014). *Developing peer assessment in postgraduate research methods training.* York: HEA.

Dweck, C. (2006). *Mindset: The new psychology of success.* New York, NY: Random House.

Hamann, E., & Wunder, S. (2013). Using a cohort approach to convert EdD students into critical friends. In V. A. Storey (Ed.), *Redesigning professional education doctorates: Applications of critical friendship theory to the EdD* (pp. 161–176). New York, NY: Palgrave Macmillan.

Jones, S. J. (2013). Critical friends groups and their role in the redefinition of the online EdD in Higher Education administration at Texas Tech University. In V. A. Storey (Ed.), *Redesigning professional education doctorates: Applications of critical friendship theory to the EdD* (pp. 145–159). New York, NY: Palgrave Macmillan.

Kamler, B., & Thomson, P. (2006). *Helping doctoral students write: Pedagogies for supervision.* Abingdon: Routledge.

Miller, F. (2013). Foreword. In V. A. Storey (Ed.), *Redesigning professional education doctorates: Applications of critical friendship theory to the EdD* (pp. xiii–xvi). New York, NY: Palgrave Macmillan.

Murray, R. (2015). *Writing in social spaces: A social processes approach to academic writing.* London: Routledge.

Page, D. (2013). The recruitment and transition of construction lecturers in Further Education: The perspective of middle managers. *Educational Management Administration and Leadership, 41*(6), 819–836.

Storey, V. A. (Ed.). (2013). *Redesigning professional education doctorates: Applications of critical friendship theory to the EdD.* New York, NY: Palgrave Macmillan.

14

Indigenizing the EdD in New Zealand: Te Puna Wānanga EdD

Jenny Bol Jun Lee

Introduction

In New Zealand the doctor of education (EdD) is not a new pathway for doctoral study. Currently the EdD is offered at four of the eight universities in New Zealand.[1] Whereas the other EdD programs are "mainstream" or generic, the EdD at Te Puna Wānanga (School of Māori Education; TPW), Faculty of Education, at the University of Auckland, pioneers a new space—a Māori and Indigenous-focused EdD program. Launched in March 2014, the inaugural TPW EdD increased the number of Māori doctoral students in our school fivefold, and nearly doubled the number of Māori students enrolled in an EdD nationally.[2] The TPW EdD is one of the most significant initiatives to support Māori doctoral growth and development to date at the University of Auckland.

While Māori specific pathways are not uncommon in the New Zealand educational landscape, the development of the TPW EdD has not necessarily been easy or straightforward. Māori-led educational initiatives have usually been in response to the overt assimilationist aims of education since Western-style schooling was established in New Zealand nearly 200 years ago. The colonization of Māori people was to be achieved through the "civilizing" mission of schooling (Simon & Smith, 2001) that served to privilege Western knowledge while denigrating Māori language, culture, and knowledge. The TPW EdD continues in the tradition of Māori educational initiatives that push back against the continued assimilative nature of schooling and new forms of colonization that have become normalized within our educational discourses and institutions. Subsequently, seeking to indigenize the EdD in New Zealand is part of a larger social, cultural, and political imperative driven by kaupapa Māori, a local Indigenous theoretical framework. In this chapter, I introduce the newly established TPW EdD in relation to the theoretical positioning of kaupapa Māori. I also locate this program within the dominant discourse and emphasis on "diversity" in New Zealand education and in the international arena.

Through a developing critical friend network (institutional membership of the Carnegie Project on the Education Doctorate, 2014) we have accrued benefits for both program design and for faculty teaching in the program. Although the University of Auckland's EdD is in many ways still considered in the margins in New Zealand, we have been able to find a "space" to connect with others involved and interested in the EdD for, with, and by Indigenous and marginalized minority groups. These relationships will be critical for the credibility and sustainability of EdD programs such as ours. In the spirit of a "critical friend" approach, a critique of diversity not only assists to better explain the "indigenizing" nature and aim of the TPW EdD, but also seeks to contribute to understanding the EdD "space" from an Indigenous lens.

Background

Like other Indigenous peoples who continue to suffer in the ongoing aftermath of colonization, Māori are overrepresented in New Zealand in most of the negative statistical indices measuring health and social well-being, including education. *Report on New Zealand Student Engagement* (Ministry of Education, 2005) provides a depressing but relatively accurate picture of Māori in mainstream schooling, which has changed little today. This Ministry of Education (2005) report examined data on school rolls, school leavers, disciplinary events such as stand-downs and suspension, early leaving exemptions, and attendance and absence. Based on these sets of information the report found Māori (alongside Pasifika and those from low socioeconomic backgrounds) are least engaged in schools. Māori continue to have the highest rates of suspensions[3] and stand-downs.[4] In 2006 the suspension rate for Māori students was 15.6 students per 1000, 1.4 times as high as Pasifika students and 3.8 times as high as Pākehā (White New Zealanders) students. Similarly, the stand-down rate of 59.8 students per 1000 was 1.3 times as high as Pasifika students and 2.7 times as high as Pākehā students (Ministry of Education, 2007). Measures of school leavers without qualifications show that only 42.7% of year 11 Māori students gained the literacy and numeracy requirements for National Certificate in Educational Achievement (NCEA) Level 1, as compared to 64.9% of non-Māori students who gained the same qualification in 2006 NCEA results (Ministry of Education, 2007a, p. 158). Māori are also overrepresented in the "as learners with special education" needs (Bevan-Brown & Bevan-Brown, 2001) and those students experiencing learning and behavior difficulties at school (Macfarlane, 2003). While the number of Māori participating in tertiary education has increased, both the retention and completion rates for Māori students were lower than for non-Māori in Bachelor degrees and higher qualifications (Ministry of Education, 2005a).

Despite the role schooling has played in the colonization process, and the persistence of the overwhelming negative statistics that have become a common hallmark to describe the crisis in Māori education, Māori learners, their parents, and whānau (extended families) continue to have high aspirations in education (Hutchings et al., 2012). Widely accepted and adopted as Māori educational aspirations today, Mason Durie (2001) articulates three key Māori educational goals. He says,

Although education has a number of other goals including enlightenment and learning for the sake of learning, three particular goals have been highlighted as relevant to Māori: enabling Māori to live as Māori, facilitating participation as citizens of the world, contributing towards good health and a high standard of living. (pp. 4–5)

The ability to attain a doctoral degree, regarded as the pinnacle of academic achievement, can be viewed as part of Māori educational aspirations, but not as an end in itself. To many Māori, the doctorate is not just viewed as an individual achievement, but one that belongs to the extended family, the tribe, and the community in order to facilitate transformational change to enable Māori "to live as Māori."

Māori doctoral aspirations are evidenced by the increased number of Māori doctoral enrolments in the last 20 years, from 77 in 1994, to 450 in 2012 (Ministry of Education, 2012a). Māori doctoral completions have also risen consistently in the last decade; the average number of Māori doctoral completions in the last seven years (2006–2013) was 41 students per year (Ministry of Education, 2012b).[5] Though the acquisition of a doctoral qualification is still highly celebrated, very few Māori achieve a doctoral degree. Despite the marked increase in Māori doctoral enrolments, the 2013 New Zealand Census data indicates that the national percentage of Māori with doctorates remains small at 1.8% (Statistics New Zealand, 2013).

Only a small amount of research literature pertaining to Māori doctoral students currently exists, and this literature is dominated by the challenges and complexities faced by Māori students and/or their supervisors in doctoral study. Although it is difficult to calculate Māori doctoral achievement rates (due to nature of doctoral study), Māori doctoral completion numbers indicate a high rate of attrition (Ministry of Education, 2012b). Lack of support and a sense of isolation are cited as key factors contributing to noncompletion of Māori doctoral students (Smith, 2007). It was also found that Māori students felt that they had to compromise their cultural integrity to pursue doctoral study (Kidman, 2007). Hohepa (2010) adds that "first generation" Māori doctoral students (which most Māori students are) also face difficulties trying to integrate academic expectations into their daily lives as whānau (Grant & McKinley, 2011).

McKinley, Grant, Middleton, Irwin, and Williams (2009) conducted the largest and most systematic study of Māori doctoral students to date, whereby they investigated the practice of supervision, including how to support better outcomes for students and their institutions. The study involved interviewing 38 Māori doctoral students and experienced Māori (11) and non-Māori (9) supervisors. The study identified some key characteristics of Māori doctoral students. In brief, these are:

- Māori students' studies are motivated by the desire to make a difference to their iwi and communities.
- Māori students often had a "mātauranga Māori" (Māori knowledge) dimension to their work, and experienced tensions between Māori and Western epistemologies.
- Māori methodologies such as kaupapa Māori (including spirituality) were often employed in Māori students' doctoral work.
- Students were strategic in selecting their supervisors, there was a variety of supervision arrangements, and changes in supervision were common.
- Cultural advice and support from Māori supervisors and/or advisors was important to Māori doctoral students.
- The opportunity to study at doctoral level enabled some students to develop their identity as Māori, as well as their identity as a scholar.

In sum, McKinley, Grant, Middleton, Irwin, and Williams (2011) point out that Māori doctoral students intent on maintaining and/or strengthening their cultural identity as Māori are likely to experience tension and conflict centered on "the production, ownership and use of knowledge" (p. 1). The research literature indicates a range of social, cultural, structural, economic, and political challenges for Māori doctoral students.

It is in the context of Māori educational aspirations, as well as the reality of Māori experiences of the educational organizations shared by Māori doctoral students, that this EdD has purposefully been developed by TPW. The increased enthusiasm of Māori to participate in doctoral study, as well as the widespread challenges faced by Māori students at this level resulting in small numbers of graduates, has seen various initiatives to increase completion rates and improve Māori doctoral students' experiences. Usually each university will have its own Māori educational strategy to improve Māori achievement, including at postgraduate level. The TPW EdD did not emerge in a vacuum—it is important to note that the TPW EdD pathway is only one Māori-led initiative emerging at one higher education institution.

Te Puna Wānanga EdD

It can be argued that the forerunner to the TPW EdD was the Māori and Indigenous doctoral cohort began by Professors Linda Smith and Graham Smith at the University of Auckland in the early 1990s. As an early member of this small group mainly consisting of Māori PhD students, I usually met the others once a month in the evenings and over weekends. A consequence of our frequent meetings was the growth of trust (Storey & Richard, 2013) and the development of a critical friend group. We shared our research, our doctoral journey stories, our aspirations, and in return received critical and constructive feedback of our work. The early Māori and Indigenous group has now become Te Kupenga o MAI (Māori and Indigenous Postgraduate Advancement National Network) funded and organized by Ngā Pae o te Māramatanga (New Zealand's Māori Centre of Research Excellence).[6] Since 2002, Te Kupenga o MAI has been a key player in raising the profile, growth, and success of Māori doctoral students nationally. Māori and Indigenous continues to feature a critical friends group network that supports and mentors cohorts of students mainly enrolled in PhD programs within and across institutions. In 2012, I was appointed the academic director of MAI ki Tāmaki (MAI program at the University of Auckland), after the program had lapsed for two years. Today, MAI ki Tāmaki hosts regular monthly workshops usually related to assisting students with academic skills, and/or featuring guest speakers. Māori and Indigenous also offers week-long writing retreats supported by experienced Māori academics who bring the group together for academic activities.

The other driver for the establishment of the TPW EdD was the opportunity I had as head of school of TPW, and therefore the senior leadership position I held within the Faculty of Education. Our School primarily centers on Māori education, which includes teaching at undergraduate, postgraduate, and doctoral level. TPW also features a Māori-medium pathway in primary teacher education, and Māori-medium foundation program, and large professional learning development (PLD) team (in-service providers and advisors to schools). When I was appointed in 2012, a key part of my work was focused on growing and supporting Māori postgraduate, in particular doctoral students, in our school and faculty. I took a lead in the initiatives to redress the need for increased support of Māori doctoral students, these included the relaunching and leading of the MAI ki Tāmaki program (August 2012);[7] the establishment of regular monthly TPW postgraduate workshops (May 2012); the organization of The University of Auckland's inaugural Māori doctoral dinner (December 2013); undertaking a small internally funded research project to investigate "Advancing a Māori doctoral cohort (MAI ki Tāmaki) through exploring a kaupapa Māori approach to learning technologies."[8] It was these projects that led us to embark on the most ambitious initiative in 2014, a new doctoral space for Māori students—the TPW EdD program.

The opportunity to offer a new EdD was unexpected, and the timeframe to organize and market the TPW was short. Working with Professor May, a non-Māori colleague in TPW and Deputy Dean of the Faculty, we began to develop, recruit, and enroll students all in a six-month time period to begin March 2014. We designed and promoted the TPW EdD for people working in Māori and Indigenous education and social policy contexts, especially those interested and involved in leading change for Māori and Indigenous communities. The response from Māori and other students was encouraging; many showed interest in joining a cohort of this nature. In the past few years, previous EdD cohorts had only attracted an intake of four or five students, so it was a significant turning point for the faculty to enroll 12 students (10 of whom are Māori) to the TPW EdD.

The program itself does not differ in its structure to the faculty's EdD. In brief, the EdD program comprises two parts. Part one is a part-time two-year program whereby the students are expected to produce a research portfolio consisting of four supervised research projects. These are: a critical literature review, a methodology project, a paper for publication, and a detailed proposal. Part two may be undertaken part-time or full-time to complete the thesis.[9] Throughout the year students attend four two-day workshops, which, as the program's co-leaders, Professor May and I mostly teach. In addition to the conventional faculty EdD, the TPW EdD has also structured into the program two optional writing retreats, and additional support workshops for assignment and abstract writing. While the program is primarily delivered face-to-face, the e-learning component encompasses engagement through regular facilitated discussion forums, planned Skype meetings with lecturers and supervisors, and one-to-one online feedback.

The TPW EdD program not only makes a huge impact on Māori doctoral numbers increasing the Māori doctoral in our School fivefold, but shifts the focus from the "supervision" of an individual Māori student to the pedagogical aspects of a cohort-based approach to doctoral study. Given the previously mentioned challenges identified in the research for Māori doctoral students, a cohort approach has the potential to better address feelings of isolation and navigate the cultural processes of the institutions and expectations of the academy. In the development of the TPW EdD we were acutely aware that, as Shulman (2005) points out, the EdD must utilize pedagogies that not only measure up to the standards of the academy, but to the professions in which the students work. However, the TPW EdD as an Indigenous focused program has an added challenge: the pedagogies must have a cultural integrity that enables Māori to think, perform, and act, or in Durie's (2001) words "to live" as Māori. Therefore the TPW EdD does not merely focus on Māori and Indigenous content, nor is it merely a grouping of Māori and Indigenous students. Rather the TPW EdD seeks to make transformative change with, for, and by Māori and Indigenous people by utilizing a "culturally located pedagogy" (Hohepa, 2010)—in this program this requires a kaupapa Māori approach.

Kaupapa Māori

Kaupapa Māori has been used by academics to refer to Māori theoretical positioning (Jenkins, 2000; Pihama, 2001; G. H. Smith, 1997; L. T. Smith, 1999) and research philosophy (Bishop, 2005; Mead, 1997; Pihama, Cram, & Walker, 2002; L. T. Smith, 2005). The word "kaupapa" refers to philosophies or a foundation (Pihama, 2001). Smith (2006) proposes that kaupapa Māori is a social project; it often refers to activities, events, or endeavors in which Māori (people, language, culture, and/or issues) are at the "center." Explicitly locating the TPW EdD as a kaupapa Māori initiative assumes a program in which Māori cultural values, beliefs, and practices are largely the "norm." To understand that Māori are at the center of an initiative such as this also presupposes a political edge—in our case, a level of Māori leadership and control. While the students or university itself may not identify the TPW EdD as political, asserting Māori control, practicing and valuing Māori language, culture, and customs is not a neutral act.

Guided by kaupapa Māori, the TPW EdD creates a "space" for mātauranga Māori to be explored, sustained, and developed. Kaupapa Māori promotes the validity of Māori epistemological and ontological constructions of the world based on the "taken for granted" position of Māori language, knowledge, and culture (Pihama, 2012; G. H. Smith, 1997). According to Tuakana Nepe (1991), kaupapa Māori originally derives from a metaphysical realm that takes shape as a body of knowledge. She says, "This kaupapa Māori knowledge is the systematic organization of beliefs, experiences, understandings, and interpretations of the interactions of Māori people upon Māori people, and Māori people upon their world" (p. 4). Kaupapa Māori has always been integral to the development of Māori ways of conceptualizing, interacting, and theorizing in our own environment (Royal, 2002). The TPW EdD undertakes to continue in this tradition.

The naming of kaupapa Māori as theory coincides with the Māori-driven educational practice in our communities such as Kōhanga Reo (Early childhood Māori language nests) and Kura Kaupapa Māori (Māori immersion primary schools). Kura Kaupapa Māori (KKM) is a well-known and often-cited kaupapa Māori social change initiative. KKM are total immersion Māori language primary schools that are based on Māori philosophies, pedagogies, and practices. In the mid-1980s there was an overwhelming disillusionment and mistrust felt by Māori parents toward the education system. Poor achievement outcomes and the denigration of Māori language and culture were common experiences. This resulted in groups of Māori parents withdrawing their children from state schools to begin an alternative Māori-centered school. G. H. Smith (2000) describes the establishment of KKM outside of the state system without government funding, resources, or support as an anticolonial resistance initiative that was both positive and proactive. The exercise of tino rangatiratanga (absolute self-determination) was seen as a key element in the popularity and growth of KKM among Māori communities, in a desire to address the dual crisis of educational underachievement and language loss (G. H. Smith, 1997). Through the assertion of KKM, Māori were able to determine the overall culture of the school—curriculum, pedagogy, assessment, administration, governance and daily routines, and expectations.[10]

While there are many articulations of kaupapa Māori (including theory, research, and practice) within whānau (extended family), hapū (subtribe), iwi (tribe), and communities, G. H. Smith (1997) has developed six key principles of kaupapa Māori based on an analysis of KKM as a Māori intervention initiative. Although these principles are not intended to be definitive or prescriptive, they have come to represent some of the common principles said to be operating in any kaupapa Māori context, including the TPW EdD. These are:

1. Tino rangatiratanga (relative autonomy principle);
2. Taonga tuku iho (cultural aspirations principle);
3. Ako Māori (cultural preferred pedagogy);

4. Kia piki ake i ngā raruraru o te kainga (mediation of socioeconomic and home difficulties principle);
5. Whānau (extended family structure principle);
6. Kaupapa (collective vision, philosophical principle).

Each principle is expressed in each initiative in particular ways, and varies depending on the purpose of the group, individuals, and context. In the TPW EdD context, each principle finds expression within the pedagogical dimensions of the program, but in the theorizing kaupapa Māori.

In sum, kaupapa Māori theory refers to Māori-centered philosophies, frameworks, and practices. As noted in the first of Smith's principles above, critical to this work of kaupapa Māori adherents, including scholars, is notion of tino rangatiratanga (absolute self-determination), and the Treaty of Waitangi (Bishop, 1994; Nepe, 1991; G. H. Smith, 1997). Signed in 1840 by independent Māori tribes and representatives of the Crown, the Treaty of Waitangi confirms Māori sovereign rights as tangata whenua (Indigenous people). The political edge of kaupapa Māori theory is emphasized by Cherryl Smith (2002): "Kaupapa Māori theory emerges out of practice, out of struggle, out of experience of Māori who engage struggle, who reject, who fight back, and who claim space for the legitimacy of Māori knowledge" (p. 13). Therefore, while kaupapa Māori theory makes "space" for Māori scholarship there is also an expectation that such an approach understands the political space it seeks to demarcate. In the case of the EdD and other Māori educational initiatives in mainstream institutions, it is critical to understand the wider space and discourses in operation. I have chosen to locate the TPW EdD as an Indigenous kaupapa Māori initiative within the broader discourse of diversity, a common response to our EdD by others who are trying to understand why such a program has been developed. Furthermore, "claiming space" within the discourse of diversity clarifies the way in which we are seeking to "indigenise the EdD."

Disrupting Discourses of Diversity

One of the dominant discourses the TPW EdD disrupts that has become increasingly popular in New Zealand educational settings is the discourse of diversity. Diversity as a broad descriptor for a range of student differences in New Zealand education is showcased in the Ministry of Education's BES *Quality Teaching for Diverse Students in Schooling* (Alton-Lee, 2003).[11] Alton-Lee (2003) states:

> Diversity encompasses many characteristics including ethnicity, socioeconomic background, home language, gender, special needs, disability, and giftedness. Teaching needs to be responsive to diversity within ethnic groups,

for example diversity within Päkehä, Mäori, Pasifika, and Asian students. We also need to recognise the diversity within individual students influenced by intersections of gender, cultural heritage(s), socio-economic background and talent. (p. v)

The concept of diversity developed here relates to ethnicity, language, social class, gender, disability, and giftedness or talent. Heterogeneity in every group of learners is the norm, and within each diverse group every individual student is different; the intersection of social class, ethnicity, and gender (among other categories of difference) influences individual worldviews, practices, and experiences. Diversity purports to recognize a plethora of intersecting diversities; the diverse student represents every person as a uniquely different individual. Diversity as individual identity that is multilayered and multidimensional produces complex and limitless manifestations of human diversity; it resists stereotypes and the essentializing of ethnic and cultural group members to a predetermined set of attributes or qualities. In its broadest sense, diversity acknowledges the infinite range of difference that exists within humanity and potentially presents an interminable litany of descriptors (Kalantzis & James, 2004).

While the Ministry of Education's (Alton-Lee, 2003) definition of diversity positions Māori as only one part of the mosaic of difference, it simultaneously attempts to accord Māori a primary place. The synthesis reads:

It is fundamental to the approach taken to diversity in New Zealand education that it [BES] honours Articles 2 and 3 of the Treaty of Waitangi.[12] (Alton-Lee, 2003, p. 5)

Unsurprisingly, exactly what the Treaty of Waitangi is supposed to mean, given the ways diversity is espoused in the BES, is not clarified. The recognition of Māori is most likely to occur when the discourse of diversity meets with the Ministry of Education's focus of reducing disparities, usually by identifying the "gaps" between the highest and lowest achievers. According to Jones (2005), diversity is often employed as the "new code" (p. 10) for addressing inequality, the latest way to describe the students who require specialist educational programs, services, and extra attention. Ironically, diversity used in this way refers to Māori, but at the same time disguises the extent of the educational disparities and needs of Māori, masking the reality of poor educational outcomes and the social inequalities that exist. Within the discourse of diversity and disparity, Māori (students, teachers, parents) inevitably fade into the diverse surroundings alongside all other groups and "different" individuals. Rather the "problem" is located in the teaching of *all* students—the focus is on better teaching to improve student outcomes for all (diverse) children.

Although the definition of diversity in New Zealand education is fragmented, it often and inadvertently subsumes Māori needs and dismisses the Indigenous status of Māori and cultural being within the grand mosaic of difference. Māori become neutralized to a state of "sameness" (because we are *all* diverse)—an assimilation of kind takes place, resembling the drive for multiculturalism in education previously experienced by Māori popularized in the 1970s in New Zealand education.

In brief, multiculturalism seemed advantageous to Māori because it endorsed Māori culture as a legitimate culture to be celebrated (not assimilated or integrated as previously advanced). In the same way diversity seeks to acknowledge the multiplicity of differences that exist between and within cultural groups, multiculturalism was also a positive advance from ignoring and/or stereotyping cultural members into essential ethnic identities. However, a multicultural approach that only focused on celebrating cultural differences and social harmony also failed to address structural issues and inequalities (May, 1994). Multiculturalism in practice did not take into account factors such as sociohistorical issues, socioeconomic analyses, structural and institutional constraints, and unequal power relationships. Neither did multiculturalism acknowledge the inequitable allocation of power and resources to Māori, the status of Māori as tangata whenua, or the resulting educational and social outcomes.

Māori critics rejected multiculturalism as a device (like diversity) that diverted attention away from the Māori-Pākehā Treaty of Waitangi-based issues. Macfarlane (2003) points out that any multicultural approach in New Zealand that is not based on bicultural partnership runs counter to the Treaty of Waitangi. Described as a "Pākehā cop-out" and "mask for Pākehā hegemony" by Māori commentators (Verbitsky, 1993, p. 45), multiculturalism concealed the operation of the dominant group's culture as if it was just a universal cultural norm. May (1999) concurs that multiculturalism in education that obscures the power and the culture of the dominant group produces a "charade of universalism and neutrality" (p. 31). While studying other cultural groups, the dominant culture was the major frame of reference for interpreting difference that remained hidden, yet thoroughly embedded in every sphere of schooling (Bishop & Glynn, 1999).

Diversity, too, dodges the issue of the powerful and pervasive presence of the dominant culture by including and identifying Pākehā as a diverse group, as if their difference is insubstantial. Alton-Lee (2003) argues that diversity explicitly rejects the notion of a "normal" group and other minority groups of children. While a discursive shift in language occurs, it is largely superficial because diversity is not a characteristic in itself, but draws meaning from relationships of difference. These relationships are neither neutral nor equal; they determine how differences are framed. Diversity provides an ideological mask to hide the privilege of the dominant group because it ignores institutional and cultural structures and power. The glaring disproportionate and persistent numbers of Māori underachievers clearly illustrates that some markers of difference are more negative than others. Māori are often racialized, stereotyped, and portrayed in harmful ways whether it is in institutions including schools, or via the media.

Despite which definition of diversity one adheres to, discourses of diversity (like multiculturalism) tend to homogenize cultural and other identities in a way that is manageable (by the dominant group) and reduces differences to a collective level of essential sameness. Jones (2005) describes this process of diversification as the collapsing of difference into the familiar—"a contradiction," she says, "which is misunderstood for equality" (p. 13). The discourse of diversity as a panacea to the problem of difference, based on the idea that everyone is an individual and therefore also diverse, conceals relationships of power and does a disservice to the differences that impact negatively on people's lives. The notion that "we are all one people" (in diversity) is the same rhetoric of multiculturalism (and integration and assimilation) that again echoes in diversity. However all cultures or differences are not equal in terms of their political and economic status, the value of each group is determined by the group with the greatest power.

Rather than mutliculturalism, biculturalism has been forwarded by Māori based on the principles of partnership envisaged in the Treaty of Waitangi. Māori have demanded the meaningful inclusion of Māori language and culture in all spheres of schooling in an attempt to achieve positive educational outcomes for Māori students. Biculturalism was to be secured before entertaining multicultural ideals. In this way, the TPW EdD can be viewed as an articulation of biculturalism in our faculty— there is a particular space or EdD that is recognized, accorded, and given status alongside the other Treaty partner. In comparison, diversity manages to sidestep the call for biculturalism because the discourse of diversity reduces difference to the level of personal attributes and extends beyond the bounds of culture. The logic of attaining biculturalism as a way to reach multicultural ideals no longer makes sense within this discourse. Even when the Treaty of Waitangi is acknowledged within Alton-Lee's (2003) BES report, the promise that Māori as tangata whenua is "fundamental" to diversity is not evident, and an explanation of how diversity honors the Treaty is not provided. In this respect, diversity represents a dangerous discourse for Māori. Māori become barely visible as Indigenous people, and the unique relationship and responsibilities of the Crown to Māori, as guaranteed in the Treaty of Waitangi, becomes blurred.

In the international setting, discourses of diversity also differ, and there is no clear agreement about what diversity in education means. In the United States, diversity in education became more pronounced as the proportion of the population of people of color increased when compared to the mostly white, monolingual, female teaching corps (Zeichner, 1993). *Diversity* is associated with issues of cultural difference (multiculturalism) and disproportionately low educational achievement among ethnic minority groups, in particular Native American, Black American, and Latino students. In the United States, the discourse of diversity has developed into a distinctive branch of multiculturalism in an effort to achieve more equitable educational outcomes for all students (with a focus on students of color)—various approaches can be categorized in the diversity category. These include culturally relevant (Ladson-Billings, 1994), culturally responsive (Gay, 2000), culturally congruent (Au & Kawakami, 1994), as well as diversity pedagogy (Sheets, 2005) and others. Proponents of these approaches recognize the centrality of social and cultural factors implicit in teaching and learning, and aim to modify classroom culture to align more positively with the culture of the home, and develop culturally responsive content, processes, and practices in an effort to ensure equity and excellence for all students (Phuntsog, 1999).

In Canada, talk of diversity in education is closely linked to "integrative inclusivity" or "inclusive schooling." There are again, however, multiple explanations of what constitutes a diversity approach. According to Dei, James, Karumanchery, James-Wilson, and Zine (2000) literature related to theorization of inclusive schooling can be described in two main categories "diversity as a variety perspective" and "diversity as a critical perspective" (p. 14). Much like the Māori experience of a multicultural approach in schools, the first approach is focused on valuing difference through fostering cooperation, tolerance, and respect for others. According to Dei et al. (2000):

> This approach to inclusion does not lead to equity, nor does it challenge power identity or representational issues in education. In fact, the approach fails to rupture difference as the context for power and domination in schools and society. (p. 14)

Similar to the ideals and experiences of multiculturalism, "diversity as variety" acknowledges and even celebrates difference, but creates no real change nor does it make any advances for subordinated groups.

262 JENNY BOL JUN LEE

The second approach falls within the purview of diversity as the critical examination of difference and power. Power and domination are used as a key to understanding and interpreting social and structural relations. Instead of essentialist or romanticized versions of the other, this perspective purports to enable an exploration of different histories and experiences of oppression in plural communities, as well as cover issues such as identity, equity, and representation. Dei et al. (2000) writes:

> The dynamics and relational aspects of difference (race, class, gender, sexuality, language and ability) are critically explored to illustrate how difference and power converge and intersect to shape the schooling experiences of minority youth. The emphasis is on transformative educational practices, which would ensure that students are equipped to challenge and resist dominance and oppression in the multivariant forms of racism, sexism, heterosexism, classism and abilism. (p. 15)

Diversity goes beyond acknowledging students' diverse realities to problematizing the social disparities that are transmitted via schools, and attempts to intervene through various pedagogical practices.

In a similar vein, Australian educationalists Kalantzis and James (2004) argue: "Difference, the insistent reality becomes diversity the agent of change" (para. 7). Diversity is promoted as inevitable, unavoidable, and normative. In doing so, it becomes a mobilizing site where difference forms the basis of a social program that seeks equitable outcomes—the redistribution of power, wealth, and resources underpinned by ideals of social justice, pluralism, and equality. From this perspective the aspirations of diversity encourage ideals of inclusive schooling and align with other social movements such as critical multiculturalism that aims for emancipatory educational politics (May, 1999). Diversity is presented as not just an acceptance of difference, but a frame for analysis of existing social structures that includes power relationships to advance social justice for all. Kalantzis and Cope (1999) describe this approach as a culturalist, pluralist form of multiculturalism (or "postprogressive" pedagogy), one in which an explicit pedagogy for inclusion and access is advanced and multiculturalism is considered a core social and educational value.

Whether diversity is expressed as an aspiration (to recognize all diversity) or a problem (to solve disparities), nationally and internationally approaches to diversity vary in social, cultural, structural, and pedagogical breadth and depth. Regardless of the diversity design, in the New Zealand context Māori are positioned as only one of the many diverse groups. This is not to say that the critique of diversity (such as "diversity as an agent of change") and educational approaches that recognize the centrality of culture in teaching and learning is not useful in helping Māori and other learners. Such approaches align with a kaupapa Māori who seeks to address power relationships in the classroom and in the school, as well as establish strong learning relationships to better engage students in learning (Bishop & Glynn, 1999). However, in a *diversity* setting all groups are treated with equal status, and Māori and Indigenous merely become another group contesting for recognition, acknowledgment, access, and social equity.

It is in the diversity in education context the TPW EdD as a Māori and Indigenous oriented program finds more meaning. For Māori, the notion of diversity is not a neutral descriptor in education, but represents an ideological shift with its own implications away from Māori as the Indigenous group with a unique relationship with the Crown and special status in New Zealand. For Māori, diversity must take into account, what May (1999) terms as, "historical and cultural situatedness" and "cultural specificity" (p. 31). While Māori acknowledge the undeniable diversity among learners, families, communities, and schools, they inevitably destabilize the politics of diversity by asserting tangata whenua status as set out in the Treaty of Waitangi. The TPW EdD is a case in point, as it demarcates a kaupapa Māori space that is not only culturally and pedagogically determined, but politically charged. The privileging of Indigenous rights in New Zealand over other forms of difference represents a division in difference that challenges the common bonds of diversity.

Conclusion

The inaugural TPW EdD at the University of Auckland is focused on Māori and Indigenous education and social policy development and leadership. Increasing the number of Māori EdD students, and improving their doctor experiences through an EdD cohort-based program, is not the extent of or what is meant by "indigenizing" the EdD program. Rather, such a program requires a culturally located pedagogy that is grounded in the place, space, and people of whom it claims to serve. In this regard the TPW EdD is underpinned by a kaupapa Māori approach, a framework that guides the pedagogy and seeks transformative change for our communities. A kaupapa Māori framework calls to attention the politics a Māori-centered program like the TPW EdD creates within discourses such as diversity in education. The TPW EdD builds on the previous Māori-led doctoral initiatives as well as kaupapa Māori educational activities already operating in New Zealand. In this way, the TPW EdD is a small part of a kaupapa Māori and Indigenous movement that is about the reclamation of language, culture, and knowledge for the sustainability of our people—articulated in Māori educational aspiration "to live as Māori." Incremental, transformational changes for our communities will not only be facilitated through the work and success of the students, but by challenging normative and dominant discourses by being, teaching, and living a Māori EdD.

Glossary

Hapū	Subtribe
Iwi	Tribe
Kōhanga Reo	Early childhood Māori language nests
Kura Kaupapa Māori	Māori immersion primary schools
Māori	Indigenous people of New Zealand
Mātauranga Māori	Māori knowledge
Pākehā	White New Zealanders
Tangata whenua	People of the land/Indigenous people
Tino rangatiratanga	Absolute self-determination
Whānau	Extended family

Notes

1. The other New Zealand universities currently offering an EdD program are Massey University, University of Otago, University of Waikato, and Auckland University of Technology.
2. In 2013, the Ministry of Education records 15 Māori students (and 111 of all students) enrolled in an EdD program nationally. Personal Communication, Senior Data Analyst, Ministry of Education, September 2, 2014.
3. Suspended students are not allowed to attend school until the board of trustees (of that particular school) either lifts the suspension (with or without conditions), extends the suspension, or expels the student from the school. If the student is expelled, the student would then have apply to attend another school.
4. The school principal is able to stand-down a student from school (not allowed to attend) for up to five school days, after which the student is able to return to school.
5. There was a significant increase (80%) in Māori doctoral completions from 2012 to 2013, whereas the increase in total number of completions was 14.4% (Pākehā 10.3%) see Domestic students completing qualifications by ethnic group, age group, and qualification level 2006–2013 (Ministry of Education, 2012a).
6. Ngā Pae o te Māramatanga (NPM) is New Zealand's Māori Centre of Research Excellence (CoRE) funded by the Tertiary Education Commission (TEC) and hosted by the University of Auckland.
7. For more information about the Māori and Indigenous see http://www.mai. ac.nz/contact-us

8. Funded by Te Wharekura, The University of Auckland, completed August 2013.
9. The EdD thesis is assessed at the same level as the PhD in Education and includes an oral examination.
10. KKM became state-funded in 1989 and have since been accountable to government policy and pressures.
11. The synthesis aimed at presenting ten evidence-based characteristics of quality teaching for diverse students reviews relevant research in primary, intermediate, and secondary schools. Quality teaching, using Alton-Lee's (2003) definition, should engage heterogeneous groups in learning that is related to curriculum goals.
12. In short, in Article 2 of the Treaty of Waitangi (Māori version), the Queen of England guarantees Māori tribes their "tino rangatiratanga" (the absolute chieftainship) over their lands, homes, and treasure possessions (including culture and language). In Article 3, Māori are accorded all the rights equal to those of the people of England.

References

Au, K. H., & Kawakami, A. J. (1994). Cultural congruence in instruction. In E. R. Hollins, J. E. King, & W. C. Hayman (Eds.), *Teaching diverse populations: Formulating a knowledge base* (pp. 5–23). Albany: State University of New York Press.

Alton-Lee, A. (2003). *Quality teaching for diverse students in schooling: Best evidence synthesis*. Wellington, New Zealand: Ministry of Education.

Bevan-Brown, J., & Bevan-Brown, W. (2001, December). How are Māori learners with special needs faring? Paper presented at the *International Conference of the Australian Association for Research in Education*, Fremantle, W.A., Australia.

Bishop, R. (1994). Initiating empowering research? *New Zealand Journal of Educational Studies, 29*(2), 175–188.

Bishop, R. (2005). Freeing ourselves from neocolonial domination in research: A kaupapa Māori approach to creating knowledge. In N. K. Denzin & Y. S. Lincoln (Eds.), *The Sage handbook of qualitative research* (3rd ed., pp. 109–138). Thousand Oaks, CA: Sage.

Bishop, R., & Glynn, T. (1999). *Culture counts: Changing power relations in education*. Palmerston North, New Zealand: Dunmore Press.

Carnegie Project on the Education Doctorate. (2014). Retrieved from http://cpedinitiative.org/consortium-work

Dei, G. J. S., James, I. M., Karumanchery, L. L., James-Wilson, S., & Zine, J. (2000). *Removing the margins: The challenges and possibilities of inclusive schooling*. Toronto, Ontario, Canada: Canadian Scholars' Press.

Durie, M. (2001). A framework for considering Māori educational advancement. *Opening Address at the Hui Taumata Matauranga*, Turangi, New Zealand.

Gay, G. (2000). *Culturally responsive teaching: Theory, research, and practice*. New York, NY: Teachers College Press.

Grant, B. M., & McKinley, E. (2011). Colouring in the pedagogy of doctoral supervision: Considering supervisor, student and knowledge through the lens of indigeneity. *Innovations in Education & Teaching International, 48*(4), 365–374.

Hohepa, M. (2010). "Doctoring" our own: Confessions of a Māori doctoral supervisor. In J. Jesson, V. Carpenter, M. McLean, M. Stephenson, & Airini (Eds.), *University teaching reconsidered: Justice, practice, inquiry* (pp. 129–138). Wellington, New Zealand: Dunmore Publishing.

Hutchings, J., Barnes, A., Taupo, K., Bright, N., Pihama, L., & Lee, J. (2012). *Kia puāwaitia ngā tūmanako: Critical issues for whānau in Māori education.* Wellington, New Zealand: New Zealand Council of Educational Research.

Jenkins, K. (2000). *Haere tahi tāua: An account of aitanga in Māori struggle for schooling.* Unpublished PhD thesis, The University of Auckland, Auckland, New Zealand.

Jones, A. (2005). Pedagogy of the gaps: Lessons on evidence, from the beach. In B. Webber (Ed.), *The Herbison lectures, 1999–2004* (pp. 7–33). Wellington, New Zealand: NZCER Press.

Kalantzis, M., & Cope, B. (1999). Transforming the mainstream. In S. May (Ed.), *Critical multiculturalism: Rethinking multicultural and antiracist education* (pp. 245–276). London: Falmer Press.

Kalantzis, M., & James, P. (2004). Introduction. In *The Fourth International Conference on Diversity in Organizations, Communities, and Nations*, Altona, Victoria, Australia.

Kidman, J. (2007). *Engaging with Māori communities: An exploration of some tensions in the mediation of social sciences research.* Auckland, New Zealand: Ngā Pae o te Māramatanga.

Ladson-Billings, G. (1994). *The dreamkeepers: Successful teachers of African American children.* San Francisco, CA: Jossey-Bass.

Macfarlane, A. H. (2003). *Culturally inclusive pedagogy for Mäori students experiencing learning and behaviour difficulties.* Unpublished PhD thesis, The University of Waikato, Hamilton, New Zealand.

May, S. (1994). *Making multicultural education work.* Clevedon, UK: Multilingual Matters.

May, S. (Ed.). (1999). *Critical multiculturalism: Rethinking multicultural and antiracist education.* London: Falmer Press.

McKinley, E., Grant, B., Middleton, S., Irwin, K., & Williams, L. R. (2009). Supervision of Māori doctoral students: A descriptive report. *MAI Review, 1*(6), 1–12.

McKinley, E., Grant, B., Middleton, S., Irwin, K., & Williams, L. R. T. (2011). Working at the interface: Indigenous students' experience of undertaking doctoral studies in Aotearoa New Zealand. *Equity & Excellence in Education, 44*(1), 115–132.

Mead, L. T. T. R. (1997). *Ngā aho o te kākahu mātauranga: The multiple layers of struggle by Mäori in education.* Unpublished PhD thesis, The University of Auckland, Auckland, New Zealand.

Ministry of Education. (2005). *Report on New Zealand student engagement.* Wellington, New Zealand: Ministry of Education.

Ministry of Education. (2005a). *Māori in tertiary education: A picture of the trends.* Wellington, New Zealand: Ministry of Education.

Ministry of Education. (2007). *Stand-downs and suspensions from school.* Retrieved December 15, 2007, from www.educationcounts.edcentre.govt.nz/indicators/student_participation/schooling/stand-downs_and_suspensions_from_school

Ministry of Education. (2007a). *2006/2007 Ngā haeata mātauranga: Annual report on Māori education.* Wellington, New Zealand: Ministry of Education.

Ministry of Education. (2012a). Māori Tertiary Education Students 2012. Retrieved from https://www.educationcounts.govt.nz/statistics/maori-education/tertiary-education

Ministry of Education. (2012b). Domestic students completing qualifications by ethnic group, age group and qualification level 2006–2013. Retrieved from www.educationcounts.govt.nz/__data/assets/excel_doc/0010/16300/Gaining-qualifications.xlsx

Nepe, T. M. (1991). *E Hao Nei E Tenei Reanga, Te Toi Huarewa Tipuna: Kaupapa Māori, an Educational Intervention System.* Unpublished PhD thesis, The University of Auckland, Auckland, New Zealand.

Phuntsog, N. (1999). The magic of culturally responsive pedagogy: In search of the Genie's lamp in multicultural education. *Teacher Education Quarterly, 26*(3), 97–111.

Pihama, L. (2001). *Tihei mauri ora: Honouring our voices.* Unpublished PhD thesis, The University of Auckland, Auckland, New Zealand.

Pihama, L. (2012). Kaupapa Māori theory: Transforming theory in Aotearoa. *He Pukenga Korero, 9*(2) 5–14.

Pihama, L., Cram, F., & Walker, S. (2002). Creating methodological space: A literature review of Kaupapa Māori research. *Canadian Journal of Native Education, 26*(1), 30–43.

Royal, T. A. C. (2002). Indigenous worldviews: A comparative study. *Report for Ngati Kikopiri, Te Wānanga-o-Raukawa, Te Puni Kokiri, Fulbright New Zealand, Winston Churchill Memorial Trust.* Retrieved from http://static1.squarespace.com/static/5369700de4b045a4e0c24bbc/t/53fe8f49e4b06d5988936162/1409191765620/Indigenous+Worldviews

Sheets, R. H. (2005). *Diversity pedagogy: Examining the role of culture in the teaching-learning process.* Boston, MA: Pearson Education.

Shulman, L. S. (2005). Signature pedagogies in the professions. *Daedalus, 134*(3), 52–59.

Simon, J., & Smith, L. T. (2001). *A civilising mission? Perceptions and representations of the New Zealand Native School system.* Auckland, New Zealand: Auckland University Press.

Smith, C. (2002). *He pou herenga ki te nui: Māori knowledge and the university.* Unpublished PhD thesis, The University of Auckland, Auckland, New Zealand.

Smith, G. H. (1997). *The development of Kaupapa Māori: Theory and praxis.* Unpublished PhD thesis, The University of Auckland, Auckland, New Zealand.

Smith, G. H. (2000). Protecting and respecting indigenous knowledge. In M. Battiste (Ed.), *Reclaiming indigenous voice and vision* (pp. 209–224). Vancouver, British Columbia, Canada: UBC Press.

Smith, K. (2007). Supervision and Māori doctoral students: A discussion piece. *MAI Review LW, 1*(3), 4.

Smith, L. T. (1999). *Decolonising methodologies*. London: Research and Indigenous Peoples Zed Books Ltd.

Smith, L. T. (2005). On tricky ground: Researching the native in the age of uncertainty. In N. K. Denzin & Y. S. Lincoln (Eds.), *The Sage handbook of qualitative research* (3rd ed., pp. 85–107). Thousand Oaks, CA: Sage.

Smith, L. T. (2006). Fourteen lessons of resistance to exclusion: Learning from the Māori experience in New Zealand over the last two decades of neo-liberal reform. In M. Mulholland (Ed.), *State of the Māori nation: Twenty-first-century issues in Aotearoa* (pp. 247–260). Auckland, New Zealand: Reed.

Statistics New Zealand. (2013). *NZ Census 2013: Quick stats about Māori*. Wellington, New Zealand: 2013 Census.

Storey, V. A., & Richard, B. (2013). Carnegie Project for the Educational Doctorate: The role of critical friends in diffusing doctoral program innovation. In C. A. Mullen & K. E. Lane (Eds.), *Becoming a global voice—the 2013 Yearbook of the National Council of Professors of Educational Administration*. Ypsilanti, MI: NCPEA Publications.

Verbitsky, J. E. (1993). *Models of political development in Mäori educational policies*. Unpublished PhD thesis, The University of Auckland, Auckland, New Zealand.

Zeichner, K. M. (1993). *Educating teachers for cultural diversity. NCRTL special report*. East Lansing, MI: National Center for Research on Teacher Learning.

Epilogue: Lessons Learned from a Global Examination of the Doctorate

Karri A. Holley

Generations from now, observers will likely look back at early twenty-first century higher education and note a chaotic system in a state of change. Evidence of this chaos abounds. The funding structure of higher education remains in flux, regardless of national context, as countries seek to balance public and private contributions to postsecondary learning. Colleges and universities are encouraged to participate in a global conversation, while simultaneously increasing their commitment to their local community. Issues of staffing, particularly among full-time faculty, raise concerns about professional stability and engagement. More students are pursuing higher education, bringing with them a diversity unmatched in previous generations. These students are part of the deepening conversation regarding lifelong learning (Schuetze & Slowey, 2013). Not only are higher education institutions expected to facilitate critical thinking and intellectual openness, but they are also responsible for the provision of educational opportunities over the course of an individual's life (Stephenson & Yorke, 2013). Taken as a whole, these changes require higher education institutions to more deeply examine the ways in which they define knowledge and enable its dissemination (Christensen & Eyring, 2011).

As the chapters in this volume have indicated, the evidence of change in twenty-first century higher education is particularly noteworthy in graduate and doctoral education (Nerad & Heggelund, 2011). While the doctorate degree has been traditionally associated with the PhD, along with its associated standards and norms, the doctorate is increasingly delivered in multiple and variable formats. The progression of the doctorate is not necessarily new, which is evident by its varying forms of existence in multiple countries. For example, American audiences may be most familiar with the education doctorate, given its history and visibility in the United States, whereas in Germany, the doctorate has long reflected the specific academic discipline rather than a philosophy designation. Furthermore, Russian universities offer both a candidate and a doctor of sciences, of which the latter may also be named for the discipline in which it is awarded. Among the academic disciplines, and around the world, doctorates in business administration, technology, science, and divinity (among others) proliferate, representing historical efforts by the academy to recognize and differentiate between multiple forms of knowledge, curricula, and student interests in ways specific to the regional context. The professional doctorate in particular illustrates the symbiotic relationship between higher education and the professions (Taylor & Storey, 2013). As professions such as medicine, law, social work, and nursing evolve to meet contemporary social needs, so should the terminal degree as a means to recognize a mastery of knowledge within the field.

It is the question of recognition that remains central to issues of the changing doctoral degree. Multiple stakeholders play a role in this process. While members of the profession must obviously embrace the degree as a benchmark of professional status, so must employers, the university, federal and state governments, members of the public, and so on. These multiple perspectives shape the doctorate, and its credibility relies on its acceptance (Wellington, 2013). The question of how academic institutions lead and support the development of the doctorate is significant. How are faculty trained to teach in doctoral programs? How are doctoral students supported financially? What relationships exist between the academic institution and industry? The chapters in this volume offer insight in organizational change, faculty learning, student engagement, and community partnerships, underscoring the complex issues related to the evolving doctoral degree. In this epilogue, I consider the chapters as a whole and offer three lessons learned from a global examination of the doctorate in its many forms:

1. *A changing social, economic, and political culture requires changes to the ways in which higher education institutions structure and deliver a curriculum.*

Across highly developed economic societies, the doctoral degree is frequently conceptualized as a strategic tool designed to provide larger benefits. Policies of innovation and economic growth are constructed with the doctorate at the center. The doctorate is presumed to open avenues toward scientific advancement that benefit society at large. When a lack of domestic students who are qualified and interested in doctoral education exist, international students are recruited, furthering the exchange of knowledge across national boundaries as well as the imbalance between advanced and emerging economies. Change in higher education credentials can be in part attributed to changing governmental and national priorities. In Chapter 2, for instance, Charles Mpofu provides evidence related to the growth of psychology and medicine professional doctorates in Australia and New Zealand with fluctuating governmental policies designed to facilitate economic growth. On the one hand, this approach privileges experimentation. National and state governments are willing to provide additional inputs, such as financial or other instrumental resources, in exchange for increased outputs, such as knowledge workers trained through innovative, applied curricula. On the other hand, the symbiotic relationship between the academy and the state emphasizes the challenging illusion of an autonomous higher education, where institutions prioritize student learning and knowledge production independent of external interests. Decisions are rarely, if ever, made simply for the sake of knowledge. Knowledge spills over institutional boundaries into multiple external arenas, requiring faculty and administrators to carefully balance the needs of the student, the institution, and society at large.

The changing nature of the doctorate is apparent in both the process and product of graduate education. Although the doctorate has been nurtured in different institutional and national contexts over an extended period of time, shared expectations do exist related to its key features. An examination of the different traits associated with doctoral education include critical and independent thinking, strong communication skills, a depth of knowledge related to the discipline, and the ability to generate and apply new knowledge (Nerad & Heggelund, 2011). Additional traits more recently identified include the need for translational or soft skills, and the ability to work as part of a team. As the path to the academic profession becomes increasingly complicated, and degree recipients choose more varied professional positions compared to previous generations, these transferable skills assume greater importance. Traditionally doctoral students are those who engage in full-time, on-campus study. Contemporary doctoral students are likely to be enrolled in a low-residency or online program, or experience a cohort-structured curriculum, expanding our notions about student learning in the classroom. Students may only interact with their peers via distance. Instead, their network of professional colleagues assumes an enhanced role in student persistence and degree completion. The variability of the dissertation process is directly related to the variability of the product while the dissertation is still considered by many observers to be the apotheosis of the doctoral experience, other forms such as the portfolio, the group project, action research and/or community engagement, digital scholarship, and the article collection prosper. At times, lost in the debate regarding the validity of these multiple forms of doctorates is the relationship to new forms of knowledge needed (and indeed, prioritized) by external stakeholders. Storey and Maughan contribute to this necessary conversation in Chapter 12 with considerations of how a practice-based doctoral capstone experience defines the practitioner-scholar. As the doctorate changes and evolves over time, so should one of its most distinctive, authoritative elements, the dissertation. "The research university is not simply a content delivery device," suggests Wellmon (2015, p. 3). "It is an institution unique in its capacity to produce and transmit knowledge that is distinct and carries with it the stamp of authority." Alternative forms of the dissertation recognize the need for such work to be socially relevant.

Related to these shifts is the increasing prominence of interdisciplinary knowledge. In Chapter 11, Pulla and Schissel consider how interdisciplinarity influences the core of the university, the faculty. Interdisciplinary initiatives have rippled through higher education for decades; indeed, in many countries, interdisciplinarity was the hallmark of innovation for undergraduate learning in the twentieth century. For doctoral education, the interdisciplinary challenge runs much deeper. The emergence of the contemporary doctorate is closely connected to the development of the disciplines (and their organizational form, the academic department). The disciplines allowed scholars to manage the vast nature of knowledge, encouraging depth and specialization. Disciplinary identity is related to a shared sense of community with like-minded scholars. As observers proclaim interdisciplinarity to be a necessity for twenty-first century challenges, its impact on the doctoral degree, faculty, students, and academic institutions is unclear. What does interdisciplinary knowledge look like as part of a doctoral curriculum? What skills should graduates of an interdisciplinary doctoral program possess? To which academic community do interdisciplinary scholars belong? What impact do doctoral recipients trained in an interdisciplinary program have on the larger society, and how does this impact compare to more traditional disciplinary-based efforts?

2. *Innovations should be sensitive to the local, institutional, and national context, although these variations make it a challenge to define the degree and wholly grasp its impact.*

The last two decades have witnessed a growth in the number of earned doctoral degrees around the world, including research and professional degrees. In the first decade of the twenty-first century, the number of earned doctorates in OECD countries increased by a staggering 38%, a growth unparalleled in previous decades (Organization for Economic Cooperation and Development, 2012). The growth of earned doctorates provides evidence of the belief that advanced, specialized knowledge plays a crucial role in a healthy society. Yet as a higher education community and a group of scholars focused on doctoral education, we are cautioned to look beyond the increased numbers of doctorates and consider the content of the degree, student experiences in these programs, and the degree's impact on larger society. This task is not an easy one. The multiple ways in which the doctorate is accomplished makes the task of defining and disseminating best practices difficult, while the balance between local needs and global scholarship is not always easily negotiated. Such balance is complicated by the influences of marketization and globalization, where academic institutions strive to climb the ladder of elite, prestigious research universities.

Although the doctorate is a shared degree, recognized across national boundaries, it is also uniquely the outcome of the context in which it is produced. In Chapter 14, Lee's discussion of the Te Puna Wānanga EdD reveals how academic institutions balance local culture and organizational behavior. The chapter also underscores how pedagogy that privileges local ways of knowing might uniquely impact social policy. In addition to local influences, evidence of global cooperation in doctoral education can also be found. In Chapter 10, Kochhar-Bryant discusses the challenge of cross-national cooperation, or the ways in which academics in different national contexts might develop and deliver a doctoral curriculum. These partnerships may reflect shared economic, political, or cultural concerns between nations. Innovative doctoral programs are defined by international networking opportunities, in addition to industry exposure, an attractive institutional environment, interdisciplinary research options, and a focus on transferable skills (European Commission, 2011). One example is Russia's Skolkovo Institute of Science and Technology. Skolkovo, in cooperation with the Massachusetts Institute of Technology (MIT), was established in 2011 to produce leaders prepared to engage in innovative practices, advance knowledge, and apply new technology to global issues not only in Russia, but around the world. Other partnerships utilize classroom settings around the world as a way to engage students in global conversations. The Global Executive Doctor of Education program at the University of Southern California requires students to meet in California, Hong Kong, and Qatar, as well as online, while the IESE Business School at the University of Navarra (Spain) encourages doctoral students to complete research abroad and earn the designation "international doctor."

While these markers of innovation may signal new avenues for doctoral education, many of the social issues which have plagued the degree still exist. Of significance are patterns of inclusion and exclusion that exist among student groups around the world that have long-term effects on doctoral recipients. From a global perspective, men far outpace women in the science and engineering workforce (UNCTAD, 2011). Women also have less access to the Internet, and hold fewer leadership positions in business and government, which contribute to a gender divide in the knowledge economy. This divide persists even among men and women who have received a doctoral degree. Though smaller than the gap between men and women who do not hold a doctorate, female doctoral recipients also experience bias related to salary, wage, and employment rates (OECD, 2012). The issue of mass versus elite education only adds to the complexity of these patterns. While the hierarchical nature of higher education is not necessarily new, the implications as part of a market-driven culture are.

Marginson (2006) referred to higher education as a "positional market," suggesting that the value of a good is in part determined by its exclusivity. "The steeper the distance between elite universities and others, the more that society values elite universities and the less it sees of their benefits," he concluded (2006, p. 6). Who pursues higher education, and how is a country's education system designed to support this pursuit? Is the impact of the doctoral degree magnified by an increased number of recipients, or is it diluted? When a national system supports the development of a doctoral curriculum for the academically elite, who is included in that process?

3. *An application of the critical friends approach requires recognition of multiple communities of practice, including the profession that supports the degree.*

Numerous theories have been employed to better understand the doctoral experience, including theories of socialization, identity development, as well as career and/or professional trajectories. The chapters in this volume expand our understanding of doctoral education by evoking the critical friends framework, suggesting a network of partners who provide candid critique and ideas in order to collectively strengthen doctoral education. This framework illustrates how multiple stakeholders are involved in the doctoral process, including students, faculty, administrators, industry, government, and the public. An evolving doctorate changes the ways in which faculty and students interact with each other as well as with other institutional stakeholders. For instance, extant research has documented the significant role that peers play in the experience of doctoral students. A lack of integration among a student's peer group results in a reduced chance for degree completion (Gardner, 2008), as peers can serve as vital resources in student learning. When students learn at a distance, engage in a virtual learning environment, or visit campus infrequently for a low-residency program, peer relationships change. We do not yet fully understand how these relationships influence alternative degree programs; however, these integrative processes have served to be beneficial to student learning outcomes. Therefore, communities of practice extend beyond the traditional face-to-face learning approach that dominated twentieth-century higher education. Advanced, deep, and significant learning can occur in a variety of contexts, ranging from the workplace to a virtual online environment.

These communities of practice also influence the development of the doctoral curriculum. Multiple chapters in this volume have illustrated the nature of the curriculum as a social artifact, reflective of a unique community and its priorities, norms, and beliefs. Through the transmission of knowledge from one generation of scholars to the next, the curriculum becomes an ever-evolving reflection of disciplinary culture. Uncertainties exist as to what role the profession plays in the doctoral curriculum, and how the discipline and the profession exist in a symbiotic relationship. For example, in Chapter 5, Smythe, Rolfe, and Larmer suggest that a successful health professional doctorate places the health client, or patient, at the center of learning. How might a curriculum shift to a more active, applied focus, and what implications are there for student learning? The doctoral degree has historically prioritized the discipline, or discipline-specific knowledge, at its center. For North American universities, students participate in a progressive curriculum designed to deepen their understanding of how the field is structured. This approach also ensures that doctoral students are socialized to seminal authors, ideas, and theories of the discipline, further strengthening the disciplinary community. The changing nature of the curriculum is indicative of shifts taking place between different knowledge boundaries. In Chapter 9, Nikolou-Walker illustrates the power of work-based learning; rather than starting from the norms of the academic discipline, such programs develop a learning agreement responsive to the individual candidate and his or her workplace setting.

A frequently unacknowledged partner for doctoral education is the job market. American economist Anthony Carnevale suggested, "Graduate and professional education contributes to the creation of a new class of global workers that heightens the conflict between local, national, and global perspectives on its proper economic role" (CGS, 2009, p. 32). The knowledge economy transcends national boundaries. While knowledge workers may be part of a local or regional community, they are also members of a globalized group. Doctoral students leave one country to study in another, conduct research in an international setting, or assume employment in locations other than their home country. The complex doctoral student population reinforces the challenges of a global job market. The push for more doctoral degree recipients is weakened without a market to magnify their talents. While not all knowledge exists toward utilitarian ends, contemporary rhetoric privileges knowledge, which possesses extrinsic value. In conclusion, perhaps the biggest challenge facing doctoral education in the future is maintaining the integrity of the degree while being open to innovation, change, and new directions. This edited volume provides an important step in collecting information on the range of doctoral programs around the world, revealing how the forces of globalization are influencing multiple higher education systems. The preparation of scholars for this reality requires attention to the doctorate in its many forms.

References

Christensen, C., & Eyring, H. (2011). *The innovative university: Changing the DNA of higher education from the inside out.* San Francisco, CA: John Wiley & Sons.

Council of Graduate Schools (CGS). (2009). *Graduate education in 2020: What does the future hold?.* Washington, DC: Council of Graduate Schools.

European Commission (2011). *Report of mapping exercise on doctoral training in Europe.* Brussels: European Commission.

Gardner, S. (2008). Fitting the mold of graduate school: A qualitative study of socialization in doctoral education. *Innovative Higher Education, 33*(2), 125–138.

Marginson, S. (2006). Dynamics of national and global competition in higher education. *Higher Education, 52*(1), 1–39.

Nerad, M., & Heggelund, M. (2011). *Toward a global PhD?: Forces and forms in doctoral education worldwide.* Seattle, WA: University of Washington Press.

OECD. (2012). *Careers of doctorate holders.* Paris: Organization for Economic Co-operation and Development.

Schuetze, H., & Slowey, M. (Eds.). (2013). *Global perspectives on higher education and lifelong learners.* London: Routledge.

Stephenson, J., & Yorke, M. (Eds.). (2013). *Capability and quality in higher education.* London: Routledge.

Taylor, R., & Storey, V. (2013). Leaders, critical friends, and the education community: Enhancing effectiveness of the professional practice doctorate. *Journal of Applied Research in Higher Education, 5*(1), 84–94.

UNCTAD. (2011). *Applying a gender lens to science, technology, and innovation.* New York: United Nations.

Wellington, J. (2013). Searching for 'doctorateness'. *Studies in Higher Education, 38*(10), 1490–1503.

Wellmon, C. (2015). *Organizing enlightenment: Information overload and the invention of the modern research university.* Baltimore, MD: Johns Hopkins University Press.

Notes on Contributors

Hilary Burgess is Professor of Education at the University of Leicester. Previously, she was a senior lecturer in the Faculty of Education and Language Studies (FELS) at the Open University where she was Director for Postgraduate Studies in the Centre for Research in Education and Educational Technology (CREET). She was also Academic Coordinator and leader of the Open University's Research Careers Advisory Team in the Research School with a university-wide remit for research career support and training. Her research and publications have focused on professional doctorates and teacher professional development in terms of mentoring and learning communities. Funded projects include research into the impact of undertaking a professional doctorate and a TEMPUS project on developing capacity in teacher professional development, the practicum, and action research with several universities in the Middle East and North Africa. She is regularly invited to submit papers at conferences including American Educational Research Association, British Education Research Association, and European Educational Research Association and has jointly written a key book for doctoral students: *Achieving Your Doctorate in Education*. She is the editor for BERA's publication *Research Intelligence*.

Eleanor Doyle is Senior Lecturer in Economics and Head (Acting) at the School of Economics, University College, Cork. She is the director of the practitioner-oriented, developmental doctoral research program—DBA (business economics). She is developing a Competitiveness Institute at the school. Her teaching and research relate to the integration of professional and organizational development and its impact on the environment for business and in turn on economic development and prosperity.

Denise Hawkes is the EdD program leader at the Institute of Education, University of London. She is an economist and has published widely on topics in applied social and education economics. Recently she has started to apply her experience with research students into writing about program development for EdD students.

Karri Holley is Associate Professor of Higher Education at the University of Alabama. Since 2013, she has served as the coordinator for the higher education program. She holds a BA from the University of Alabama, and a Med and PhD from the University of Southern California. Her research interests include organizational change in higher education, graduate and doctoral education, interdisciplinarity, and qualitative inquiry. She wrote a monograph on interdisciplinarity in higher education for the ASHE-Jossey Bass monograph series, and recently edited *Increasing Diversity in Doctoral Education* as part of the New Directions in Higher Education series. She teaches courses for masters and doctoral students at the University of Alabama as well as for participants in the Executive EdD in Higher Education program. Her teaching focuses on higher education administration and governance, organizational change, and qualitative inquiry. She has held several leadership roles in national associations, including chair of the AERA Doctoral Education across the Disciplines Special Interest Group and member of the program committees for both ASHE and AERA.

Carol A. Kochhar-Bryant is a professor and senior associate dean of the Graduate School of Education and Human Development at the George Washington University, Washington, DC. For 28 years she has developed and directed advanced graduate and doctoral leadership preparation programs in education, and guided the introduction of PhD programs. She has served on standards boards such as the NEA Great Schools Indicators Project and the National Board of Professional Teaching Standards Exceptional Learners Panel. She consults with public school districts, state departments of education and federal agencies, and nonprofit organizations that seek to improve services and supports for children and youth with disabilities in education, employment, and independent living. She has been invited to collaborate in special education research with the World Bank, and by the US Department of Education to lead evaluation teams for the six federal resource centers. Kochhar-Bryant is widely published in areas of disability policy and practice, leadership development, interagency service coordination, transition to postsecondary, and employment for special learners. She is past president of the Division on Career Development and Transition of the International Council for Exceptional Children.

Peter Larmer is an associate professor and the head of the School of Clinical Sciences, which has combined seven clinical practice disciplines. His professional background is physiotherapy. He was an early student of the doctor of health science and came to see the value of a wider exposure to philosophy and the nature of health systems. He co-leads a paper called practice and philosophies with Elizabeth Smythe, and takes a particular interest in leadership. His mixed-method thesis is a showcase of the value of exploring an issue through different perspectives.

Jenny Bol Jun Lee belongs to the subtribe of the Waikato tribe in Aotearoa, New Zealand. From 2012 to 2015, she was Head of School of Te Puna Wānanga (Māori Education) in the Faculty of Education, University of Auckland. During her term as Head of School she initiated the inaugural Māori and Indigenous EdD in 2013. Previously a Māori language secondary schoolteacher, Jenny Lee has worked in the community, tertiary, and business sectors with a focus on teaching and learning and Kaupapa Māori research. Jenny Lee is a speaker of the Māori language, has a strong reputation in Māori research, and is a respected member of the Māori education community. Her teaching and research interests include Māori and Indigenous education, Māori pedagogies and effective teaching, and pūrākau (Māori story-telling) as narrative inquiry.

Gareth Lewis is a research associate with the University of Leicester. He was a teacher of mathematics for ten years at two secondary schools in the United Kingdom. Following his teaching career he moved to develop a career as a leadership and organizational development consultant. More recently, Gareth undertook doctoral research investigating disaffection with school mathematics. He has published widely on issues related to affect in mathematics education and is involved in a range of research activities in the School of Education at Leicester.

Margaret Malloch is Director Research Training in the College of Education, Victoria University, Australia. Her role includes working in the doctoral programs. Her research focuses on workplace learning and professional practice. She has several years' membership and is a past chair of the Executive Committee of the Workplace Learning Special Interest Group of the American Educational Research Association and is a link convenor of the European Research Network on Vocational Education and Training Special Interest Group of the European Education Research Association. Malloch has researched women in vocational unions and women in education and change, as well as worked more recently on the capable organization and vocational education and training, specifically on employers' views of competency-based qualifications. She has undertaken international workplace training consultancies and programs in the Asia Pacific region. Malloch has worked in the school, further education, and higher education sectors in Australia.

Bryan D. Maughan served as the director of the professional practices doctorate program in the Department of Leadership and Counseling at the University of Idaho, Idaho Falls. Previously he served as a faculty member at Eastern Idaho Technical College where he taught students in technical and technology degrees in medical, mechanical, and business-related industries. As a research fellow at the Idaho National Laboratories, he studied the effects of interpersonal relationship training on scientists, engineers, and members of management who served as mentors to university interns. He served as the CEO and president of Sentire Mentoring, a professional consulting company focused on the activity of knowledge transfer and management through mentoring in the workforce. He was the director of International Language Programs (ILP) in Russia and Taiwan where he was instrumental in founding and developing two ESL schools. His current research interests include organizational analysis, agentic learning and complexity, heutagogy, tacit knowledge transfer, and action and translational research.

T. W. (Tom) Maxwell coordinated the University of New England (UNE) EdD for a decade until the early 2000s. During that time he became interested in the potential of professional doctorates to make a difference in the workplace. He led the development of UNE's Prof D (Industry and Professions) and co-convened five international conferences on professional doctorates (1996–2004). He has a range of publications related to professional doctorates and doctoral education. His experience extends to higher education work in Bangladesh, Bhutan, Fiji, Laos, the Maldives, Vietnam, Uganda, and Zambia. Maxwell is now an adjunct professor, having retired in July 2010.

Charles Mpofu is a lecturer in the Faculty of Health Sciences at the Auckland University of Technology in New Zealand. He has been teaching health professionals since 2004 in the areas of health promotion, professional development, health and lifestyle, and developmental psychology. His research interests in professional regulation and health policy have led him to be involved, in 2008, in a national forum on registration of overseas-trained doctors in New Zealand. This work has since continued to his current research focus on comparing working conditions of medical doctors in New Zealand and Australia. He developed an interest in such comparative studies while doing his doctorate in medical education in Australia at James Cook University's School of Medicine and Dentistry.

Elda Nikolou-Walker is a senior lecturer in the Institute for Work-Based Learning in Middlesex University, London. She has made a new contribution to the growing body of literature in the field of work-based learning with her book *The Expanded University: Work-Based Learning and the Economy*. The format of the book and its range of theoretical models and approaches assist in applying new insights and thinking to the vast array of work-based situations that might be encountered. Nikolou-Walker is continuously publishing in the area of Work-Based Learning.

Siomonn Pulla is an associate professor in the Office of Interdisciplinary Studies at Royal Roads University, Victoria, Canada, and one of the core faculty in the Doctorate of Social Sciences program. He is committed to innovative interdisciplinary research and teaching, with an emphasis on seeking solutions to real-world issues. His primary focus is on participatory and collaborative research, corporate–Indigenous relations, and indigenous learning systems. Pulla is especially passionate about ensuring that indigenous cultures have access to adequate and appropriate tools for learning. An important aspect of his research is the emerging intersections between technology and educational programming, especially in the delivery of curriculum and programs to remote, rural, and underdeveloped communities.

R. Martin Reardon holds an MEd in Mathematics Education from Queensland University of Technology and a PhD in Educational Policy, Planning, and Leadership from the College of William and Mary in Virginia. Reardon spent three years as the inaugural chair of Leadership Studies at Marian University before moving to Virginia Commonwealth University (VCU) in 2005. He played an integral role in establishing and eventually directing the EdD program aligned with the Carnegie Project on the Education Doctorate (CPED) before moving to East Carolina University (ECU) in 2013 and collaborating with his ECU colleagues to successfully apply for CPED membership and redesign the EdD accordingly.

Gary Rolfe is Professor of Nursing in the College of Human and Health Science at Swansea University. He qualified as a mental health nurse in 1983 and has an academic background in philosophy and education. He teaches reflective practice, practice development, and action research and has published ten books and over one hundred journal articles and book chapters on philosophical aspects of practice, research methodologies, practice development, and education. He has been invited to speak at conferences across the world, including keynote presentations in the United States, Canada, Australia, New Zealand, and throughout Europe. Since moving to Swansea University in 2003 Rolfe has worked with practitioners across West Wales to establish a number of practice development units. He holds visiting chairs at Trinity College, Dublin, and Canterbury Christ Church University, Kent, and is Professor of Innovation and Development with ABMU Health Board.

Gail Sanders is Professor of Management Education and Development at the University of Sunderland and is program leader for the university's professional doctorate. She has a particular interest in management education and development through work-based learning with a focus on professionalism and professional identity. She is leader of the research cluster for leadership and professional practice.

Bernard Schissel is a professor and the program head of the Doctor of Social Sciences Program at Royal Roads University, Victoria, Canada. In general, his research focuses on the marginal position that children and youth occupy in Western democracies and how such institutions as law, education, medicine, the political economy, and the military exploit children and youth in very subtle, politically acceptable, and publicly endorsed ways. His current books are *About Canada: Children and Youth*, *Marginality and Condemnation: An Introduction to Critical Criminology* (with Carolyn Brooks), *Still Blaming Children: Youth Conduct and the Politics of Child Hating*, and *The Legacy of School for Aboriginal People: Education, Oppression, and Emancipation* (with Terry Wotherspoon).

Joan Smith is Lecturer in Education at the University of Leicester. She is currently the program leader for the EdD (Doctorate of Education), a professional doctorate designed for full-time teachers and educational leaders who wish to combine full-time work with part-time study. Smith was a secondary school teacher in the English Midlands for almost 20 years, holding a range of middle and senior leadership roles. She then worked in Initial Teacher Education at the Universities of Canterbury Christ Church, Nottingham, and Leicester before taking up her current role. Her research interests include gender and leadership, teachers' lives and careers, and pedagogical research focused on developing postgraduate students' criticality and methodological understanding. She is a member of the British Educational Research Association, the British Educational Leadership Management and Administration Society, the Society for Research in Higher Education, the Society for Educational Studies, and the British Psychological Society, including the specialist sections Qualitative Methods in Psychology and the Psychology of Women Section. She is a fellow of the Higher Education Academy.

Elizabeth Smythe is a professor within the Faculty of Health and Environmental Sciences at Auckland University of Technology. Her professional background is nursing and midwifery. She is currently the program leader of the Doctor of Health Science, which draws students from a wide range of health disciplines. She co-leads the practice and philosophies paper, which encourages students to examine the assumptions underpinning research methodologies and to discern insights from their own experience of leadership. Her research expertise is hermeneutic phenomenology.

Valerie A. Storey is an associate professor in the School of Teaching, Learning and Leadership, College of Education and Human Performance at the University of Central Florida. She has served as director of EdD educational leadership programs grounded on the working principles of CPED, and of a PhD educational leadership program. Storey earned her doctoral degree in Educational Leadership and Policy at Peabody College, Vanderbilt University. She serves as the chair of the Carnegie Project on the Education Doctorate Dissertation in Practice Award Committee.

Jacqueline Taylor is an artist, writer, researcher, and lecturer. She was awarded her art-practice-research PhD in 2013 at the Centre for Fine Art Research, Birmingham City University. She continues to work there as a research fellow and as a researcher developer at the University of Worcester. Her research examines poetic interrelations between writing and painting, fine art research practice, and the student experience and pedagogy in art and design doctoral study. She regularly exhibits, publishes her work, and speaks at conferences and symposia nationally and internationally.

Sue Taylor is course leader for the Institution Focused Study, the first research component of the EdD at the Institute of Education, University College, London. She is also program leader for the postgraduate diploma in social science research methods, an access route for widening participation into doctoral studies for nontraditional students. Her primary research foci are on adult professional learning and development and on curriculum design for developing generative learning. Recently she has focused on the use of andragogy through blended learning, particularly in relation to doctoral students.

Sian Vaughan is an art historian by training whose research interests and publications concern the interpretation and mediation of engagement with contemporary art and design through the modalities of public art, arts research, and the archive. Recent work has questioned the conceptualization and methodology of the archive in relation to creative practice, and prompted a wider consideration of doctoral student experience in art and design. Vaughan is a senior research fellow and the keeper of archives with the Faculty of Arts, Design and Media, Birmingham City University. As an art historian, she has previously taught art and design history in further and higher education in the United Kingdom.

Philip Wood teaches across a range of master's degrees focusing in particular on work with distance and international students, and also supervises several EdD and PhD students. Wood is a member of the Society for Research in Higher Education, the Collaborative Action Research Network, and the Society for Educational Studies. His research interests focus on pedagogy in higher education and he was a founding member of the Lesson Study Research Group within the School of Education. He is also a teaching fellow of the University of Leicester, UK.

Index

CPSIA information can be obtained
at www.ICGtesting.com
Printed in the USA
LVOW04*1013260316
480891LV00005B/201/P